VOTERS, PARTIES, AND LEADERS

Jean Blondel, who disclaims any connexion with the *trouvère* who practised lyrical politics outside Richard Coeur-de-Lion's prison, was born at Toulon in 1929 and later grew up in Paris. The rigours of a French education in a Jesuit grammar school set him wondering what made it all tick, and he went on to the Institut d'Études Politiques to find out. When St Antony's College, Oxford, awarded him a scholarship in 1953, he came to Britain. At Oxford he was repeatedly asked: 'What are you reading?' and this led, owing to an unfortunate failure to appreciate the logic of English pronunciation, to his completion of a two-years' survey of the political life of Reading. In 1955 he took his B.Litt.

The French Army still had claims on his services but after these he returned to Britain where, at Manchester University, he studied the relations between central and local government and in 1958 became a lecturer in the Department of Political Institutions at the then University College of North Staffordshire, now the University of Keele. Early in 1964, after a visit to the United States, he took up the post of first Professor of Government at the newly created University of Essex in the city of Old King Cole. Jean Blondel, who is married and has two daughters, has never advocated (openly) government by professors, nor stated (in print) that Britain is the world's leading political asylum.

J. BLONDEL

VOTERS, PARTIES, AND LEADERS

THE SOCIAL FABRIC OF BRITISH POLITICS

PENGUIN BOOKS

Penguin Books Ltd, Harmondsworth, Middlesex, England
Penguin Books Inc., 7110 Ambassador Road, Baltimore, Maryland 21207, U.S.A.
Penguin Books Australia Ltd, Ringwood, Victoria, Australia

—

First published 1963
Reprinted (with revisions) 1965, 1966, 1967, 1969
Reprinted 1970, 1972

—

Copyright © J. Blondel, 1963, 1965, 1966, 1967, 1969

—

Made and printed in Great Britain
by Cox & Wyman Ltd,
London, Reading and Fakenham
Set in Monotype Imprint

Preface

MUCH research has been done, since the end of the Second World War in particular, on the social aspects of British politics. This book is based to a large extent on the result of this research. I have mainly tried here to put the material together and to present a general picture. In doing so, I have often been obliged to summarize and I hope that I have not too often given a distorted image of the more detailed findings.

I relied so heavily on printed material that I had to decide what to do about quoting my sources. For the sake of not over-burdening the text, I decided to limit footnotes to the barest minimum and to refer the reader to the fairly long bibliography which will be found at the end of the book. However, in a number of cases where my argument is based on a single piece of research, I have mentioned my source while going along. I take the opportunity to acknowledge here Messrs Routledge and Kegan Paul's permission to reproduce tables or parts of tables which appeared in G. D. H. Cole's *Post-War Condition of Britain*, in Benney, Gray, and Pear's *How People Vote*, in R. K. Kelsall's *Higher Civil Servants in Britain*, and in an article published by Dr Eysenck in the *British Journal of Sociology* in 1951. I also acknowledge the Oxford University Press's permission to use material appearing in J. D. Stewart's *British Pressure Groups* and to reproduce a table appearing in M. Stacey's *Tradition and Change, A Study of Banbury*, Messrs MacGibbon and Kee's permission to reproduce a table appearing in C. Jenkins's *Power at the Top*, the Conservative Political Centre's and Dr M. Abrams's permission to reproduce a table appearing in *The Future of the Welfare State*, the Hansard Society for Parliamentary Government's permission to reproduce two tables from H. C. Mackenzie and R. S. Milne's *Marginal Seat*, and Political and Economic Planning's permission to quote from a table appearing in the survey of trade union membership published in *Planning* in July 1962.

Although I borrowed so much from many sources, I am, of course, responsible for the general line of the argument. I was

7

very much helped, however, by the advice and comments of many of my colleagues at Keele, not only of those who read the manuscript in its final stages, but also of those with whom I discussed some of the problems with which this book is concerned. I would like in the first place to express my warmest gratitude to Professor S. E. Finer, who encouraged me to undertake this work and helped me all along with his comments. I would like to thank Dr J. Eros, Mr H. B. Berrington, Mr A. Angell, and Mr A. Hall who went patiently through the draft and discussed it with me. I would also like to say how grateful I am to Mr P. M. Williams, of Nuffield College, Oxford, who took great pains to make this book less imperfect both in style and in content, and to Professor P. W. Campbell, of the University of Reading, who suggested some lines of research and whose comments on the final draft were of great value. I would like to thank Sir Michael Fraser, of the Conservative Research Department, and Mr S. Swingler, M.P., for their help at various stages of the preparation of the book and for their comments on the manuscript.

I would like to thank particularly Dr H. Durant and his staff of the British Institute of Public Opinion for their invaluable help; not only did they open their archives to me, but they were ready to undertake some calculations especially for this book and they never showed any sign of impatience at my repeated requests.

Finally, I do not really know how to thank my wife who had to bear the burden of listening to the various drafts and whose encouragement and help were invaluable.

J.B.

Keele, July 1962

Note for the revised edition

This edition includes substantial updating of the tables and other material which constitute the bases of the analysis. Yet, despite major fluctuations in party support and some substantial changes in the social structure, the broad characteristics of the social fabric of British politics remain the same: oscillations have had a greater amplitude in the 1960s than in the 1950s, but the centre of gravity has not significantly moved.

Colchester, January 1969

CHAPTER ONE

Introductory

THIS book is concerned with the relationship between politics and society in contemporary Britain. But politics is taken here in a broad sense. We seem sometimes to think that politics is a very special game played in a peculiar way by small groups of politicians. It is true that politics is a job which has its rules and its code of conduct like any other job. But politics is also, in our societies, the concern of almost all members of the community. Millions of people vote. Even though many may say that, between elections, they are not interested at all in politics, they are, at least once every four or five years, important players in the political game. Millions are, moreover, members of organizations, such as trade unions, professional associations, or trade associations, which are, from time to time, involved in politics. Depending on their traditions, they may react vigorously against the government or they may prefer to use quieter methods and behind-the-scenes pressure to obtain better consideration of their claims by the ministers. But they all have to engage in politics to some extent.

There are thus at least three aspects of the relationship between politics and society which we have to examine in somewhat greater detail. First we have to look at the political divisions of the electorate and see how far they reflect the social structure of the nation. Then we have to consider the life of the parties, since parties are social groups as well as political groups. Finally we have to survey the activities of some other social groups, such as the unions or the business groups, in order to see what part they play in the political life.

Social structure and political divisions

Everyone knows that there is some connexion between the way people vote and the social groups to which people belong. Many even assume a closer connexion than the one which exists in fact. Our views on this question depend to a large extent on our prejudices and on the number of cases which we have come across, but very few people would go to the extreme of saying that voting has nothing to do with class, or with religion, or with family background, or with environment. We may know that some people do change the way they vote in the course of their life. We know that the relative support received by the parties is not static; fluctuations have affected the Liberals as well as the major parties. But we also know that voting behaviour is often sufficiently stable among many sections of the population to enable us to look for broad associations between the social structure and party allegiance.

If we want to find these associations, however, we need to obtain more precise data than the ones which we might casually gather from impressions. We need to correlate voting with the social structure of the country in general. But it is not possible to obtain first-hand information on voting behaviour, since the vote is secret: we have to rely mostly on surveys, which are accurate within certain limits only. Moreover, we have to correlate voting behaviour with a large number of social characteristics of the electors, quantitative as well as qualitative. All these characteristics contribute to form the social structure of the nation, but we have to analyse them one by one when we want to test the influence of each of them on voting behaviour. This is why the next chapter will be devoted to an outline of the social structure of Britain, although such an outline has here to be both summary and selective. As only a few pages could be devoted to an analysis which would require a volume to be given the treatment which it deserves, I have concentrated on the aspects of the social structure which seemed to have a particularly strong influence on political life.

Once we start examining the social characteristics of the electors of the parties, it becomes necessary to consider also the social characteristics of the members and leaders of the parties. It is important to know from which social groups the nation draws its M.P.s and its ministers. It is also important to compare the social background of the electors of a political party with the social background of its leaders. If the M.P.s of a party were drawn from a narrow social group while the electors of that party were not, most people would probably argue that there was something wrong with that party, that its leaders were 'unrepresentative'. It is as if, in a democracy, M.P.s of a party had to be, at least up to a point, a cross-section of the supporters of that party. Of course, this is not what is meant in law by 'representation'. Juridically, a 'representative' does not have to be drawn from the same social group as the people whom he represents. Representation means only that there must be a correspondence between the views of the representative and those of the electors. Indeed, that correspondence does not need to be very precise: in British political theory, representatives are not delegates and they do not have to follow instructions. Yet, in practice, it is sometimes commonly said or unconsciously assumed that a representative ought to belong to the same social groups as the majority of his constituents or to have at least some experience of life within these groups, in order to be able to understand and feel the basic attitudes, motivations, and desires of the members of these communities. In practice, a 'representation of social groups' cannot, of course, be mathematical, but that representation is not usually entirely ignored.

Life of the parties

The social background of electors and politicians is thus the first problem which we have to examine. When we come to consider members of parties and professional politicians, however, we are not concerned only with their social background. We are concerned also with the life of the political organizations to which they belong. Professional politicians – and in particular M.P.s – are at the apex of the pyramid of the political parties. But there are also large numbers of members who devote much of their time to political activities, although they may not be professional politicians. All over the country, thousands of people play a modest or influential part in the life of the constituency organizations. Some are content to be members; others belong to committees and have greater influence. There are also scores of active party workers in regional offices and national headquarters. Some of them are full-time politicians, as the M.P.s are; others have other activities as well. There is thus a hierarchy of power and influence in the political parties, both inside and outside Parliament. Political parties are like other organizations: they have a pyramidal structure and power is concentrated towards the top.

Hence the second problem. Parties are not just collections of M.P.s and semi-professional politicians. They are social groups; they have a corporate life. They encounter the problems which other social groups encounter as a result of that corporate life. We cannot, therefore, examine only the social background of the individuals who compose them. We must also examine the collective developments which take place in them. From which sections of the parties do leaders emerge? How long do they stay in office? Do executives represent the various groups which exist in the rank-and-file? What kind of bond is there between members and leaders? Are party 'élites' responsible to the rank-and-file or are they, despite a democratic façade, rather closed oligarchies? These are some of the points which have to be investigated.

The social life of the parties cannot be entirely divorced from the ideology and general political attitudes of the electors, members, and leaders of the political parties, however. Up to a point, one can analyse the life of the parties as one would analyse the life of any other organization: one can, for instance, measure the smoothness and efficiency of the machine without reference to political attitudes. But it becomes more difficult to do so if one wants to see whether the machine is 'democratic'. Representation, as we said, means that the views of the representatives correspond to some extent to the views of those who are represented. Efficiency is thus only one of the aspects of the life of the parties which has to be analysed; another is the problem of communication of ideas and attitudes between the bottom and the top. We have to see whether the views which are held by the leaders are also held by the rank-and-file. The leadership may be an 'oligarchy', it may manage to remain in office for long periods, it may even not be socially representative of the rank-and-file. Yet if this oligarchy tries to – or has to – be responsive to the views of the rank-and-file, it clearly will not bear all the stigmas normally attached to oligarchies.

Social background, power structure, and political views are thus profoundly linked. It becomes difficult to analyse each of these problems separately. This is why, in this book, it seemed preferable to examine each level of the political parties as a unit. We shall look at the constituency parties and associations, at the national parties, at the parliamentary parties, and, in each case, we shall consider the social background and the attitudes of members and leaders in conjunction with the life of the organization.

Interests, bureaucracy, and politics

After having examined the social background of politics and the social life of political organizations, we have to consider the influences to which politicians are subjected. These influences are often exerted by people whose main activities are not political and who do not primarily aim at playing politics when they put their case to the politicians. Broadly speaking, the men and the organizations which have such dealings with politicians belong to two main groups. There are, on the one hand, the numerous social and economic interests; there are, on the other hand, the members of the civil service. Interests and bureaucracy have different functions and a different place in society. The ways in which they exercise influence are also very different: while civil servants exercise their influence on ministers only, at least in this country, interests try to put pressure on a much wider range of political people, including even in many cases the whole of the electorate. Yet both interests and bureaucracy are at least similar in this respect: that they exercise influence on politicians. This is sufficient to give them an important place in a general picture of politics. The picture cannot be complete, unless we look at the life of these groups, at their methods of action, and at the social background of their members.

Interest groups

An important distinction has to be made at the outset among the interests. Some are interest *groups* formally constituted into associations, while others have a much looser organization and

13

much more informal means of influence. Interest *groups* are created for the defence of some particular section of the population or for the promotion of a cause. When workers complain about the pay pause, they do not only write letters to their M.P.s or lobby them at Westminster. They use their trade unions. Indeed, the leaders of these trade unions do not wait and see whether the workers are going to react; they take the initiative and they are expected by the workers to do so. They use all the means at their disposal, or, at any rate, those of the means at their disposal which they think will be most appropriate in each circumstance. Their aim is to influence the government, to make it change its policy. In this respect, the interests of the workers are thus more clearly in the hands of the unions than in those of the parties, although strictly speaking unions are not political organizations.

Of course, in this country at any rate, many unions are affiliated to one party, the Labour party. It can be claimed with some justice that these unions are, as a result, partly political. Yet, although there is indeed often close cooperation between unions and the Labour party, the main spheres of activity of the political and industrial sections of the Labour movement remain different. In any case, these unions are not the only organizations which fight for the interests of members whom they represent. Many unions are not affiliated to the Labour party. Many associations defend the interests of professional people and are not even in sympathy with the general ideas of the Labour party. The general sympathy of some of them lies with the Conservatives; others are entirely neutral. The National Farmers' Union, the British Medical Association, the National Union of Teachers, and the Automobile Association defend their members and 'represent' them, as other unions do, alongside the political parties. Other associations defend the interests of corporate bodies, of firms, of public authorities. Some of them have a complex 'federal' organization. The Confederation of British Industry, for instance, is composed of a large number of individual firms, which are already affiliated, and of trade associations grouping firms engaged in the same branch of industry. In the case of these associations of corporate bodies, the 'representation' may not be a direct representation of individuals as it is, for instance, in trade unions; it is, none the less, a representation. In the last resort, these associations of corporations indirectly represent the interests of individuals.

These interest or pressure groups differ in many ways from political parties. They bring together people who have the same interests, or at any rate one interest in common. They all try to influence governmental policy, although they do not all use the same means to exercise this influence: some have access to the government, or to the civil service, or to M.P.s, while others can try only to influence the public. But, unlike parties, they rarely, if ever, compete in elections, although they may try to exercise pressure on candidates and even 'sponsor' some of them. They do not aim to 'take power'. They do not aim to constitute a government. This is partly because their field of activity is usually narrower than that of parties: they want to force parties and politicians to accept their claims on specific points only. Some of their members and even some of their leaders may individually be politicians: this might indeed help the group. Collectively, however, as organizations, they do not wish to achieve political power.

Yet interest groups resemble political parties in one important respect. They are representative, or at least claim to be, of a very large rank-and-file. They are not always representative in the same way as political parties are. Usually and normally they cater for a clearly circumscribed section of the community: their membership may for instance be open only to people engaged in a certain manual occupation, to members of a certain profession, to certain types of firms. But even this is not always so. The interest groups which we have mentioned up to now are protective groups, in which people of a certain social section join forces to defend their own interests. Others are of a promotional character and open their membership to anyone who is interested. Some groups promote or defend causes, such as the National Council for Civil Liberties or the Council for the Preservation of Rural England; others, like the National Society for the Prevention of Cruelty to Children, defend sections of the community which cannot organize themselves for their own defence. These promotional groups are representative in the same way as political parties are.

In practice, the technical differences between the nature of representation in interest groups and in parties are not very important at this stage. What is important is that *a* form of representation should thus exist outside the political parties. There are two lines of representation which, broadly speaking, fulfil the same function, because, through them, the views, ideas, or prejudices of the people at large are channelled. It is pointless to remain on a formal plane and argue that one line is 'political' and the other is 'economic and social'. Both reach for the same aim. If the members of the cabinet want to remain in power, they have to take into account the views of interest groups as they have to take into account the views of their party and to some extent the views of the opposition party. This means that a sociology of politics has to concern itself with interest groups. Because they are numerous and vary greatly in size, in organization, and in aims, one cannot hope to do more than outline the general pattern of representation which they achieve. But this pattern of representation must at least be compared to that of the political parties.

There is one difference, however. Interest groups do not have official representation in Parliament. They have official representation on many advisory bodies, but these bodies are only advisory. In order to become influential, these interest groups have to associate or align themselves with the political parties. The association may be close or even permanent, as with many trade unions, or the alignment may be much more informal, as for most other groups. But in all cases there must be some kind of link, either with the parties, or with the government, if these interests are to achieve their aims. Thus we must not only see how interest groups are run and whether their rulers are responsible to the rank-and-file; we must also try to find out at which point there is a bridge between the interest groups and the political parties, whether it is in Parliament, at Cabinet level, or elsewhere.

Informally organized interests: civil service

Some interests may exercise influence although they are not formally organized in interest groups. Their power does not come from the fact that they have a large rank-and-file. It comes from their economic strength, from their traditional status in the nation, from the ties which may exist between their leaders and the ministers. This is what happens, or can happen, for very large businesses. Leaders of large businesses do not have to be heads of an interest *group* in order to exert influence on the government, although they may think it useful to play some part in an interest group. The role of their business organizations in the economic life of the country may be such that their advice will be sought as a matter of course. The same also obtains in other fields. In the churches, in the universities, prominent individuals exercise influence although they are not leaders of groups: the very notion of a pyramidal representation, if it exists at all in these organizations, is much more imprecise than it is, for instance, in political parties or in interest groups. The same also applies, in a different way, to some higher civil servants. Civil servants give advice to ministers and implement ministerial orders. They can, in this way, exercise influence. Yet they are not representative of any group but are, on the contrary, deemed to be both above factions and subservient to the representatives of the people.

The case of the civil service is indeed a special one. 'Controllers' or large economic interests and leading individuals in the social and cultural fields may have a personal influence. But this type of influence remains somewhat abnormal; it is an exception which runs against the general pattern of representation. One may or may not consider that big business is very influential, but care is always taken to explain or justify the amount of influence which big business might have, as if this influence contradicted the principles of representative and democratic government. The same cannot be said of the bureaucracy. The influence of the civil service is not meant to be, nor is even usually considered as being, an exception to a prevailing system of representation. It is considered as being consistent with this system, as well as necessary to modern industrial societies.

The influence of the civil service appears consistent with the representative system because civil servants are deemed merely to implement ministerial decisions. This traditional theory, however, does not strictly correspond to the reality. Now that administrative burdens have become heavy, ministers cannot be expected to take alone even all the important decisions, and the technical character of the administration has forced them to rely heavily on experts. Yet the theory is still generally upheld, although most people know that the influence of higher civil servants is large and although they also know that it is unrealistic to look for a marked decline of this influence in the future. Indeed, this influence is even reinforced by the fact that the representatives of the interest groups and the leaders of the large interests use the civil service as their channel of communication with the ministers. It is to the higher civil servants that the grievances of the groups are conveyed in the hope that these grievances will be more carefully considered by the ministers if they are channelled in that way. Civil servants thus become a necessary link between interests and government, although they are technically outside the sphere of politics.

The question would only have academic importance if the civil service were an abstract entity. But, like the political parties, the interest groups, the interests in general, the bureaucracy is composed of men and women who may or may not have certain ideas in common, who may or may not belong to the same social groups, who may or may not be a 'representative' cross-section of the nation. Their social origins are of some importance, since each party and each interest group tends naturally to be more associated with some social groups than with others. However impartial civil servants may be, however much they are trained to be impartial, they may react, if they are drawn from some social groups rather than from others, in the way most members of these social groups are commonly known to react. They may be unconsciously more favourable to some claims and to some policies than to others.

We shall therefore have to examine the bureaucracy, and particularly the higher civil service, after we have considered the political parties and the interests. We shall have to see how the representatives, the individual leaders, and the civil servants influence each other in contemporary British politics. We shall have to examine whether, or to what extent, the influence of one group on the other or of some men on others is exerted through official bodies, is centred upon Parliament, or upon Whitehall. We shall have to see what importance can still be attributed to personal contacts, old friendships, or a common background. Some argue that, in modern Britain as in the past, the privilege of running the country still firmly remains in small, fairly closed, and tightly knit social groups in which there may be occasional differences of opinion but where there is a common attitude and a common approach to major problems. This is the question of the 'ruling class' and of more modern versions of the same type of theory. One must examine this question, although in the scope of such a small book one cannot do much more than draw some conclusions from the alliances and oppositions which can be noticed in the political world. In many respects, the answers to such a question are liable to be modified, perhaps very rapidly, in the future. The old and traditional forces in finance and in industry are being replaced by more modern 'technocratic' forces. The relationship between the social and economic forces has perhaps never been more fluid and more open to extensive modifications.

The general plan of this book is thus simple. In the next chapter, we shall outline the social structure of Britain. The following three chapters are devoted to the parties, and chiefly to the two main parties, because, at any rate at present, the influence of the Liberal party on the inner circles of politics remains very limited. We shall start with the electors and move upwards from the members to the politicians and the leaders. We shall then turn briefly to the representation of interests and to the social structure of the bureaucracy. We shall afterwards consider how parties, interests, and bureaucracy work with each other and against one another. We shall examine the points of contact and try to see to what extent contacts simply develop because the same people belong to two or more groups. Finally we shall try to see whether these contacts produce a number of independent circles of power, or are one single large ruling circle, whose members are often in agreement despite the differences of opinion which exist in the country.

CHAPTER TWO

The Social Structure: an Outline

POLITICS is probably affected by all the forces which shape the social structure of a country. But some aspects of the social structure have a more direct impact on political life. Since we are concerned here with general characteristics, it seems appropriate to consider briefly, in the first place, in what way British society differs from other industrial societies. It is very homogeneous – although, of course, seen from the outside, differences between the North and the South may often seem glaring. It is heavily urbanized. Tradition still plays an important part in determining many of its aspects. Secondly, since politics is commonly associated with class, the purpose of this chapter is to look at some components of the British class system and, in particular, at the influence which occupations and education seem to have in determining it.

A homogeneous country

Britain is probably the most homogeneous of all industrial countries. It is homogeneous because it is small, but this is not the only reason, for some smaller countries, like Belgium or Switzerland, have more social diversity than Britain. Moreover, sources of diversity are also present in Britain, as is shown by the division of the United Kingdom into four countries, England, Wales, Scotland, and Northern Ireland. What makes Britain appear homogeneous is the fact that the population is not uniformly spread in these four countries but highly concentrated in a small area. In the early part of the nineteenth century, the population of England became much greater than that of the three other countries combined and a century later Southern Ireland seceded from the United Kingdom. As a result, over 80 per cent of the whole British population now reside in England.

Nor is this all. Even in England, one would find more

diversity if the population were uniformly spread over the 50,000 square miles from Land's End to Margate and from the Isle of Wight to Cumberland. In fact, the population is concentrated in a strip of territory of about half the total area of England. This strip, roughly 300 miles long and less than 100 miles wide, contains the main centres of population. Outside this strip, in the extreme North, in the South-West, in East Anglia, densities are lower. In the twenty-five geographical counties which form the thickly populated area, there live thirty-five million people, or 80 per cent of all Englishmen and two-thirds of the population of the British Isles.

Table 1. *Population (millions)*

	1801	1841	1901	1951	1966 (est.)
England	8·8	14·9	30·5	41·1	45·4
Wales	0·6	1·0	2·0	2·6	2·7
Scotland	1·6	2·6	4·5	5·1	5·2
N. Ireland	1·4	1·7	1·2	1·4	1·5
TOTAL	11·9	20·2	38·2	50·2	54·8
Percentage England	69	74	80	82	82·8

(from *Census* reports. For 1801, Porter, *Progress of the Nation*, J. Murray, 1847, p. 8. For 1966, Annual Abstract of Statistics, 1967, pp. 7–11)

The population is not only heavily concentrated in the centre and South-East. It also came to be agglomerated in large conurbations on a scale which has not been achieved in other industrial countries. The inhabitants of the central strip do not live in small villages and medium-sized towns as does the population of Belgium or Holland. They are not scattered over the area: they crowd into huge urban areas which spread tentacles over miles of road and often come very near to joining each other. Moreover, many other large towns lack the distinctive character which cathedral towns, for instance, have. No industrial country has such a large proportion of its population concentrated in so few urban areas. While almost two-fifths of the British people live in the seven major conurbations and almost one-fifth in the largest of all, the Metropolis, the rural districts house a mere 20 per cent of the population. Indeed, many of those who live in 'rural' districts are commuters who belong to the large centres and have simply 'overspilled', by taste or necessity, into the neighbouring countryside.

This is not, of course, the whole picture. At the extremities of the country, in South-West England, Wales, Northern Scotland or Northern Ireland, large towns are rare. Only 29 per cent of Welshmen, 44 per cent of Scots (two-thirds of these in Glasgow and Edinburgh) and 32 per cent of Ulstermen (nine-tenths of these in Belfast) live in towns of 50,000 inhabitants or more. The largest town in Cornwall has only 37,000 inhabitants and one-tenth of the total population of the county. Overall, however, large urban areas weigh much more in the social structure of Britain than they do in that of France, Italy, or even Germany. So much population and so many economic activities have been concentrated in the central part of England that the other parts have had, willy nilly, to follow the lead.

Within the central part of England the predominance of London increases the homogeneous character of the country. Germany never really had a capital; Italy has two; the supremacy of Paris has had to be imposed. London did not become the political, social, economic, cultural capital of the country as a result of a decision taken by some seventeenth- or eighteenth-century monarch. It has long been unchallenged, even though its predominance may still be resented in many parts of the provinces. Its location is such that it is within easy reach of the large majority and can easily service large masses of people. At least half the British people can go to London on business and return home on the same day. Things might have been different if, as Paris is to most Frenchmen, London had been as distant to most British people as it is to the Scots.

Hence the centralization of business, of the administration, and of the media of mass culture in the Metropolis. Hence the unique development of a national press covering all Britain daily and offering the same national news at the expense of regional and local information. Radio and television may have helped to centralize even the most diverse countries; nowhere except in Britain is it possible for the citizens of a country of fifty-five million inhabitants to go from one part of the country to another and find, as a matter of course, their favourite newspaper on their breakfast table. If a Frenchmen or a German moves 200 miles, he will realize anew, every day, that he now belongs to a new community, because he will have to read a regional newspaper. An Englishman may find, while talking to his new colleagues, to his neighbours, that the accent has changed, that some customs are different; he might be treated as a 'foreigner'. At least one thing remains solid, and that is the mass culture which he absorbs every day.

The absence of a 'peasant class'

Britain is homogeneous not only because of its conurbations and because of London. It is also homogeneous because it does not possess, like other European countries and even North America, a 'peasant class', living independently from the rest of the community and having developed its own traditions.

In the first place, Britain has a small agricultural population. Agriculture diminished so rapidly in the course of the nineteenth century that, around 1930, it seemed on the point of disappearing altogether. The fall has been halted, largely because of the panic caused by the Second World War: agriculture is now well protected and it is in no danger of losing its present position in the economic life of the country. But there has been no movement of workers back to agriculture and increased production has been almost entirely due to mechanization. No large country in the world has a smaller proportion of its population working on the land. While agriculture employs one man in ten or even one man in five in other industrial countries, it only employs one man in twenty in Britian.

The agricultural community is not only smaller than elsewhere; it is different. It is much more integrated to the social structure of the nation than it is in other countries. This is because, while English agriculture was transformed by an economic revolution in the eighteenth and nineteenth centuries, the type of social revolution which took place on the land in other parts of Europe never took place in Britain. After 1789, in France and in many parts of Western Europe, agrarian reform was one of the main political battles. Tension between landlords and farmers mounted. Landlords were forced to abandon their rights in some areas; in others they voluntarily renounced them. Almost everywhere in North-Western Europe the traditional hierarchy between landlord and farmer was broken.

In Britain, at any rate in much of England, this pressure on the landlords did not materialize. In fact, the landlords were often the originators of the economic revolution of the eighteenth century. They introduced new methods. Stock raising and sheep farming were often substituted for agriculture proper. Manpower was saved and many rural workers were forced out of the land. The farmers who remained were not only probably more prosperous than their counterparts on the Continent; they also continued to accept the traditional social hierarchy of landowners, farmers, and labourers. The landed gentry succeeded in keeping, if not its privileges, at least its social status.

As a result, a *peasantry* did not develop in Britain, while it developed in many continental countries. Independent smallholders – independent, but usually not well-off – formed, and still form, a class of their own in France, as they also do, although to a more limited extent, in many parts of North-Western Europe. They also form an independent class in the United States. These peasants are at the margin of industrial societies. They are self-employed; in a sense, they might even be said to be 'capitalists'. But they are 'capitalists' living in precarious conditions. They often distrust the 'organization' of modern industrial societies and attack the State on semi-anarchistic grounds. They are sometimes ideologically radical. But their radicalism does not lead them necessarily to ally themselves with the industrial workers. Agrarian 'populism' does not go hand in hand with socialism. Russia and the Communist countries of Eastern Europe never really integrated the peasants in their new society and they have been repeatedly embarrassed by the agricultural problem. Peasants really and truly constitute a class of their own. They often form parties. They reject the centralization which modern societies impose. They loathe

the bureaucracy which is the instrument of that centralization. They have an individualistic approach to politics. In Britain, where the rural population is small, where the economic conditions under which it lives are different, where the social structure on the land has remained more traditional, these disruptive tendencies have been avoided. Society did not have to reckon with the members of the farming community as an element apart. Political parties have dealt with them as if they were engaged in an 'occupation' or an 'industry' like any other.

British society is therefore much more integrated than most societies on the Continent. Despité regional differences and apart from the extremities of the country which are out of reach of this uniform culture, Britain is essentially a homogeneous nation in which the major distinctions are not based on geography, but on social and economic conditions. One cannot begin to describe the structure of France, Germany, the United States, or even Belgium or Switzerland, without first considering in detail profound regional differences which are sometimes as important as national characteristics. These differences cut across nation-wide social and economic problems. But, in Britain, national class differences are the main divisions of society. The British class system may be complex, although it is perhaps no more complex than the class system of other industrial countries. It may be different, as it clearly is in some of its aspects. It is, at any rate, the main line of division between the British people. One of the differences between Britain and other countries is perhaps that class divisions play a much greater part in the structure of British society simply because, elsewhere, local characteristics often unite people of all classes to an extent which is rarely attained in Britain.

Components of the class structure: class and status

We must pause a moment, however, because we will have to use the word 'class' on almost every page of this book and class requires an element of explanation. In ordinary language, everyone uses 'class' in a very loose fashion and the definition changes according to different situations. 'Scientific' language is unfortunately not much more precise. It would be much easier if we had a simple and clear definition, but the only one which fitted this description was the marxian formula and it is no longer adequate. Marx divided the population of industrial capitalist societies into two classes, bourgeois and proletarian, and he defined the bourgeois as being those who owned the means of production. This distinction presupposed that those who *owned* the means of production were also those who *controlled* them: this assumption was legitimate in principle, since one of the main rights of an owner is that he can use his property. However, with the growth of joint-stock companies, ownership and control of the means of production became more and more divorced. Large quantities of people acquired shares without being interested in the control of the companies of which they legally owned a portion. They simply considered these shares as means of acquiring dividends or, more recently, as means of making capital gains.

Control often fell into the hands of directors who had only small fractions of the capital and even in the hands of salaried managers who did not own any capital at all. Marx had realised the importance of control alongside ownership. He did foresee the development of the managerial class. He did not, and could not, envisage the extent of the change which was about to take place. Even if he had envisaged it, he could not have saved his definition by substituting control for ownership, because control is so vague that, if one substitutes one notion for the other, the simplicity of the definition – and thereby its clarity – disappears in the process. One simply cannot use 'control' as a means of distinguishing classes *in general*; one can examine the cases of individuals and conclude that these men control a certain industry. But control does not have a precise legal meaning: it cannot be used *a priori* to divide society into groups and to separate the sheep from the goats.

Meanwhile, it became clearer and clearer that there was more than one component entering into the definition of class. Class has a multitude of aspects, economic as well as social. One may distinguish these components for the purpose of analysis; one must always remember that they are not independent of each other and that each of them reverberates on all the others. An economic component such as *income* depends on occupation. *Occupations* do not have an economic aspect only, since status and social values, as well as material benefits, are attached to them. Occupations largely depend on education. *Education*, which plays a part in determining class independently of the occupation and income which it may provide, is also dependent on other factors, particularly on the *family background*. Yet neither income nor occupation are entirely dependent on education, nor is income always closely related to occupation: in the same occupation, people may earn different incomes and the variations can often be large. Apart from income, occupation, education, family background, a host of other social characteristics seem to play a large part in determining class divisions: language, manners, general social education seem sometimes to play a larger part in conversations about class, at any rate in Britain, than some other components.

However, in this country at least, occupation and education are probably the two most important criteria. They are the only two criteria about which a large amount of information is readily available. Detailed information about incomes is difficult to obtain. Family background and social manners are often unknown. Hence, partly for practical reasons, partly because of the undeniable influence which they have, we shall very often limit the analysis of the social background to occupations and to education. This should not be taken as meaning that class can be defined in terms of these two only, and we shall indeed introduce other factors when the detailed examination of a section of society requires it specifically.

We have mentioned, up to now, the *objective* components of class. The population of the country can be subdivided into various categories by looking at tables of incomes, tables of occupations, or educational tables, although we do not ask people whether they agree with these classifications or not. The categories may often be difficult to draw. There are many problems at the borderline, particularly when occupations are considered, since occupations are numerous and have to be grouped together: these groupings are always somewhat arbitrary. Yet one can make some classifications. One could even classify people on the basis of their accent or manners if one took the trouble to interview a sufficiently large sample of people.

These objective criteria are not the only ones, however; *subjective* criteria can also be very important. It is not sufficient to know whether people should be classified in a certain way; one must also know whether people feel that they should be classified in that way. Marx insisted on the fact that one of the criteria of class was the consciousness which people had of belonging to the same class. The left has often emphasized the need for developing 'class-consciousness' in the proletariat. If there is a need for developing class-consciousness, it is clearly because the consciousness, the realization that one belongs to a certain class, is not as widespread as it might be. We may classify people into categories; they might not necessarily agree with our type of categories and they might prefer their own. Experiments have been conducted along these lines, particularly where occupations were concerned. In the late 1940s, J. Hall and D. Caradog-Jones made a survey in order to find how different people 'scaled' occupations. The great bulk of the respondents agreed on a broad scale. But there were variations from the 'norm'. Moreover, it has been argued from later inquiries that the measure of agreement would have been smaller if the sample had contained more manual workers: it seems that manual workers often place manual occupations much higher on the scale of occupations than non-manual workers do. This is not simply because most people tend to upgrade their own occupation, but more generally because people are divided on the social usefulness of manual labour, management, and professional activities. People thus do not place themselves and others at the point one might have expected. Whether they are right or wrong is irrelevant, because this subjective ranking may be as important a guide to the understanding of human behaviour as the objective and apparently 'scientific' ranking which can be produced by sociologists.

Subjective elements are not confined to the ranking of occupations. In reality, differences in the ranking of occupations indicate profound disagreements about the structure of society and about what society should be. Problems raised by the subjective approach are thus so distinct from problems raised by the objective approach that it has sometimes been argued that two different words should be used. Objective components of the social structure would constitute the *class* system, while subjective elements would constitute the *status* relationships. But the vocabulary has rarely been strictly adhered to and we can only say that there are both objective and subjective components in the social structure of any society.

One of the reasons why it is difficult to distinguish between the two concepts is because the objective and subjective components have an obvious influence on one another. We saw already that 'objective' classifications of occupations are somewhat arbitrary and depend to some extent on a subjective ranking. Conversely, the subjective ranking is partly the consequence of objective criteria. Surveys use a simple method which consists in asking persons who are interviewed to state the social class to which they assign themselves. One does find that this 'self-assigned social class' or 'status' follows to some extent the occupational divisions, although there are appreciable variations. Most manual workers assign themselves to the working class, but many consider that they belong to the middle or lower middle class, as the Table 2 indicates.

About a third of the manual workers who voted Labour and half the manual workers who voted for other parties assigned themselves to various subdivisions of the middle class. Occupations do, therefore, influence 'subjective social class' to some extent. Education and income probably also play a part. A study of Woodford showed that manual workers who owned their house or owned a car were less likely than others to consider themselves part of the 'working class'.

There are many difficulties, however. Much depends on the wording of the question. An American survey used the expression 'lower class' instead of 'working class' as an alternative to 'middle class'. This resulted in a surprisingly large proportion of 'middle class' people, simply because respondents found it difficult to consider themselves as belonging to a 'lower class'. Moreover, we do not know exactly what people mean when they answer that they are 'middle' or 'working class'. If one wants to know what people really think about their own class and that of other people, one must ask more than one question and indeed be prepared to let people speak without forcing them to answer ready-made questions. Depth investigations have to be conducted. Those which have been undertaken in the United States and in Britain, both in village and suburban communities, did show that 'status' relationships are, as one might have expected,

Table 2. '*Self-assigned class*' *of* manual *workers only* (percentages)

	Labour voters	Other voters
Upper middle class	–	3
Middle class	14	31
Lower middle class	16	16
Total middle	30	50
Skilled working class	27	28
Labouring working class	40	18
Total working	67	46
Don't know	3	4
	100	100

(from M. Abrams and R. Rose, *Must Labour Lose?*, Penguin Books, 1961, p. 18)

infinitely more complex than the straightforward 'subjective' assessments of the type mentioned in the previous table seem to suggest. The difficulty, however, is that these depth investigations require long interviews and cannot easily be applied to a 'sample' of a community. The answers which are obtained are qualitative, not quantitative, and therefore cannot be easily compared. One often runs the risk of generalizing from a few examples and it is usually impossible to find out whether the answers are 'typical' or 'average'. Until we have the means of multiplying inquiries of this kind, we shall not have a general picture. However important these documents may be, they will probably have to be considered as 'case-studies' for a long time to come.

Occupation, income, and social class

Let us now return to the objective components of class, and particularly to the most important ones which are occupation (plus income) and education. There is more than one way of classifying occupations, but, if one is concerned with defining classes, one will naturally try to group together, irrespective of industry, all those who have the same degree of skill, all those who are in the same supervisory capacity, etc. This is not easy, and indeed somewhat arbitrary, as we saw: it was in order to avoid ranking occupations in an arbitrary fashion that Hall and Caradog-Jones preferred to use a scale given by a sample of respondents. This method is not fool-proof either, not only because respondents rank occupations somewhat differently, but also because there are so many occupations that one cannot ask respondents to rank all of them. One of the greatest difficulties occurs at the borderline between 'manual' and 'non-manual' jobs. Some 'non-manual' jobs are so routine that they resemble unskilled manual jobs. The distinction seems to be sometimes based on 'status' more than on an objective assessment of the manual component of the work.

Let us assume that these difficulties are overcome. Even if many routine jobs are classified as 'non-manual', Britain still remains mainly populated by manual workers. The Census of 1961 drew two tables for England and Wales: one divides the population into five classes, but it is very unsatisfactory for the middle groups, because it lumps routine non-manual workers with skilled manual workers, and even for class 1, which includes many small shopkeepers as well as big businessmen. The other table divides the working population into seventeen 'socio-economic groups' and it gives a much more precise picture of the situation.

The division into socio-economic groups clearly indicates that manual workers greatly outnumber non-manual workers. The former constituted about two-thirds of the working population in England and Wales in 1961. The white-collar section may seem very large, perhaps because white-collar workers flock every morning into the centres of the main cities while manual workers are dispersed along the industrial belt of the large towns. In reality, the working population of Britain is still predominantly composed of manual workers.

Admittedly, with one-third of the working population engaged in non-manual jobs, the white-collar revolution is well

Table 3. *Distribution of the male working population in England and Wales, 1961*

Classes		Socio-economic groups		
1 Professional, proprietorial	4	Proprietorial and managerial		12·5
2 Intermediate (non-manual)	15	farmers	2	
3 Skilled manual and white-collar routine	51	employers, managers (large)	3·5	
4 Partly skilled (manual)	21	employers, managers (small)	6	
5 Unskilled	9	professional (self-employed)	1	
	100	Other non-manual		20·5
		professional (employees)	3	
		intermediate	4	
		junior non-manual	12·5	
		personal service	1	
		Manual		63·5
		foremen and supervisors	3·5	
		skilled	31·5	
		semi-skilled	15	
		unskilled	8	
		own account	3·5	
		agricultural workers	2	
		Armed forces		2
		Indefinite		1·5
				100

(from *Census* of England and Wales, 1961)

under way in Britain. Not only underdeveloped countries, but even many developed countries do not have such a large middle and lower middle class. It has been shown that, in industrial societies, the sector of production of raw materials (mining, agriculture), known as the primary sector, gradually shrinks and that the sector of manufacturing and allied industries (secondary sector) first increases and eventually also shrinks. The great winner is the tertiary sector, that of services, transport, administration. While these developments take place, the proportion of manual workers gradually decreases. In Britain, one can still note the increase of the secondary sector, but the primary sector is diminishing.

The white-collar group increases, and it increases quickly. White-collar workers formed only 4 per cent of the working population in 1901; they formed 10·5 per cent of the working population in 1951. This 250 per cent increase in percentage is startling. Yet, despite their increase in numbers and in pro-

Table 4. *Employment in various industries in Britain in 1966*

	Numbers in 1966 (thousands)	Increase (+) or decrease (−) between 1956 and 1966
Agriculture, forestry, fishing	478	− 642
Mining and quarrying	580	− 282
Manufacturing	9,056	− 472
Construction	1,725	+ 147
Gas, electricity and water	431	+ 48
Transport and communication	1,629	− 186
Distributive trades	3,035	+ 113
Professional, finance, miscellaneous	5,468	+ 1,220
Central and local government	1,381	+ 47
Armed forces	417	− 334
Unemployed	281	+ 64

(from *Annual Abstract of Statistics*, H.M.S.O., (1964), p. 107 and (1967), p. 109)

portion, white-collar workers are still far fewer than manual workers. Moreover, this 250 per cent increase has not been produced entirely at the expense of the manual workers or at the expense of the primary and secondary sectors only. White-collars jobs have been filled by women much more than by men: women were not more than one-eighth of the clerical workers in 1901; they are now in a majority. This increase coincided with

34

a sharp decline in the numbers of people employed in domestic services: yet domestic servants belong to the tertiary sector.

Two conclusions seem to emerge fairly clearly: manual workers, particularly male manual workers, are likely to remain in a majority in the working population for many years to come. If the present rate of growth of non-manual jobs remains the same as it was in the last few decades, at about 1 or 1·5 per cent of the working population per decade, the manual workers are not likely to be overtaken by the other groups before three-quarters of a century. At the same time, the merging between people in manual and non-manual jobs, at the bottom of the scale, is likely to increase rather than decrease. The proportion of non-manual workers among women is greater than among men; the absolute numbers of women are even greater than those of men in some branches of the tertiary sector. In concrete terms, this means that many women who work in non-manual 'lower middle class' jobs are the wives or the daughters of men who work in manual jobs. As a result, from the point of view of an objective assessment of class, the division between manual and non-manual jobs is not likely to be very meaningful in many occupations where women are employed in large numbers. Tradition places the 'working class' under the 'lower middle class': the validity of this hierarchy may soon no longer be so apparent.

This breakdown of the hierarchy is a slow process, however, and large sections of the lower middle class continue to feel that they belong to a different world from that of the working class, particularly when the husband's job (and not just the wife's job) is a white-collar one. This feeling of superior status has indeed recently been exacerbated in some sectors because many members of the lower middle class no longer have – or think that they have – as many material advantages as they used to have. They have retained some advantages: the conditions of work are more pleasant, pensions are more common, many earn salaries and not wages and enjoy some material benefits and a higher status as a result. However, the gradual equalization between these salaries and the manual workers' wages is often bitterly resented. Certain detailed studies have showed that the differentials have indeed sharply diminished. Average earnings of men in industry were over £18 in 1964 and £20 in 1966; already in 1960 over 10 per cent of the manual workers had earned wages of £25 a week or more: people in white-collar jobs, under the level of manager, do not seem to have better prospects. They may earn more regular salaries, they may even gradually increase their earnings over the years while the manual workers see their wages diminish when they are older. The over-all size of the earnings and the prospects of good salaries – in the form of four-figure incomes – are probably little if at all better in white-collar jobs.

Table 5. *Estimated classification of family incomes by ranges of income before tax*

Incomes	Percentage of the total number of incomes in each group for each financial year		
£	1954–5	1959–60	1964–5
Under 300	23·0	12·6	2·0
300–499	32·5	22·0	17·7
500–799	31·5	35·7	26·0
800–999	6·6	14·0	16·9
1,000 or more	6·4	15·7	27·4
	100	100	100

(from *Annual Abstract of Statistics*, H.M.S.O., (1967), pp. 286–7)

It is therefore no longer clear whether white-collar workers can claim to be 'in the middle', between manual workers, who constitute the majority, and managerial and professional people, who constitute a very small minority, perhaps not much more than 4 or 5 per cent of the population. These 4 or 5 per cent have normally much larger incomes – except perhaps at the very beginning of their careers – than either manual or white-collar workers. Their influence in decision-making in all sectors of the economic and social life of the nation is unquestionably very large. Even if we leave aside the question of the recruitment of the members of these groups, it is undeniable that this small minority has many advantages, material and otherwise, which members of the other two groups do not have. Admittedly we should distinguish various categories within this minority: we shall do so to some extent in the following pages. Yet the managerial and professional 'class' as a whole appears very different from the other two 'classes' which, on the contrary, resemble each other more than is sometimes said. Many manual jobs have become less tiring and, if not always positively agreeable, at any rate less disagreeable. Work in extractive and heavy manufacturing industries may not have changed markedly in character in recent years, but there are more jobs in light engineering which may be boring but are not dirty. At the same time, white-collar and other routine non-manual workers do not enjoy the same status as in the past and they do not receive as many material advantages. Members of the managerial and professional groups do not enjoy all the advantages they did in the past, but, on the whole, they remain above members of the two other groups, while the position of white-collar workers becomes less different from that of manual workers.

Education and social class

We have said already that occupation and education were probably the two most important objective components of the social structure. Yet, broadly speaking, the division of the country on educational lines seems to repeat and underline the division of the country on occupational lines. Manual workers are early school leavers. Those who stay at school after sixteen normally enter white-collar, managerial, or professional jobs. Although the proportion of children who stayed at school after fifteen has increased markedly since the war, it is still a very small minority from which very few manual workers will be recruited.*

Because most manual workers have left school at an early age, education does not help us very much to understand differences

* We are concerned here with the education of those who are now manual workers, not with the opportunities which sons of manual workers may have. This last question is considered later in this chapter.

between them. But, at the other end of the social scale, educational differences can be of great importance, particularly in Britain, for two main reasons. Firstly, education is often the means by which the non-manual groups come to be subdivided into their clerical, managerial, and professional sections. Secondly, because public schools exist, education has, in this country, a definite impact on social stratification over and above occupations, and it accounts for the existence of informal links between men living in different walks of life. Some values have also been maintained which otherwise might not have subsisted. The more one goes up the social structure, the more education, rather than occupation, helps to define subtle boundaries between groups and informal connexions between individuals.

Table 6. *Education in England and Wales*

| | 1938 | | 1958 | |
	Numbers (thousands)	Percentage of age group	Numbers (thousands)	Percentage of age group
To 14	5,247	86·7	6,939	93·9
15	99		243	
16	50	6·1	125	14·7
17	19		55	
18 and over	10		22	
	5,425		7,384	

(from *Annual Abstract of Statistics*, 1960, H.M.S.O., p. 85)

State education is divided into primary, secondary (grammar and modern), and university education. Compared with the first of these three groups, the second and the third look ridiculously small. About a fifth of the children aged fifteen to nineteen stay at school: they are mainly those who go to grammar schools and technical schools. This is already a small proportion, but numbers fall very quickly between sixteen and seventeen: less than 15 per cent of the children complete their grammar school education. Yet only about half these children find their way into a university. Although the universities have doubled their intake of the forties and fifties, they still absorb only 4 or 5 per cent of the young men and women in the age groups eighteen to twenty-two. This is a much smaller proportion than the one attained in many European countries and in the United States, and it is likely to remain smaller in Britain than elsewhere for many years to come. Oxford and Cambridge, which have not increased their intake in the same proportion as the other universities, take only about one-eighth of the total student population. At the present rate, only about one out of every hundred children can expect to enter one of the older universities.

The cultural gap between the large majority who went to secondary modern schools and the small minority who went to grammar schools is too often stressed to need further analysis. Yet the public schools superimpose a further distinction in the education system which is surely no less important and which is peculiar to this country. Abroad, outside the State education system, one finds usually private schools only: children are sent to these schools for religious reasons or because they have failed the State examinations. In Britain, *private* schools may be used in similar situations, although the State system includes also a large number of aided schools which have a definite religious character. The middle-class élite is formed, however, not through the private schools, but through the public schools.

The importance of the public schools bears little relationship to the numbers which go through them. The principal girls' schools and the boys' schools which are listed as Headmasters' Conference schools take between them no more than 4 or 5 per cent of the total numbers of boys and girls in each age group and this percentage remains static: the bulk of the increase in full-time education after fifteen has taken place, and will continue to take place, in State supported schools. While three-quarters of the children who were at school after fifteen in the early 1960s were in a maintained school, this percentage had grown to over four-fifths by the late 1960s.

General figures are misleading, moreover, because they are obtained by lumping together all the public schools, whatever their prestige and their educational value may be. Admittedly this overall classification gives an idea of the percentage of parents who are prepared to send their children even to a minor public school on the grounds, presumably, that any public school education is a better passport to life than even the best of the grammar schools. Yet the inner circle of the public schools, most of which are boarding, constitutes the really important phenomenon. These public schools explain the existence of the others: if they did not exist, the others would probably be relegated to the status of private schools and would have no greater prestige than private schools in other countries. This inner circle, represented by the nine Clarendon schools, has an

Table 7. *Pupils on the registers of schools, England and Wales, 1966*

| | Under 15 | | Over 15 | |
	Numbers (thousands)	Percentage	Numbers (thousands)	Percentage
Maintained	7,183	91·9	641	81·8
Special	76	0·9	10	1·3
Direct grant	117	1·5	42	5·4
Independent	309	3·9	77	9·8
Other	141	1·8	13	1·7
	7,826	100	783	100

(from *Annual Abstract of Statistics*, 1967, H.M.S.O., p. 85)

intake of no more than 2 per cent of the total grammar school population and it caters for about a third of a per cent of the total British population in each group.*

Public schools, even the best known ones, are not really old. But they have been so integrated in the British social system

* These nine schools – Eton, Harrow, Rugby, Winchester, West-minster, Charterhouse, Merchant Taylors', Shrewsbury, St Paul's – are known as 'Clarendon' because they were the object of the investi-gation of a Royal Commission headed by Lord Clarendon in 1864. Since many studies have taken these nine schools as examples of 'ex-clusive' public schools, we shall have to follow suit, but the division between Clarendon and non-Clarendon does not in fact exactly corres-pond to the division between 'exclusive' and 'less exclusive'.

that they seem to be as old and well-established as such immemorial institutions as the monarchy and Parliament. It is difficult to distinguish between the reality and the myth when public schools, particularly the best ones, are concerned. It is also difficult to distinguish between their intrinsic academic value and the social value which the best ones give to those who have gone through them. It is even difficult to disentangle reality from appearance in the case of these contacts. Most of the boys who go to the best public schools are sons of professional and managerial people; many belong to the upper strata of these groups and to the aristocracy. The latter, at any rate, have many contacts with other members of the same groups and would probably have no difficulty in finding a job through their families.

Yet some of these advantages are more than just a myth. The public schools have greater academic – particularly scientific – facilities. Boys and girls are taught and educated on a more individual basis. They acquire friends coming from a wide range of middle-class groups. Without the public schools, sons of managerial and professional people would meet only occasionally. If they did not go to boarding schools, they would not know each other so well. If they went to grammar schools, they would meet children from other social groups, lower down the social scale, and they would not have so many friends among children at the same level in the social hierarchy. The only children from the same level in the social hierarchy whom they would come to know would be, in most cases, children from the same section of the middle class as the one in which their father happens to be. At the public schools, they meet children coming from all sections of the middle class or upper middle class. An integration of the upper strata of society is realized at the expense of a wider variety of contacts with children lower down the social scale. The social hierarchy, as well as the closely knit character of the British middle and upper middle class, is more easily perpetuated.

Public schools help to create 'two nations'; indeed, since State schools are divided into grammar and secondary modern schools, the whole system of education helps to create three nations. At the same time, public schools have succeeded in shaping a socially integrated élite. They have helped to perpetuate some of the power and many of the values of the middle and upper classes. They have also prevented, to some extent at least, the upper levels of the middle class from breaking up into well-defined and antagonistic sections. If, as seems likely, school children educated at grammar schools or at minor public schools come to acquire a greater proportion of the managerial and professional jobs, this integrated character of the upper middle class might diminish in the future. Indeed, similar changes may affect the whole middle class, if comprehensive schools become numerous gradually. Both developments may ultimately transform the fabric of politics.

Mobility, hierarchy, and equality in British society

Education, even at grammar schools, and more so at public schools, is to a large extent the product of family background. Careers depend partly on education and partly on family contacts. Incomes depend on careers, at least in broad terms. Meanwhile, large incomes enable parents to send their children to better schools and therefore to give them better career prospects. The social structure seems condemned, as a result, to perpetual immobility. Indeed, one can add to these automatic influences of income, occupation, and education a number of subtle, yet important, psychological pressures: workers and their children often consider higher education as an unknown world; they do not know the opportunities existing in the managerial sphere. These children often want to start earning money early in life for their own enjoyment or in order to relieve their parents from financial burdens. The lack of mobility from one social class to another is not, as a result, very surprising. Only a trickle of children are likely to be able, and indeed to be willing, to move up the social ladder.

Such tendencies are general: they are not peculiar to Britain. In fact, the British record of social mobility does not seem to be one of the worst in modern industrial societies. An inquiry, admittedly a partial one, showed that mobility was rather greater in Britain than in the United States, and markedly greater than in France and Italy. The numbers of school children from the working class who go to Eton are clearly not large, but the proportion of school children who go to grammar schools has markedly increased. It progresses sufficiently quickly to make it possible to envisage a period, in the fairly near future, when children of manual workers will no longer be under-represented in grammar schools. In universities, the numbers of undergraduates coming from manual workers' homes has increased, although they do not correspond to the proportion of manual workers in the community. Partly as a result, the proportion of white-collar workers coming from working-class homes has also increased: it has moved from one-third to about half in recent decades. Taken together, these increases indicate that opportunities are no longer as unequally distributed as in the past. They will probably be more equally distributed in the future.

Table 8. *Social background of children in grammar schools and of undergraduates in universities* (percentages)

	Working population (1951)	Grammar schools (1957)	Universities (1957)
Professional and inter-mediate	12	18	29
Clerical	13	19	14
Skilled manual	40	41	24
Semi-skilled and un-skilled	33	10	5
Unknown	2	12	28
	100	100	100

(from *15 to 18*: Crowther report, Part 2, pp. 13 and 62)

These changes concern the society of tomorrow. They are probably already giving rise to the development, at the top of the social structure, of a managerial class which does not come from the traditional upper middle class. Yet, for the time being, the social structure of Britain retains its traditional façade. New members are introduced, on an individual basis, into a compact and well-integrated upper middle class group. As we saw, this integration is more than partly maintained by the public schools. It has also been maintained because British society has been isolated from the revolutions and other upheavals which have shaken Continental countries. While elsewhere the aristocracy has almost disappeared or has been relegated to irrelevant corners of society, it still continues to have its place at the top in Britain.

Whether the monarchy buttresses the aristocracy or whether the aristocracy buttresses the monarchy is a matter for academic discussion. The general point is that, in contemporary Britain, there are both a monarchy and an aristocracy, and that the monarchy is not conceived of as being 'democratic', nor as having to be 'democratic', by the mass of the people: it is conceived of as being the apex of a social pyramid. Likewise, the aristocracy has its place earmarked at the top of the pyramid. Admittedly the composition of the aristocracy is flexible and always has been; admittedly also, the aristocracy may no longer play, as of right, an important part in the economic life of the nation. Yet its very existence indicates that a pyramid of status is officially recognized by the State; this official pyramid is also accepted, if not by the whole nation, at least by large sections of the middle and upper middle class.

The aristocracy thus perpetuates a hierarchy in British society. It helps also to integrate the top sections of the community. What public schools do for sons of the upper middle class early in their life, the peerage and the House of Lords do for many successful men at a later age. The House of Lords is more than a mere symbol; it is a concrete proof of the permanence of a social hierarchy in Britain; it is even to some extent a meeting place for people belonging to different branches of the managerial and professional worlds. The title counts, but also the club itself. The Upper House provides a platform not only for the more prolix or less busy generals, businessmen, lawyers, administrators, and politicians who have become peers, but even for the others, because it enables them to defend their point of view or their interests if their views are attacked or these interests threatened.

The upper sections of society are thus both integrated and hierarchically organized. The places in the hierarchy are defined while at the same time there are many clubs which enable people coming from various lines of activity to meet and to know each other. At the other end of society, however, Britain contains another and much larger section in which the notion of hierarchy is almost totally absent. Accent, breeding, or education in the social sense have an importance within the compass of the middle and upper middle class. Among manual workers, problems are different. The feelings of hierarchy are certainly absent from large fractions of the working class, even though deference is not entirely unknown in some sections. It is perhaps because so many British workers do not have a feeling of inferiority towards the upper classes that the British working class as a whole does not seem to have the sense of frustration which is so often conspicuous among working classes on the Continent.

In Britain, a complex equilibrium has generally been maintained between the rulers and the ruled, the 'establishment' and those who do not belong to it, the predominant groups and the 'underdog'. Britain is perhaps not peculiar in having developed a form of constitutional government in the middle ages: in other parts of Europe similar developments were taking place at the same period. But Britain is peculiar in never having been dominated by one political or social group. Some form of opposition always existed. This does not mean that toleration was always practised or that some forms of opposition did not have to go underground. But, generally speaking, the rule of a group was never complete. The Roman Catholic church had to go underground, but the Established church was quickly challenged by various protestant groups. Factions opposed each other on the political front. One cannot speak, as one could perhaps for pre-revolutionary France, of *an* élite governing the country almost without challenge, at least without recognized challenge. There have usually been gaps in the pyramid of power and those who were at the top were never sufficiently strong to be able to extend their political and social rule over the whole of the community.

These gaps have existed in the social pyramid as well as in the political pyramid. The social pyramid was – and still is – based on hierarchy. But the groups which did not fit in the system rejected the very notion of hierarchy as well as the leaders who embodied it. The nonconformist chapels of the eighteenth and nineteenth centuries operated against the established hierarchy and they came to be based on social values which emphasized, not hierarchy, but equality or perhaps more specifically fraternity and solidarity. This was of course part of their creed, but this happened to be necessary for their very survival. Because they were not crushed, these chapels helped to maintain a sense of solidarity and equality within the many protestant dissenters. The British people are divided into more religious denominations than the people of other European countries; but the sense of fraternity within each of these groups is probably greater than it is in the more massively supported churches of the Continent.

Table 9. *Membership of the various denominations* (thousands)

England and Wales		Scotland	
Anglicans:		United Church (1966)	1,234
baptized (1964)	27,500	Episcopal Church (1967)	94
confirmed (1964)	9,700	Roman Catholic (1965)	810
full members (1959)	2,495		
Roman Catholics (1965)	4,000	Northern Ireland (1961)	
Methodists: full members	948	Anglicans	345
Presbyterians ,, ,,	68	Roman Catholics	498
Congregationalists:		Presbyterians	413
full members	198	Methodists	72
Baptists ,, ,,	290	Others	98
Quakers ,, ,,	21		
Others	15		
Jews (U.K.)	450		

(from the *Statesman's Yearbook*, Macmillan, 1968, pp. 77, 78 and 129)

The same spirit of solidarity was taken over by, or passed on to other 'underdogs', particularly to the industrial workers. It might have developed in the rural minority, had the 'peasant' class been sufficiently numerous, although the independence of mind of the 'peasant' might not have been a good ferment for such a solidarity. The spirit of fraternity developed among industrial workers, where trade unions had, originally at any rate, some of the characteristics of religious chapels. Slowly, the trade unions grew. They were not crushed, because industrialization was too widespread: their early beginnings were difficult, but probably not as difficult as elsewhere in Europe. Solidarity between the workers was perhaps greater; the traditional upper class was not so opposed to them as the rising middle classes and the traditional upper class was still partly in command. Of course, many of the early characteristics have disappeared. Trade unions have now to be classified, like the British Medical Association or the Institute of Directors, as 'interest groups'. Yet they are still based, as they were originally, on a certain sense of fraternity. This did not always mean equality; in many cases, it meant and sometimes still means profound inequalities between members of different trades and workers with different skills. However, the spirit of fraternity gradually extended to the whole of the working class and it became slowly intellectualized in the form of equality. This feeling of equality and of fraternity was and still is juxtaposed with the ideas of hierarchy prevalent in the upper middle class. The two traditions continue to remain alive. They never dramatically clashed; one never entirely superseded the other.

By accident or by a mysterious sense of its long-term interests, the British upper class accepted infiltration by people of the middle class. It also accepted, in the religious and industrial fields, coexistence with large groups which did not agree with its values. Neither side tried very consistently to eliminate the other. As a result, there are two types of attitudes in contemporary Britain. They are perhaps only manifest in extreme cases, but they can be seen and they can be more clearly differentiated than in other countries. There is an accepted – and not imposed – hierarchy at the top, which is materialized in the aristocracy. There is much real, profound, traditionally embedded sense of fraternity and equality in the masses. One cannot hope to explain the mysterious way in which these two attitudes coexist. Let it simply be noticed that these two profoundly different types of values do coexist and that this coexistence is probably one of the major sources of equilibrium, not only within the 'top' groups and within the mass of the people, but also within the whole of British society.

CHAPTER THREE

The Electors

IRONICALLY enough, after great precautions have been taken to ensure the secrecy of the ballot in modern democracies, great efforts are now made to find out – admittedly for 'scientific' purposes only – how people vote. Interest in electoral behaviour began to grow after electors started voting in secret, but the process was a slow one, particularly in Britain. The analysis of voting behaviour began in France in 1913, in the United States in the interwar period; it was a postwar development in Britain. This is probably because the requirements of the election law made studies more difficult in Britain than elsewhere. Since all the ballot papers of a constituency have to be mixed before being counted, one cannot, in Britain, examine voting results by polling station. In other countries most of the early work was done by comparing results by polling districts; this technique was ruled out in Britain and electoral analysis had to wait for the development of a new technique.

The deadlock was broken by the use of the survey, which indeed quickly proved to be a much more fruitful method of investigation than the detailed analysis of polling district results, although it is, admittedly, a much more expensive technique. Instead of simply comparing results, one could ask questions and obtain information on a wide range of political questions. Provided one selected a representative sample, the answers which one obtained were known to be those of the whole population from which the sample was drawn: the margin of error is very small. Numerous criticisms were at first levelled against the methods on grounds of inaccuracy, but they quickly died out when it was found in practice that the findings of the surveys corresponded with only small variations to, for instance, general election results. Politicians and public opinion came to accept surveys and some indeed became addicts of the 'Gallup polls'.

Criticisms are still voiced in some quarters, on a different plane. What is doubted is not so much the accuracy of the sampling methods as the validity of the conclusions drawn from the questions. Persons who are interviewed are often asked to give a straight Yes or No answer, when they might have preferred to give a more qualified answer; they are asked to reply quickly, on the spot, to a large number of complex questions about which they have little or no knowledge. There is a danger that people might be unintentionally pushed into answering, one way or another, in order to get the whole business out of the way. These criticisms are serious and they are clearly not groundless: questions must be drafted with great caution and results must be examined with great care. An element of danger will probably always remain. Yet the criticisms are directed, not at the method, but at the use which is made of it. The survey has made it possible to have a picture of the electorate which is incomparably more detailed and more precise than the one which we had in the past. Nobody would deny that we have gained, through the survey, a wealth of valuable information.

Two lines of investigation: voting and opinions

The survey has opened two lines of investigation, and the major criticisms which are now voiced are limited to one of these two lines. The first type of investigation, which we can call *objective* analysis of voting, has been concerned with collecting the largest number of social and economic data about the electors of the parties. Who votes and who abstains? Are Labour supporters primarily composed of manual workers and in which proportions? How do Anglicans or Roman Catholics divide their vote? Other social conditions being equal, does one find regional variations in voting behaviour? Who are the electors who switch from one party to another between two general elections, the famous 'floating voters'?

The other type of analysis is that of *subjective* factors. It is concerned not with finding social or economic data about the persons who are interviewed, but with views and opinions about political issues, the parties, individual politicians. There are, of course, an infinite number of such questions. One can ask people whether they would like to see Britain enter the Common Market, whether they think that the Labour party is the party of the 'working class', or whether they like the prime minister. All these questions have, however, one thing in common: they are concerned with the personal views of the respondents on one problem, and not with a fact, such as their age, their sex, or their occupation.

The answers to these questions are clearly important for the understanding of the political behaviour of the electors. They have to be treated with great caution, however. The risks of misinterpretation are large: some people may have been forced into categories into which they would not, on reflection, place themselves. It is also necessary always to remember that one never finds the *why*, but only the *how*, when one asks such questions. If it is found, as in 1959, that there is a correlation between voting Labour and wanting to see old age pensions increased, one is not permitted to conclude that some people voted Labour *because* they wanted to see old age pensions increased: for all we know, it may be the other way round. One does not want to enter the field of the theory of motivation: the only thing which is essential to remember is that motivations are never simple and cannot be reduced to the form of A is the cause of B.

Yet, at the same time, it is vital to examine opinions if one is to understand political behaviour in a less superficial fashion. We all know that in Britain people do not express their political views directly by referendum. They express them indirectly by voting, technically for a man, in practice for a party. However, it is assumed, in current political language, that while voting for a party, they express confidence, not only in its leaders, but in a programme which this party puts forward at the election. In some cases, as in 1910 on the House of Lords and in 1923 on free trade, it is even argued that the election amounted to a referendum, because the issue was alleged to be of crucial importance. Since the Common Market question has been raised in Britain, it has sometimes been argued that there should be an election *on* the Common Market. Of course, literally speaking, there cannot be an election *on* the Common Market: elections are fought on men and on parties. Since, however, there is a connexion between parties and programmes, it is essential that we should try to know what this connexion is. If a party A puts forward issues a, b, and c, do electors who vote for that party approve all these issues, or only some of them, and in what proportion? Have they even always heard of these issues?

This is not all. One may want to have this information for its own sake, but one may also want to go further. If it is found that people vote for a party *and* know and approve of the main points of the programme of that party, one might be able to conclude not that people vote *because* of that programme, but that there is a clear correlation between issues and voting. If it is found, on the contrary, that there are many voters who vote for a party but do not approve of some important points of its programme, one will clearly have to reconsider the general problem of the nature of voting. At the outset, we do know already that there is a considerable discrepancy between views and voting. In 1959, the nationalization question was, among other reasons, particularly in the news because a poll, known as the Hurry poll, was conducted in 129 marginal constituencies in order to test opinion on it. Nearly two million people were interviewed and a majority of Labour voters was found to be opposed to further nationalization. This was not, in reality, a discovery: other polls had already shown that this was the case. For the student of politics, the important point is that the 1959 election demonstrated that many voters voted Labour *although* they disapproved of steel renationalization. The nature of voting behaviour is at stake and we cannot avoid examining 'opinions' as well as 'objective data' on voting when we consider the sociology of the electorate.

Voting and non-voting

Let us consider the 'objective data' first. The first which we encounter is the overall rate of voting: it is over 75 per cent but not often over 80 per cent at general elections and much lower at most by-elections and at local elections where it falls to 50, 40, and even 30 per cent. It is not surprising that the turnout at general elections should be high: it could easily be higher. In some countries, Germany for instance, it is much higher, even without compulsory voting.

Table 10. *Turnout since 1945* (percentages)

1945	73·5	1959	78·7
1950	84·0	1964	77·0
1951	82·5	1966	75·8
1955	76·7		

Admittedly the abstention rate is always artificially swollen because it is calculated by reference to a register which is necessarily somewhat out of date. The register is compiled in October, comes into force in the following February and is then used without modifications between one February and the next (except for the fact that new voters become entitled to vote in October and not in February). Meanwhile, some electors will have died and a few will have moved out of the country. In principle, those who are ill, who have moved out to another constituency, or who are away on business can ask for a postal vote; in practice they can only do so if the illness, the move, or the cause for travel do not occur on or before the last qualifying date for a postal vote, which has naturally to be a few days before the election. At least 5 per cent and probably 7 or 8 per cent of the electors either should no longer be on the register when the election comes or are unavoidably prevented from voting. To assess the abstention rate realistically this percentage should be deducted; the further from February an election takes place, the greater the percentage which should be deducted.

Yet real abstention remains. Since the abstention rate is usually around 20 per cent and since only about 5 to 8 per cent should be discarded, 12 to 15 per cent of the electors could go and vote but do not. One can perhaps divide them into two groups, the 'positive' or active abstainers and the 'negative' or passive abstainers. The first group is probably the smaller of the two: these 'positive' abstainers are those who abstain because the parties or the candidates, either in the country as a whole or more often in their constituency, do not appeal to them. One might have expected this group to be larger than it is. One variety could be the cynical, who, seeing that the constituency in which they are registered is a safe seat, consider that there is no point in bothering to come out and vote. Few British electors seem to fall in this category. Admittedly the turnout is a little higher in marginal than in safe seats. Three-quarters of the seats where, in a straight fight, the successful candidate had a majority of 5 per cent or less of the votes cast over his opponent at the General Election of 1955 recorded turnouts of 80 per cent or more in 1959, while only slightly over two-fifths of the safer seats had such a high turnout. However, the difference is a rather small one overall. A turnout of under 70 per cent is rare, even in the safest seat; mining seats, however safe, record very high turnouts and even outside mining areas the great majority of seats have turnouts of over 75 per cent.

Table 11. *Size of majority at the 1955 General Election and turn-out at the subsequent General Election of 1959** (straight fights only)

Turnout in 1959 (%)	Total	Number of seats where the majority at the 1955 Election had been			
		under 5%	between 5 and 10%	between 10 and 25%	over 25%
under 70	26	–	1	10	15
70–75	45	7	3	15	20
75–80	102	7	15	42	38
80–85	149	38	25	53	33†
over 85	17	9	4	3	1‡
	339	61	48	123	107

†27 of these 33 seats are mining seats.   ‡Mining seat

Others might criticize the electoral system in a more serious fashion. The mass of the electors have no say in the selection of the candidates. Most fights have been straight fights, at least between 1951 and 1959: Liberals, Communists, and other minorities had no way of expressing their point of view. One might expect to find everywhere a certain number of staunch

* I am most grateful to Mr H. B. Berrington for these calculations.

Liberals as well as of other electors joining the abstention camp. There are not many of these, however. It was found in 1959 that the turnout was only 1 per cent higher in seats where a Liberal candidate stood. In 1955, the turnout fell and part of the drop can perhaps be attributed to an element of disgruntlement among supporters of all parties and particularly among Labour electors. The total drop – of 5·7 per cent – cannot, however, be solely attributed to such a disgruntlement.

The other form of abstention is much more negative. It can be occasional or persistent. These abstainers are the ones who are not interested in political matters, who either never vote or happen to vote only if it does not result in the slightest personal trouble to them. They are usually the most ill-informed of the electors. They are often found to have no opinion on current political issues. These perpetual and occasional abstainers are more likely to be found among women (not in 1964), among young and old people, among poorer people. Admittedly, there may be more artificial abstention among the members of

Table 12. *Social characteristics of abstainers* (percentages)

		Non-voters (1964)		Whole sample (1964)
SEX:	male	50	(1959: 42)	48
	female	50	(,, 58)	52
AGE:	21–24	16		8
	25–34	24		19
	35–44	16		20
	45–64	28		37
	65 and over	16		16
CLASS:	well-to-do	4	(1959: 3)	6
	middle	18	(,, 16)	22
	lower middle and working	63	(,, 63)	61
	poor	15	(,, 18)	11

(from Tables drawn in 1959 and 1964 by the British Institute of Public Opinion)

these groups than among the members of other groups: many old people are sick or invalid, many women may be prevented from voting, at the last moment, by some household chore. Some sparsely populated areas of Scotland and very large cities, in particular London, also abstain more. There may be technical reasons for this abstention too: in areas where the density of population is very low, the distance, in large towns, the fluctuations of population, are clearly factors of abstention. Yet, over and above these technical reasons, there are probably in many cases more profound social habits. It is among the less educated, the very poor, and among women that one finds the largest proportion of people who claim not to be interested in political matters. Moreover, the same characteristics seem to prevail at local elections: it has been found that women and electors in large cities are more prone to abstain.

The social pyramid and the two main parties

We all know that, roughly speaking, the well-to-do are more likely to vote Conservative and the less well-off are more likely to vote Labour. We assume that the Liberal electors are to be found somewhere in the middle of the social scale. This view seems to be confirmed by the geographical dispersion of the vote: industrial areas return Labour members, residential and farming areas return Conservative members. A majority of respondents, if asked, would probably take the view that the 'Labour party is the party of the 'working class' and that the 'working class' mainly votes for the Labour party.

Yet we also know that a large section of the working class votes for the Conservative party. The Conservatives would never be returned to office if they did not receive the support of a large proportion of the manual workers who constitute the majority of the population and who will continue being a majority, despite the white-collar 'revolution', for a good many years. Percentages of Conservative and Labour support among the various groups all indicate similar breakdowns to that found by Dr Abrams in 1958. (See Table 13.)

Table 13 shows how the members of each 'class' divide between the political parties. But one can look at the distribution of the votes from the other angle and consider what proportion there is, in each party, of the members of the various 'classes'. We have constructed a diagram from J. Bonham's analysis of voting patterns in 1950. Since it is based on 1950

tables, it is slightly out of date: in particular, the proportion of
the middle-class which votes Labour decreased during the 1950s,
but seems to have increased somewhat in the early 1960s. Yet it
gives a general idea of the distribution of the strength of the
various social groups within the electors of each party.

Table 13. *Voting and social 'class'* (percentages)

'Class'	Proportion of the population in each 'class'	Conservative	Labour	Other	Total
Solid middle class	15	85	10	5	100
Lower middle class	20	70	25	5	100
Upper working class (manual)	30	35	60	5	100
Solid working class	35	30	65	5	100

(from M. Abrams, 'Class Distinction in Britain', in *The Future of the Welfare State*,
Conservative Political Centre, 1958)

Table and diagram lead to the same conclusion: while the
professional and business classes, as well as, to a lesser extent,
the white-collar groups, very strongly favour the Conservative

Figure 1. *Distribution of occupational groups within each party*
(*1950*)

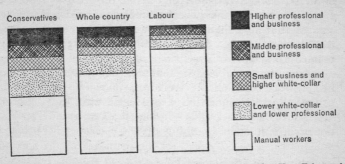

(compiled from the data appearing in J. Bonham, *The Middle-Class Vote*, Faber and
Faber, p. 130)

party, the manual workers are much more evenly divided between the two major parties. If the votes were distributed at random, the two parties should receive something like half the votes of each group: in fact the Conservatives receive one-third to two-fifths of the manual workers' vote, while Labour receives only one-fifth of the votes of the non-manual sections of the population. Furthermore, Labour receives only about one-tenth of the votes of the professional men, managers, and businessmen. Hence this strange paradox. The middle class claims not to believe in classes, yet its vote seems to uphold the classical Marxian division of society into two main classes. The manual working class is said to be class-conscious and it has at its disposal a party which mainly caters for the working class, but not more than two-thirds of its votes go to that party.*

It is because of this paradox that the Conservative party can rightly claim to be more representative of the whole society than the Labour party. As one can see from the diagram, the top sections of society are crushed in the electorate of the Labour party; on the other hand, in the Conservative party, the over-representation of the solid middle class and lower middle class does not lead to a ridiculous under-representation of the manual workers. 20 per cent of the Conservative electors are from the solid middle class; another 30 per cent, or perhaps slightly more, if one allows for the increase of the white-collar workers since 1950, come from the lower middle class. Half, or about half, of the Conservative votes come from the manual workers. If it was not for the lower middle class, which forms a sizeable, but none the less small, portion of the Labour vote, the Labour party would almost solely represent the manual workers.

It is no exaggeration to say that most of the work which has been done since the war on voting behaviour in Britain has been connected with the question of the Conservative working-class vote. Since the Conservative working-class vote is too large to be regarded as an anomaly, but as it does not easily fit with the

*The Liberal vote tends to be a mirror image of the nation although when there is an influx of new Liberal voters (as was the case in the late 1950s and early 1960s) some groups may be particularly favoured.

commonly accepted view that the Labour party is the party of the working class, it is understandable that the Conservative working-class vote should have been one of the major puzzles of voting behaviour. It is not limited to Britain: France, Germany, Belgium, and indeed all Western European countries have a sizeable right-wing working-class vote. But to say that the right-wing working-class vote is a world-wide or at any rate all-European phenomenon does not make the problem any easier to understand.

The Conservative working-class vote: factors which influence voting behaviour

There is no simple explanation of the phenomenon. No single 'cause' has been found, and is likely ever to be found. But there are several clues, some of which, unfortunately, are not as yet substantiated by much numerical evidence. Indeed, we seem to progress as much towards understanding the Labour middle-class vote (which is very small) as towards understanding the Conservative working-class vote (which is much larger).

Table 14. *Voting intention and some social characteristics* (percentages)

	Whole sample	Cons.	Lab.	Lib.	Others & D.K.	TOTAL
SEX: male	46	35	53	6	6	100
female	54	41	44	7	8	100
AGE: 21–24	6	36	51	5	8	100
25–34	17	37	50	6	7	100
35–44	21	37	48	7	8	100
45–64	37	37	49	6	8	100
65 and over	19	41	44	7	8	100
TRADE UNION MEMBERS: 25		19	69	5	6	100
RELIGION:						
Anglicans and Church of Scotland	72	42	47	6	5	100
R. Catholics	10	24	65	4	7	100
Noncomformists	10	32	49	12	7	100
Others	8	34	42	9	15	100

(from Tables drawn in 1966 by the British Institute of Public Opinion. These figures do not include Northern Ireland)

1. We find, in the first place, some associations between voting and *demographic* factors. Women are more right-wing than men by a small but sizeable proportion. Middle-aged people are more right-wing than young voters, although, in recent years, the allegiance of very young electors seems to have fluctuated markedly and the Labour vote has also started to increase among very old people. We do not know the reasons for these associations. We may say that older people, having had more experience, become less idealistic and more conservative. It may also be a question of generations and of experience gained in one's adolescence. We may say that women, most of whom still do not go out to work, do not experience the difficult conditions of life in factories and that in any case many more work in offices where work is clean and generally more pleasant. These interpretations may be correct, although we have no way of proving or disproving them. What seems to be true is that the influence of sex and age on voting behaviour is not specifically a working-class phenomenon: it may explain why the Conservatives obtain more votes in all classes than they would obtain if the suffrage had remained all male and were limited to people in the lower age groups. It does not explain, as far as one can see, why the manual workers are more prone to vote Conservative than the non-manual workers to vote Labour.

2. In the second place, we find *religion*. But, while it is a factor of crucial importance in voting behaviour in Germany, its influence does not seem to be so marked in Britain. There is a tendency for Nonconformists and Roman Catholics to be less Conservative than Anglicans, but this tendency seems to be subjected to large variations from area to area. The association between religion and voting did not seem to be very marked in Bristol and in Greenwich. It was very marked in Glossop, but the authors of the Glossop survey stressed that there were local reasons for the persistence of a religious influence on voting in the area. Religion clearly plays a much greater part in voting behaviour in Wales and Northern Ireland than it does in other parts of Britain. The least that

can be said is that, over the country as a whole, Nonconformist and Roman Catholic Conservatives are far from being exceptional.

Table 15. *Religion and voting in Bristol North-East, 1955* (percentages)

	Whole sample	Conservative	Labour	Liberal
Church of England	52·7	62·4	42·2	50·0
Roman Catholics	4·3	4·4	4·5	2·2
Nonconformists	20·5	16·8	24·2	23·9
None	22·5	16·4	29·1	23·9
	100	100	100	100

(from H. C. Mackenzie and R. S. Milne, *Marginal Seat*, published by the Hansard Society for Parliamentary Government, 1958, p. 65)

Moreover, it is difficult to distinguish the influence of religion from the influence of occupations because the followers of some religions are more likely to be found in certain social classes than in others. Middle-class people are likely to be Anglicans in England. Roman Catholics are often Irish immigrants and Irish immigrants are often manual workers. The Free Churches developed among the 'people'. Of course, one finds many middle-class people who are Roman Catholics and many who belong to a Free Church. Proportionately, however, the Church of England probably groups a larger number of middle-class voters than any other religion. If this is so, the edge which the Labour party has among the members of the Free Churches and among Roman Catholics may not come from religion, but from occupations. The precise impact of religion on voting is thus difficult to determine.

3. *Tradition* and *environment* constitute the third type of factors which are associated with voting behaviour. Tradition is a loose expression which is not very useful when one is trying to examine in detail the components of voting behaviour. Some surveys did find, however, that the vote seemed to be influenced by the social background of the parents of respondents as well as by the social background of the respondents themselves. But this type of analysis mainly applies to the lower middle class by the very nature of the question: it is in the lower middle class that

there are sons of manual workers moving up the social ladder alongside sons of middle-class and lower-middle-class parents. The influence of tradition on the voting behaviour of manual workers could only be measured if it were possible to know the political history of the family of the respondents; interviewers are unlikely to obtain reliable answers to questions of this kind.

Environment is also a form of tradition, although the tradition may be broken if one goes to a new environment. It plays probably a large part in voting behaviour. In the United States, in Sweden, in France, it has been shown to be of great moment. More precisely, environment can influence voting behaviour in three different ways. Firstly, there is the influence of what might be called the *regional* environment. People living in certain parts of the country are more likely to vote in a certain way than people living in another part. In the United States, where this form of environmental influence was at one time predominant and still is very important in some parts of the country, many detailed studies have been made to try to measure it with precision. In France 'electoral geography' has been for a long time the only form of studying voting behaviour. In Britain, unfortunately, studies of the French or American kind have been hampered by the impossibility of analysing results by polling districts and also by the general impression that such regional influences were likely to be very small in a highly homogeneous country.

However, Gallup poll investigations give a general idea of the extent of these geographical variations. Admittedly findings remain limited because the smallest area into which Gallup poll figures can be broken down is the standard administrative region: research done abroad indicates that there are often large differences in voting behaviour within regions as well as between regions. Yet calculations made by the British Institute of Public opinion especially for this book show that *in each class* voting at the General Election of 1959 varied appreciably from one region to another. Comparisons have been limited here to the two main parties and to two of the four social groups into which the Gallup poll divides the British population, because the two others are too small to be examined in detail. Overall, the Conservatives obtained 57 per cent of the votes in the 'middle class' and Labour 17 per cent, the rest going to the Liberals, minor parties, and in abstentions. The Conservatives obtained 30 per cent of the 'lower-middle-class and working-class' vote and Labour 41 per cent. But these averages concealed ample variations: the Conservative 'middle-class' vote varied from 44 to 67 per cent, depending on the region, and the Labour 'middle-class' vote from 11 to 25 per cent, while the Conservative 'lower middle-class and working-class' vote varied from 18 to 38 per cent and the Labour 'lower-middle-class and working-class' vote from 27 to 57 per cent.

Some of these geographical differences deserve further examination. In the first place, they show a general opposition between the South of England, which is more Conservative, and Wales, the North, and North-East of England, which are more Labour; Scotland, the Midlands, and the North-West are about average. Wales is a definite Labour stronghold: Labour receives almost a quarter of the middle-class vote, instead of about a sixth over the whole country, and almost three-fifths of the lower-middle-class and working-class vote, instead of about two-fifths over the whole country. On the other hand, all the three largest English conurbations are outside the areas where Labour is strongest in the working class and in the middle class; it is impossible to know, in the absence of any other evidence, whether the character of the conurbations – by contrast to the character of smaller industrial towns – is in any way responsible for this situation.

In the second place, there appear to be differences within that broad pattern. Areas of strength of one party in one class do not always correspond to areas of strength in the other class. Outside Wales, Labour's main strength in the 'lower middle and working class' is along the East coast of England, as can be seen from the map; but the Conservatives' 'middle-class' support is also stronger than average in Yorkshire and in East Anglia. The voters of these two regions seem to be more divided on class lines than the voters of other regions. The South and South-East seem to be, on the contrary, the two regions where the support for the two main parties differs least from one class to the other.

These findings refine some of the impressions which appear when one considers electoral results. They confirm the Labour strength in Wales. They also confirm the traditional Liberal strength in the South-West. In Northern Ireland, where the Gallup poll does not conduct investigations, it seems that the Conservative strength is above average: Belfast is the most Conservative city of its size in the whole of the British Isles. In

Figure 2. *Regional variations of voting behaviour in two social 'classes' in the General Election of 1959*

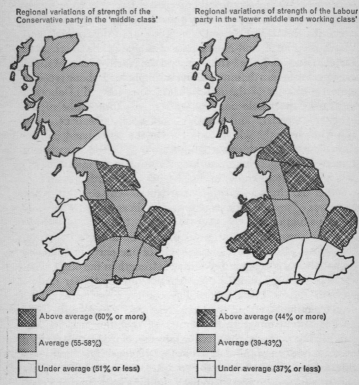

Regional variations of strength of the Conservative party in the 'middle class'

Regional variations of strength of the Labour party in the 'lower middle and working class'

Above average (60% or more)

Average (55-58%)

Under average (51% or less)

Above average (44% or more)

Average (39-43%)

Under average (37% or less)

(constructed from tables compiled by the British Institute of Public Opinion on answers given to surveys taken over several months in 1961)

Wales, Scotland, and Northern Ireland, the pattern of voting behaviour is also affected by the presence of nationalist parties. In general, if it does seem that Britain, and particularly England, shows a fairly marked homogeneity in its voting patterns, one cannot rule out regional variations altogether. The origin of these variations still remains to be known. Religion unquestionably plays a part in some areas, but there are also other factors. More detailed investigations are needed before one starts to understand – and indeed to measure adequately – the influence of geographical environment.

A second form of influence of the environment is that of *home surroundings*. It has been shown in Sweden, the United States, and France, that the more an area is inhabited by manual workers, the greater is the *proportion* of manual workers who vote for a left-wing party. People tend to conform to the predominant influence of the area in which they live. In Britain, the information is scattered, but it points to the same conclusion. People who come to new towns cease to be 'solid' Labour supporters. I have participated in an analysis of voting behaviour in Newcastle-under-Lyme, in which the voting behaviour of the electorate in different parts of the constituency was compared: in middle-class districts, manual workers were less likely to vote Labour than in working-class districts.

Yet the examination of the influence of home surroundings is complicated by the existence of a third type of environmental influence, that of the *firm*, *workplace*, or *factory*. Generally speaking, it is probable that workers in large plants are more likely to vote Labour than workers in small plants. Mrs Stacey's analysis of Banbury showed that manual workers employed in 'traditional' firms were markedly more Conservative than manual workers employed in 'non-traditional' firms: Labour received only slightly over half the votes of the former, but nearly three-quarters of the votes of the latter.

There are also probably differences from industry to industry: there seem to be more Labour supporters among miners than among any other manual workers' group.

It is difficult to decide which of these factors plays the most important part. Miners, for instance, are at the intersection of a number of pressures which all seem to work in the direction of a Labour vote. They are engaged in one of the more traditional industrial occupations, they usually live in self-contained housing estates, they are often sons of miners. Finally, they are heavily unionized and we shall see presently that trade unions are clearly one of the determining factors of a left-wing vote.

Table 16. *Voting and type of firm in Banbury*

| | Traditional firms | | Non-traditional firms | |
	Conservative and Liberal	Labour	Conservative and Liberal	Labour
Non-manual	72	13	36	18
Manual	47	54	89	233
	119	67	125	251

(from M. Stacey, *Tradition and Change: A Study of Banbury*, O.U.P., 1960, p. 46)

4. '*Self-assigned class*' is sometimes given as an element of explanation. One does find that people who describe themselves as middle class are more likely to vote Conservative than people who describe themselves as working class.* A survey found that, among manual workers, the former divided equally between the two parties and the latter favoured Labour by slightly over two to one. Yet 'self-assigned class' is not really satisfactory. Like the other factors which we have just mentioned, it accounts as much for the middle-class Labour vote as for the Conservative working-class vote. Among the manual workers, moreover, the discrepancy between the voting behaviour of those who describe themselves as working class and those who describe themselves as middle class is not sufficiently large to constitute a complete explanation. Finally, we do not know what this criterion really means. At best the difficulty is transposed rather than solved. We may not have to 'explain' any longer why people vote Conservative or Labour, but we have to 'explain' why they call themselves middle class or working class and what difference there is between a man who calls himself middle class and his neighbour who calls himself working class.

* See table p. 31.

5. The most satisfactory single element of 'explanation' is perhaps *trade union* membership, although some controversy has developed in recent years both on the extent and direction of the relationship. National surveys have shown that 'manual workers who are members of trade unions are usually three times more likely to vote Labour than Conservative'. Surveys conducted in particular areas have not always confirmed this trend, however. Moreover, it is not certain that manual workers necessarily vote Labour *because* they are members of trade unions: in some cases, it may be the other way round; in other cases both a Labour vote and trade union membership may simply be the consequence of some third factor, such as family background or environment. Finally, some groups are more reluctant than others to join a union.* However, trade union membership does help us to understand the manual workers' vote and does not only 'explain', like the other factors which we have just examined, why some categories of manual *and* non-manual workers are more likely than others to vote Conservative.

Voting behaviour in Britain can perhaps be summarized in the following way. In the non-manual occupations, the odds are three or four to one that electors will vote Conservative: the higher the occupation in the middle class, the greater the proportion of Conservative voters. Among manual workers, rather less than half are members of a trade union and these union members vote Labour in the proportion of three or four to one. The other manual workers – and perhaps the very lowest fringes of the non-manual groups – distribute their vote almost at random. In all cases, women, middle-aged people, and Anglicans are more likely to be Conservative. In some areas, the pattern of voting is disturbed by the perpetuation of particular traditions. In every ward and housing estate, the vote is probably somewhat modified by the predominant occupational group, manual or non-manual, which happens to live in the area.

Some general points are perhaps worth noting. The solid core of the Conservative vote is based on occupations (with reference to income and education as well). The solid core of the Labour vote is based on the membership of a voluntary

* See p. 169.

association, the trade union. Admittedly, in many cases, the membership of the trade union is not really voluntary: pressure is brought to bear on workers in many factories, and family up-bringing also plays its part. However, the distinction between unionized and non-unionized workers is not entirely one of occupation, rarely one of income, never one of education. The distinction between Labour and Conservative voters is largely one of occupation, of status, of income, when one comes to distinguish between manual and non-manual workers, between lower middle-class and solid middle-class people; it is largely based on the membership of an organization within the manual working class.

The electorate tends to be divided into three groups, of about the same strength: the non-manual workers, the manual workers who belong to a union, and the manual workers who do not belong to a union. In the imagery of British politics, the first group is associated with the Conservatives and the second with the Labour party. The third group, although it is as large as the two others, is somewhat forgotten. The Conservatives seem to have made more efforts to win over trade unionists than to win over non-unionized workers. Labour leaders have recently tried to appeal to the middle class more than to non-unionized workers. Each party seems to try to dissociate the rank-and-file of the other party from its social leaders: Labour attacks the 'ruling class', the public schools, and the conspiracy which the public schools are alleged to produce. The Conservatives – at least some of them – attack the leadership of the unions, which is said to constitute an equally sinister conspiracy. Except perhaps very indirectly, neither party seriously seems to try to appeal to the indistinct mass of non-unionized manual workers, perhaps because these workers form an unidentifiable group without any particular shape or form. The conflict is polarized, almost per-sonalized, around the middle-class élite and the trade union élite. This is not by accident. If it were polarized, for instance, on the churches, it would not correspond, in Britain at least, to any emotions among the electors. One may dislike the present polarization around the middle-class and trade union élites, but it does correspond to the social reality of the country.

Floating voters

Elections are won and lost by small *overall* changes in party support. In the 1940s, electoral movements have been minute on the surface. The 'swing' – the mathematical formula expressing the relative percentage gains and losses of the two main parties from one election to another – has always been small since the war.* Between 1945 and 1959 the total swing to the Conservatives was 7·3 per cent, and between 1950 and 1959, it was 4 per cent. But the swing to the left of 3·6 per cent in 1964 was sufficient to wipe out the large Conservative majority of 1959 and bring Labour back to power.

Table 17. *Voting in post-war general elections* (thousands)

	Electors	Voters	Cons.	Labour	Liberal	Other
1945	32,836	24,083	9,578	11,633	2,197	675
1950	34,270	28,773	12,503	13,267	2,622	381
1951	34,646	28,596	13,718	13,949	731	198
1955	34,858	26,760	13,287	12,405	722	346
1959	35,297	27,859	13,750	12,216	1,639	255
1964	35,909	27,650	12,002	12,206	3,093	349
1966	35,965	27,264	11,418	13,065	2,328	453

These small swings seem to confirm the Gilbert and Sullivan analysis of British politics: about 24 million – or 85 per cent of the voters – remained fixed (or appeared to remain fixed) to their allegiance since 1950. It seems all the more important to concentrate on the small band of 'floating voters' who by their fluctuations make the British system of government 'work'.

In reality, one should not use overall figures to analyse the floating vote. As soon as one comes to examine detailed results, the fixed character of voting behaviour becomes less obvious. Firstly, the electorate is partly rejuvenated at each election: the voters of a given election are not all physically the same persons as those of the previous election. Over half a million people

* The swing between two parties is calculated by adding the percentage gain of one party to the percentage loss of the other and dividing by two. This is necessary if one wants to measure the relative gain of a party compared to another, irrespective of the 'intervention' of any third party in the constituency or the country.

die every year; in the course of a decade, about a sixth of the electorate is being gradually replaced by new electors. We may say that these changes cancel each other out – which they do only to some extent. But we cannot say, if we want to be precise, that there are no movements at all.

Another difficulty comes from abstainers. Let us consider the results of the 1951 and 1955 General Elections. The Liberals had approximately the same number of votes – about 700,000. Labour lost 1·5 million votes and the Conservatives also lost half a million. If we consider only the *net* gains over the whole country, the Conservative victory of 1955 appears entirely due to movements between parties and abstention. Similarly the Labour victory of 1964 appeared due, not to a global increase in the Labour vote, but to a marked decrease in the Conservative vote combined with a large increase in the Liberal vote. Between 1945 and 1951, on the other hand, both parties gained votes, but the Conservatives gained relatively more, apparently mainly from among abstainers in 1950, from the Liberals in 1951. Between 1945 and 1969, only at two elections, those of 1959 and 1966, was the result marked *both* by an increased poll of the victorious party and a decreased poll of the other major party.

The importance of the abstainers in the composition of the floating vote can be measured with more precision, thanks to a detailed study made in Bristol North-East in 1955. In that constituency, it was found that only one-fifth of the total Conservative gain (a mathematical swing of 1·5 per cent) came from transfers of votes from Labour to Conservative. A Liberal 'intervention' in 1955 made no difference to the relative strength of the two major parties. But one-tenth of the advantage was due to new voters and *seven-tenths* were due to movements involving abstainers. More Labour voters of 1951 abstained in 1955 and more of the abstainers of 1951 voted Conservative in 1955. This was probably an extreme case; yet, in varying proportions, similar movements occur at each election in each constituency. They are simply submerged when we consider the overall figures.

One must take into account changes in the register. One must examine abstention. One must also look carefully at the movements from one political party to another. There are, in the first place, the Liberal votes: 700,000 electors voted Liberal in 1951 and 1955, but many of these electors cannot be the same ones, simply because Liberal candidates did not stand in exactly the same constituencies. Moreover, movements between the two major parties are not entirely one way. In Bristol North-East, 6 per cent of the Conservative voters of 1955 were Labour voters of 1951, but 6 per cent of the Labour voters of 1955 were Conservative voters of 1951. This was why the transfers from one major party to the other constituted such a small proportion of the total 'swing'. In every constituency, as all the surveys have shown, there are electors who switch their vote in the opposite direction to the general trend throughout the country – and in some parts of the country, in 1959, this happened rather more than usually.

If one tries to analyse the floating vote, one must analyse all the possible movements. If one analyses all the possible movements, one finds that the floating vote is a very complex reality. In a straight fight, in two successive elections, there are three possibilities open to each elector: he can vote Conservative, vote Labour, or abstain. Since he can have voted Conservative, have voted Labour, or abstained at the previous election, there are nine possible courses open to the electors of the constituency. All these courses are in fact taken. Only three of them constitute a form of 'fixed' voting behaviour; each of the other six is a form of floating vote. If the constituency has a three-cornered fight in one of the instances, there are twelve possibilities, nine of which constitute a form of floating vote. With a three-cornered fight in both instances, twelve courses out of sixteen are forms of floating vote. It may be, as Gallup polls showed, that 80 per cent of the population always voted for the same *party*; this does not mean that only 20 per cent are floating voters, because this would amount to discarding the occasional abstainers. We saw that in Bristol in 1955 their role was crucial. It is perhaps nearer the truth to argue, from the evidence of detailed constituency surveys, that as many as a quarter of the electors are in some sense floating voters, *from one election to the next*.

One finds, in each constituency, movements of floating voters in all possible directions. One should not be surprised to find also, as voting studies showed, that the floating voters are not the most rational of electors. Floating voters may play a crucial part in the British system of government. But they do not seem to be aware of their responsibilities. They do not seem to be drawn from the most politically conscious section of the community. The reasons for their change of allegiance are often trivial. They seem to be less committed, not because of a genuine independence of mind, but more out of apathy. They resemble abstainers more than they resemble the image of the perfect voter. Indeed, since many floaters are, or have been, abstainers, there is a natural similarity between the two groups. As the authors of the Bristol surveys said, they are likely to 'resemble, not Hamlet, paralysed by the pale cast of doubt, but Lancelot Gobbo' (*Marginal Seat*, p. 192).

Nor is this all. Underneath the actual floating vote, there is perhaps an even larger category of *potential* floating voters of whom the actual floating voters are only the most resolute section. When electors are asked, between elections, which party they are likely to vote for in a future election, many are uncommitted or have even decided to vote for a party other than the party of their previous choice. Some of these potential floating voters return to their traditional allegiance, but others will be prepared to cross the Rubicon. In many ways, the upsurge in Liberal fortunes at by-elections and at local elections in the early 1960s as well as at the 1964 General Election has to be analysed along the same lines.

Perhaps these floaters – and the electors who vote for another party at by-elections – are not real floaters. Perhaps their protest is not an indication of any genuine change in party allegiance. Perhaps, however, they are brought back into the party fold by the effect of the election campaign, which does seem to rally waverers more than it converts opponents. It will never be possible to know for certain. But even though many waverers come back to their party, even though the actual floating vote is much smaller than the potential floating vote, these waverers or potential floating voters must not be forgotten or dismissed out of hand. In the normal way, they rally to their respective colours when they are called, but it would be dangerous for a party to believe that they will always do so.

Are there long-term changes in voting behaviour?

We have examined short-term changes. Are there long-term changes as well? Liberals were replaced by Labour in the course of the 1920s and 1930s. The Liberal revival of the 1950s and 1960s excited much speculation. The Labour party lost votes in the early 1950s and appeared doomed; in 1963–4, the same gloomy predictions were made about the Conservative party. Can reasonable guesses be made? What is the long-term future of the political parties?

The short answer is that we do not know. Any extrapolation of recent voting changes is speculative. Clearly the Labour party lost support in the 1950s among the middle classes and, to a lesser extent, among the working classes; the 1964 recovery was partial; it was followed by a marked success in 1966: but this was in turn followed by a period of reverses. Neither the results of the 1950s nor those of the 1960s constitute evidence for a long-term trend.

One theory of long-term development is based on the impact of the white-collar 'revolution'. Since the proportion of manual workers decreases, runs the syllogism, and since manual workers tend to vote Labour in larger proportions than white-collar workers, the Labour vote is bound to decrease a little every year.

This syllogism is based, however, on the assumption that 'present conditions and present voting patterns will remain constant'. We are not, in reality, allowed to make such an assumption, because our knowledge of voting patterns is not a precise one. We know only that manual workers have a greater propensity to vote Labour than white-collar workers in general. At the boundary between the manual and non-manual groups – a boundary which is difficult to define in any case – voting patterns are not very different. A white-collar worker is not automatically a Conservative voter. Indeed, it has been found that, in the white-collar groups, sons of manual workers have a greater propensity to vote Labour than sons of non-manual workers. Moreover, the relative changes in the proportion of manual and non-manual workers are slow, as we saw in the previous chapter. The consequences on voting behaviour of these long-term changes are too small to be measured with the instruments which we have at our disposal: a one or two per cent change over a decade is within the margin of error of voting surveys. We cannot be certain of the magnitude of these long-term changes in voting behaviour; we cannot even be certain that these long-term changes exist. In fact, it seems that in the 1950s and 1960s more modifications in voting patterns occurred within each class than as a result of one class growing larger at the expense of another.

Hence the second theory of long-term development. With society becoming more affluent, manual workers cease to react like manual workers: they become integrated in the new society and abandon the old 'taboos' of class warfare on which socialist parties are based. This argument probably overestimates the amount of class hatred which existed in Britain before the Second World War. It is impossible to check the accuracy of the general impressions which one had at the time against the more sober results of opinion polls which did not exist then. The Labour party did much better at the polls in the 1950s and 1960s than it did in the 1930s, although the 1930s was the period when capitalism was at its lowest ebb. In any case, the question is not one of political temperature; the question is whether people are prepared to jump from one side of the fence to the other on the basis of some long-term social change. The answer must certainly be that we still do not know. It was unreasonable to predict the end of the Conservative party in 1945: the Conservative party did recover. It proved unreasonable to extrapolate from the movements which took place in the 1950s: the Labour party showed resilience and recovered, despite the fact that 'affluence' appeared at one point to favour the Conservatives indefinitely. Short-term movements are still those which account for electoral fortunes more easily than long-term trends.

One type of long-term movement did emerge in the 1950s and 1960s: the growth of 'independence' from traditional party allegiance. Two-party partisanship reached a high point in 1951; it has decreased fairly regularly ever since, through greater abstention, increased vote for minor parties and greater regional variations in swing between the major parties. The 'hold' of the two parties dropped from about three-quarters of the *electorate* in the early 1950s to about two-thirds in the 1960s. A marked increase of this trend would begin to threaten the position of the main parties.

The electors' opinions

With the two-party system, a vote for a party means a vote for a government and for a programme. Each party is committed to a comprehensive set of policies, which range from economic and social matters to humanitarian questions. Foreign policy cannot be defined entirely in advance. Yet, as far as is practicable, each party describes the broad lines of its foreign policy to the electorate. Moreover, a vote is as much a judgement on past policies as on future action. At Westminster, in the press, and to a lesser extent on radio and television, the Government and the Opposition parties criticize each other and endeavour to show the consistency of their action and of their proposals as well as the inconsistencies of their opponents'. Above all, everything is done to emphasize the divisions between the parties. The electors are presented with alternative policies and, in most cases, should be aware of them.

Yet, when one considers the answers given to straightforward party issues, one often does not find comparable divisions among the electors. Most electors may continually vote for the same party, but few respondents to public opinion polls show a consistent party line on all issues. This does not happen only on details. It does not concern only the 'more' or the 'less' within the framework of a general party policy. It concerns the policy itself, and main parts of that policy. The answers given to the Gallup polls show that the majority and the minority on each issue cut across party lines as much as they follow them.

We have selected twenty-two questions among those asked by the British Institute of Public Opinion during the periods 1959–61 and 1965–68. These cover a wide range of issues:

1959–61
  1 Humanitarian: capital punishment

2 Liberal: reform of House of Lords to enable peers to stand for the Commons
3 Foreign affairs: nuclear disarmament
4   opinion on South Africa
5   opinion on the United Nations
6   entry into the Common Market
7 Economic and social questions: taxes: choice between taxes and social services
8   raising the level of surtax
9   increase in N.H.S. charges
10   further nationalization measures
11   industrial relations: responsibility for cost-of-living increases with government or trade unions

1965–68
1 Humanitarian: immigration: approbation of strict limitations
2 Liberal: House of Lords: approbation of abolition of hereditary peerage qualification
3 Foreign affairs: maintenance of British nuclear bomb
4   Rhodesia: settle with Mr Smith's régime
5   admission of Communist China into U.N.
6   entry into the Common Market
7 Economic and social questions: justification of unemployment
8   sale of council houses
9   value of the comprehensive school idea
10   approbation of an incomes policy
11   responsibility for economic situation on government

Since our purpose is to *compare* the views of Conservative and Labour electors, it is important to know both what these views are and how much they differ. We thus present the answers in the form of four diagrams in Figure 3: the first two show the percentage of the supporters of each party who took a given attitude on each issue; the other two show by what percentage the supporters of each of the two main parties diverged from the average of all respondents.* In order to simplify these diagrams,

* The average which is taken as a basis for the construction of these diagrams is the average for all respondents, and the average between Conservative and Labour respondents only. The difference between these two averages is small, but it exists.

however, only one side of the answer is shown. In most cases, respondents could answer by Yes, No, or Don't Know; in some cases there were more possibilities of choice. The answer selected for the diagrams is the right-wing answer or, in the case of the Common Market, the pro-Common Market answer.

The first two answers on the left of each of the diagrams concern humanitarian and liberal matters. The general attitude of respondents is 'left-wing' on the House of Lords and 'right-wing' on crime and punishment and on immigration. Partisanship is fairly low: Labour electors are only slightly more 'left-wing' than Conservative electors; electors of both parties remain near the average for the country.

The next set of four answers concerns foreign affairs. There is relatively little partisanship, although the support for a 'right-wing' policy varies greatly from question to question: variations between the two parties exist on Rhodesia (recognizing the *de facto* situation) or on the retention of nuclear weapons by Britain, but they are much less marked than the variations which might have been expected. This 'consensus' was manifest all through the 1960s, though it appears to have diminished somewhat, but only somewhat, after Labour took office.

Even on social and economic issues, partisan cleavages remain relatively small. They seem to have been greater in the early 1960s than under the Labour government of the second half of the 1960s, although the topical questions were also of a different character. Neither housing problems (sale of council houses) nor even comprehensive schools appeared to lead to the same levels of partisanship as taxation questions, the health service or nationalization matters did at the beginning of the decade. Yet, overall, it is on social and economic questions that the Labour and Conservative curves grow further and further apart at both ends of the 1960s. If British electors are partisan, it is on these questions and on these questions only. Other questions may divide the parties at Westminster or in the constituency organizations; they do not divide Conservative and Labour electors against each other.

It is interesting to look more closely at the degree of partisanship. If electors were very partisan, one would find 100 per cent

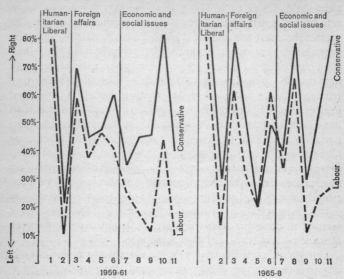

Figure 3. *Proportion of electors of the two main parties favouring a right-wing answer on individual issues*

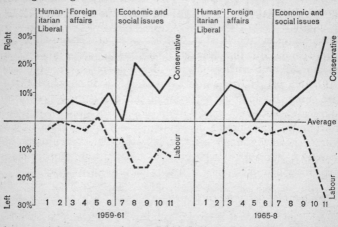

Percentage variation from the average proportion of electors favouring a right-wing answer

(constructed from answers given to British Institute of Public Opinion surveys, 1959–61 and 1965–8)

of the electors of one party but none of the electors of the other party on each side of the fence. Extreme partisanship would be reflected by a difference of 100 per cent on the bottom two diagrams, the curve of each party being 50 per cent away from the average. One cannot expect such a high degree of partisanship, even on the most burning issue. Yet it is perhaps surprising to note that the 'percentage of partisanship' is often in the 20 to 30 per cent range, even on allegedly 'burning' issues. It exceeds 40 per cent on only one of the issues shown here – and this is an issue which relates more to confidence in the government (to a party 'image', as we shall see) than to a policy in the strict sense of the word. Except where party allegiance (and, to a more limited extent, trade unions) are involved, supporters of each party are much more divided among themselves than along party lines. And these divisions among supporters of the same party appear to be of long standing: neither time nor change of party in power seemed to do much to modify this apparent divorce between attitude on issues and partisan allegiance.

One should consider in this light a matter which was of great importance in the 1950s and during most of the 1960s, the question of nationalization. It appears clear that some movement of opinion did take place between the early 1950s and the mid-1960s, in that the supporters of further nationalization measures gradually decreased in the population at large. The movement of opinion is undeniable, whether one attributes it to the record of the nationalized industries or to anti-nationalization propaganda. But this decrease did occur at large, among the electors of both parties, and not merely among some sections. Although nationalization does remain an issue on which there are some divisions on party lines, the cleavages *between* the parties are not as sharp as is often thought. Overall, on nationalization as on nuclear disarmament, on immigration as on comprehensive schools, electors of both parties have much in common. Similarities in governmental policies are more than in part inscribed in electors' attitudes on individual issues.

Opinions and party support

We already said that we do not intend to 'explain' the 'causes' of voting behaviour, because this is plainly impossible to do. Yet we cannot just note in passing the discrepancy between views and voting. Electors hold views which are not those of their party and still vote for that party. Nationalization was raised once more at the time of the 1959 General Election, partly as a result of the 'Hurry poll' which we already mentioned. But the drop in the Labour vote was very small; moreover, it is highly improbable that much of this drop was due to opposition to nationalization. As we have seen, the discrepancy occurring on nationalization is only one of a series of discrepancies, some of which are larger, some of which are smaller, than is the discrepancy on nationalization. The important point is that the electors of one party are seldom united in upholding one line; they are even sometimes divided right in the middle. Individual issues are clearly not a predominant factor in voting behaviour.

Of course, there are cases when the discrepancy occurs because the electors are not aware of the line taken by their party. The knowledge of party policies has become more widespread, chiefly as a result of the development of television which has been found to be the main instrument of political education of the average voter. Yet there are still electors who do not know what the issues are at a general election and who do not know what their party stands for. In 1959, a survey conducted in Leeds showed that 16 per cent of the electors who had seen the party programmes on television did not know what the Labour party platform was on old age pensions; the proportion was much higher among those who had not seen the party programmes.

However, those who come to learn what the party line is on an issue seem more often prepared to change their views than to modify their vote. Voting behaviour is usually more solid than opinions. When, in July 1961, Mr Macmillan stated that Britain was to seek entry into Europe, changes in attitudes occurred: Conservatives became more favourable and Labour electors more unfavourable. Conversely, support for the Common Market increased from 38 to 63 per cent among Labour electors between 1964 and 1967, while the percentage of Conservative supporters decreased somewhat. Parties thus do succeed in changing the views of their supporters over a period of time.

Moreover, many electors know that their views are not those which their party puts forward and are prepared to state this disagreement and to continue to vote for their party. Some declare that they do not know what the party line is because they prefer to conceal their apparent inconsistency to interviewers. Many plainly acknowledge their disagreement. In November 1961, large majorities of electors stated that they would continue to vote for their party even if that party eventually took, on the Common Market, a line which they opposed. Among Conservatives, only 13 per cent declared that they would change their vote and 73 per cent said that they would not; among Labour supporters, 16 per cent said that they would change their vote and 63 per cent declared that they would not. Three years before, in 1958, over 80 per cent of the supporters of each of the two main parties declared that they would carry on voting for their party even if both parties had exactly the same policy. It would be interesting to know whether they would also declare their readiness to carry on voting for their party if Labour policy became extreme left-wing or Conservative policy reactionary.

Party images

Voting cannot be explained by entirely rational criteria. At the beginning of the century, Graham Wallas showed the fairly narrow limits of the rational element in voting behaviour. Even though the two-party system enables electors to choose between two sets of programmes and only between two sets of programmes, it is not true that electors choose between programmes. It is not even true that electors, having only one vote, establish an order of priority and select one 'most important issue' on the basis of which they cast their vote. Studies which have taken place since Wallas have shown that the support which electors give to a party is linked, not with 'issues', but with much broader and vaguer general 'images' with which the party is associated. These images often coincide with a certain view of the class system in the country, particularly among Labour electors, a large majority of whom claim that their party is 'for the working class' and an even larger majority of whom claim that the Conservative party is 'for the rich or big business'. These images are also associated with some general economic and social notions, such as the 'Welfare State', 'full employment' in the past, 'free enterprise' and, now, quite often, 'nationalization'. The internal unity and the character of the leadership of the parties play a part in the formation of these images. In recent years at any rate, foreign affairs do not: respondents of whatever political views recognize that both parties are 'for peace' in a general sense. Images do not spring up either, in the minds of electors, on humanitarian and libertarian ques-

Table 18. *Party images in Bristol North-East, 1955* (percentages)

| | Images of the Labour party | |
	by Labour supporters	by Conservative supporters
For the working class	68	32
For the Welfare State	18	12
For the country as a whole	5	4
For full employment	4	2
For nationalization, controls	4	32
Impractical, extravagant	1	18
	100	100

| | Images of the Conservative party | |
	by Labour supporters	by Conservative supporters
For all classes	6	30
For free enterprise, for business	7	26
For the rich, big business	85	8
For individual freedom	–	14
For denationalization	1	5
For full employment	–	9
Capable, experienced leaders	1	8
	100	100

(from *Marginal Seat*, p. 132)

tions. To that extent, the partisanship which one finds on economic and social 'images' corresponds to the partisanship which we found earlier on economic and social issues.

Images differ from issues, but they are connected to them. Images do live. As the authors of the Bristol surveys said, some issues cross the gateway and become images, as, in recent years, nationalization; others, such as full employment, disappear in the wilderness. Images are influenced by issues in a general fashion: they are influenced by what is going on. They are also influenced by leadership and party dynamism. But they are more persistent than issues and some of them, for instance the image of class, are so persistent that they seem to be permanent. They are much vaguer than issues; they indicate that the electors have a general view of society and of the way in which the parties fit in the framework of society. One of the difficulties of the Liberal party seems to be that it does not evoke any images in the minds of the electors.

There is nothing inherently wrong in the fact that electors associate the parties with images and not with policies. We have just said that, in the long run, these images are modified and influenced; they are modified by the policies and record of the parties. Moreover, if party support was entirely rational and solely based on policies, representative government would become unworkable. The parties would never be able to count on some loyal support in cases of blunders and difficulties; nor would they ever be able to rally their supporters and thereby educate public opinion. But the decisions at election time would not become any easier, since the parties have comprehensive programmes and since a vote has to be a vote for a package deal. Voting is clearly partly an emotional affair. It is based on pre-judices as well as on a rational assessment of the structure of society in general. It is based on the view which the electors have of the future society which the parties are trying to build. It is up to the parties to modify, slowly but profoundly, these prejudices and these views. Party images are the medium through which the party conflict is resolved, every four or five years, at the general election. General elections involve the whole life of the nation. It is natural that they should be decided, not only by views on one or a few fairly specialized questions, but on the whole of the impressions which, rightly or wrongly, electors have of society and of its political forces.

The notions of right and left and the electorate

One may understand why voting cannot be directly influenced by the views which electors have on one political issue: some people may be opposed, for instance, to Labour's policy on various issues, but they may feel that the dependence of the Conservative party on big business is such that, in the present divisions of society, they must continue to vote Labour. Yet the answers to some of the questions are perhaps more surprising. It may seem surprising to see that the same majorities, in both parties, take the same right-wing stand on capital punishment and corporal punishment. It may seem surprising to note that

Table 19. *Humanitarian and 'liberal' questions and social class* (percentages)

| | Capital punishment | | Corporal punishment | | Race Relations Act | | |
	For	Against	For	Against	For	Against	Don't Know
Well-to-do	69	31	76	24	} 34	45	21
Middle	75	25	75	25			
Lower middle and working	} 79	21	74	26	27	47	26
Very poor					28	46	26

(from answers to British Institute of Public Opinion interviews in March 1960 and April 1968)

almost the same majorities in both parties are in favour of Britain keeping nuclear weapons. In all these cases, the 'left' seems to be almost as large among Conservative electors as it is among Labour electors.

Some have concluded that the traditional distinctions between a 'right' and a 'left' are purely and simply wrong, that they are the product of the imagination of sophisticated politicians, but do not have any roots in the electorate, that the 'syndrome' between attitudes on social, economic, humanitarian, libertarian, and other questions is not a real one. Indeed, if one analyses the attitudes of different social classes on different issues, one sometimes notices that the same social groups divide differently on different types of issues. On capital punishment, middle-class respondents were found to be more 'left-wing' than working-class respondents. This was not the case, however, for other 'humanitarian' questions.

Findings on humanitarian issues such as those on capital punishment led some sociologists to the conclusion that manual workers were more authoritarian and less tolerant than non-manual workers. Others have criticized this point of view on the grounds that daily experience showed that manual workers were loving parents and loving husbands and that the 'authoritarian-ism' of the manual working class was based on a confusion be-tween toughness and what the middle class would consider to be 'lack of manners'. Conducted at this level, the discussion is likely to be both endless and fruitless; it is sometimes based on entirely different premises and on emotional standpoints.

It is perhaps possible, however, to discover one flaw in the distinction between right and left. It purports to be a compre-hensive division embracing all political attitudes. But there is one way in which the opposition between political attitudes may not always coincide with right and left. Two people may have identical aims in view, and yet they may strongly be opposed to each other when it comes to considering means. In current politics, this is very often the case; it is even the case at the level of political doctrines. Communism and Fascism differ from right-wing Conservatism and from Socialism respectively, not so much because of the views or the aims, but because of the means which the upholders of these doctrines are prepared to use.

If this distinction between aims and means is taken into account, it becomes necessary to think, not in terms of one linear division between right and left, but in terms of two divisions in two different dimensions. On a slightly different plane, investi-gations have been made in order to see whether one should distinguish people according to two different criteria. Dr Eysenck suggested that electors should be 'scaled' on two different axes, one which would measure their 'conservatism' or their 'radicalism' and another which would measure their 'tough-mindedness' or their 'tender-mindedness' (Figure 4). There was indeed some evidence indicating that the variations

Figure 4. *Party supporters and the two scales of political attitudes (1950)*

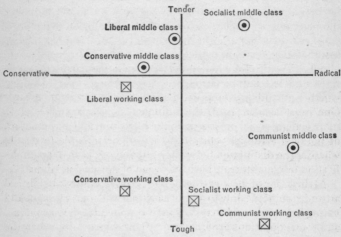

(from H. J. Eysenck, 'Primary Social Attitudes', in *British Journal of Sociology*, 1951, p. 198; also *Sense and Nonsense in Psychology*, Penguin Books, 1957, p. 303)

according to one axis did not coincide with variations according to the other.

On these scales, as might have been expected, Communists were found to be more 'tough-minded' than Conservatives and Socialists, Liberals being the most 'tender-minded' of all. On the same scales, it also appeared that, within each party, the middle-class elements were always more 'tender-minded' than the working-class supporters. The difference, in a country like Britain which is on the whole very 'tender-minded', is very small. In other countries, where people are more inclined to adopt violence as a means of achieving political aims, the differences are perhaps larger. As a result, it may be more useful to use the two dimensions in other countries than in Britain.

Such analyses have only started. They have not been followed up systematically enough to be more than indications of a possible line of research. However, the distinction between 'opinions' and 'voting behaviour' is so apparent that it becomes obvious that we must analyse 'opinions' independently from 'voting'. We have seen that, to some extent, voting can be explained by class, although we have had to add a number of other factors, of which the membership of a trade union was probably the most important. The origins of opinions have scarcely, as yet, been considered, partly perhaps because one too readily assumed that opinions coincided with voting. The 'syndrome' of political attitudes which is summarized by the expressions of right and left surely needs much rethinking. One must see whether attitudes on ends are distinct from attitudes on means. One must also measure the influence of propaganda and of more general social pressures on the formation and perpetuation of political attitudes. Only then will it be possible to decide whether the distinction between right and left is an oversimplification or constitutes a basic cleavage of political attitudes.

At this stage of the investigation, we can conclude that political attitudes coincide only to a limited extent with party images and voting behaviour and that they mainly coincide when economic and social questions are involved – more specifically, when the relative position of classes in society is involved. The basic division in the electorate is still a distinction between people who have a different view of what the 'class system' is and what it ought to be. This view of the class system does not, in many cases, amount to a 'socialist' vision of society on the part of Labour voters, though discontent may arise if the party does not bring about the 'utopia' when it is in power. The image which springs up in the minds of the electors is blurred, but for better or worse, the simple division between 'working' and 'middle class' is still very alive in many sections of the British electorate. It is the division which still contributes to the clearest cleavage in British political attitudes and in British voting behaviour.

CHAPTER FOUR

The Political Parties

POLITICAL parties occupy a peculiar position in Western democracies. They are, almost everywhere, and in particular in Britain, private associations to which the law does not give more rights and duties than to other private organizations. However, neither Britain nor any other democracy could function without parties. They are the main link between electors and their M.P.s. Without them, elections would be meaningless for the vast majority of voters who know very little about the candidates. Without them, elections would decide nothing. Parties are part and parcel of the real life of elections and of Parliament. They are not really private bodies: they perform the public function of representation. The law says that the M.P.s are the representatives; but, since the candidates owe their loyalty and their seat to the parties, the reality of the function of representation is, nowadays, more in the parties than in the M.P.s.

Parties perform this function of representation in two main ways. They do so by selecting candidates for elective posts – in local government as well as in national politics. They also do so by adopting policies which these candidates, as well as the party as a whole, propose to the electors. In order to achieve both these aims, political parties have long ceased to be, in Britain more perhaps than elsewhere, loose federations of small committees constituted in each locality; they have become large machines, with hundreds of thousands of members, with hundreds of paid officials.

This transformation was inevitable. It came as a result of various causes, among which the growth in the size of the electorate, the loss of influence of prominent individuals in the constituencies, the development of nation-wide mass-media, the virtual ending of local issues, and the overriding importance of national problems played a part in varying degrees. Moreover, the appearance of mass parties was held by many to be the proof of the democratization of politics: political organizations would no longer be run by small groups of self-appointed 'natural' leaders; the people at large – at least those who were interested enough to join the party of their choice – could play a part in the decisions.

This pious hope has not been realized at all, according to the cynics. Almost as soon as the mass parties developed in Western Europe, some observers asserted that even in the alleged democratic parties, like the Socialist parties, an 'iron law of oligarchy' prevailed. According to such critics, leaders are not really 'chosen' by the rank-and-file, but tend to be selected by a narrow group and often perpetuate themselves in office. Politics are not the result of the consensus of opinion of the local militants, but the fruit of the personal whims of these oligarchs.

Students of politics have since introduced nuances to both these theories and probably no one would seriously hold that either of these extreme models fits the British political parties, although it is sometimes alleged that the Conservative party closely resembles the 'oligarchical' one. In fact, as we shall see, the situation is rather more complex, although we still know too little of the inner workings of the parties to be able to pronounce definite judgements. British parties are so large that no honest judgement can be a simple one. If one is to pass judgement, one must at least examine the organization and life of the parties at the various levels. (1) One has first to consider the ordinary members: are they, or are they not, representative of the electors? Do they come from the same social classes, do they hold the same views? (2) One has to look at the local leaders who constitute the first and crucial level of the political 'élite' since they choose the parliamentary candidates and form a large part of the local councillors. (3) One has to examine regional leaders, although regions have less influence: regions are the connecting link between the national and local organizations. (4) One has of course to examine the national leaders and see how far they represent the rank-and-file and the local leaders or how far they constitute a world of their own. One must see which part M.P.s play in the composition of the ruling bodies. Only then will it be possible to pass a tentative judgement on the 'democratic' or 'oligarchical' character of the parties. One should not be surprised to find that the same conclusions do not equally apply to the various levels of these 'pyramids'.

Rank-and-file members

British political parties are among the largest in the world. The Conservative party has about 2·8 million members; Labour with its trade union members is 6·3 million strong and its individual members alone number 800,000. Of course, it is probable that these figures are somewhat inflated: in the Labour party, many members are counted twice, through the constituency parties and through the trade unions; in both parties, local organizations are not always up to date with their membership figures. However, even if the real figures are somewhat below the official ones, the totals are very large by comparison with the totals obtained in many other European countries. They are particularly impressive on the Conservative side, because right-wing parties usually have much smaller membership totals than left-wing parties. One out of four or five electors of the Conservative party is a member, while only one out of thirteen or fourteen electors of the Labour party is an individual member. The individual membership of the Labour party is slightly larger than the individual membership of the German Socialist party, but the number of its electors is also slightly greater. The Conservative party has fewer electors than the German Christian Democratic Union of Dr Adenauer, but it has ten times more members. In the late forties and early fifties, the Conservatives achieved the remarkable result of trebling their membership, while the Labour individual membership remained almost static – indeed, declined a little – during the 1950s: Labour's big increases in membership were earlier, in the period just before and just after the 1945 General Election.

There has not yet been a general study of the membership of any British political party. Since 1950, however, several local parties have been examined in some detail and, from the facts which have been collected in such different places as Greenwich, Glossop, Stretford, Gorton (Manchester), Banbury, and Newcastle-under-Lyme, we begin to have some idea of the social structure and of the political views of rank-and-file members. Many of the results point to the same general trends and from these trends we can perhaps draw a few conclusions about the character of the membership of British political parties.

Generally speaking, the social structure of the membership of each of the two main parties seems to correspond to the social structure of its electorate, with one important reservation concerning the Conservative party. One finds little difference between the age groups of the members and the age groups of the electors, although members are perhaps slightly older than electors. One finds little difference in the distribution between the sexes. The Conservatives have more women among their electors as well as among their members, but women do not overwhelm the membership of local Conservative associations: they may, as it is often said, do all the work, but male members are almost as numerous as female members. There are more men among Labour members, but there are more men among Labour electors as well; only one survey, that of Greenwich, found male members to be disproportionately numerous in the Labour party.

The only really striking difference concerns the occupational structure of the members of the Conservative party. If the various 'classes' were to be represented among the membership in the way they are in the electorate, the Labour membership should be overwhelmingly composed of manual workers and the Conservative membership should be almost equally divided between manual and non-manual workers. Labour members are generally distributed in that way; Conservative members are not: they come from non-manual groups more than they 'should' if they were to reflect the distribution of the Conservative votes among the various classes. Non-manual groups constituted, for instance, three-fifths of the Conservative members in Glossop, but only half the Conservative electors. The working-class Conservative is easier to find among Conservative electors than among Conservative members.*

Views of rank-and-file members

One is often led to believe that party members are extremists

* See diagrams, p. 98.

and do not 'represent' the views of a balanced cross-section of each party. This is said to be the case in both parties. Conservative members are thought to be die-hards and Labour members extreme Socialists. One refers perhaps more, admittedly, to the active members than to the whole rank-and-file; but when this is the case, one often opposes the 'activism' of the 'militants' to the more sedate views of the whole rank-and-file. The views of the whole rank-and-file need to be examined in either case.

Conservative members do not seem to be particularly extreme in their views, as far as one can see from the small amount of evidence which is available. Comparisons with the results of the Gallup polls are not usually possible, but the authors of the Glossop survey examined the views of Conservative members in some detail and they did not find them to be to the right of the government. By large majorities, the rank-and-file was opposed to nationalization, to increases in food subsidies, and to the raising of the school-leaving age, but it was also opposed to further increases in National Health Service charges (1953). On humanitarian matters, Newcastle-under-Lyme members were not more right-wing than Conservative electors throughout the country. The evidence is still small. It does not suggest that Conservative members are 'die-hards'; it seems to indicate that they react rather like Conservative electors. They are united on a right-wing, but not on a reactionary, economic policy and they are more divided on other questions.

Conservative members probably hold the same views as Conservative electors but they are not distributed among the social classes in the same way as Conservative electors are. Within limits, the situation is reversed in the Labour party. Manual workers are proportionately as numerous among Labour electors as among Labour members, but left-wingers seem to be more numerous among members than among electors. In Glossop and Stretford, majorities, and sometimes large majorities, of members favoured the nationalization of many industries. Supporters of unilateral nuclear disarmament were numerous in the rank-and-file of the Newcastle-under-Lyme Labour party.

Even in the Labour party, however, 'extremism' is not as

widespread as it is perhaps sometimes thought to be. The membership is generally divided: the constituency parties which have been investigated have been found to be divided into two almost equal parts on many contentious issues. Moreover, the left-wing 'syndrome' is usually not complete. This is not only because members are often found to support policies to the right of the official line, such as the sale of council houses, but also because attitudes on leaders do not always coincide with attitudes on policies. It is surely exaggerated to contend that all Labour party members are extreme Socialists. Many are, and there are more of them among members than among electors. Many others are not. A general study throughout the country would probably show that the two 'wings' of the party are fairly evenly balanced. It would probably also show that, in many cases, the division between 'right' and 'left' is not as clear-cut among members as the division between 'activists' and 'ordinary rank-and-file members' sometimes seems to imply that it is.

Active and passive members

Most members are not active. In reality, apart from paying their dues, they *never* participate in any activity, whether political – including electoral – or social, of the party which they have joined. Most members of political parties behave like members of other social bodies: they do not exercise the right – or the duty – which membership entails.

The proportion of active or of not totally inactive members seems higher in the Labour party than in the Conservative party. At least two-fifths and perhaps more of the Labour members seem to play *a* part in the activities of their party, most of them admittedly very spasmodically. In the Conservative associations the figure is probably around a fourth or a third. Even if these proportions are not in fact the correct ones over the whole country, a difference between the two parties seems to exist, since the same difference has been found in all the constituency parties where the question has been examined. As a result, the size of the manpower which is at the disposal of the parties, at general elections for instance, is not as different as the total figures of membership would suggest. The disparity between the two parties is, on paper, one to three; it is probably only one to two or one to two-and-a-half in reality.

It is difficult to know whether these differences in the percentage of active members are indicative of any difference in the nature of the bond which links the members to their party. In the first place, 'active' is taken here in a rather negative sense: it merely means that these members are not completely foreign to the activities of their party. In the second place, since Conservative associations have more members, it is perhaps logical that the proportion of active Conservative members should be smaller. Conservative associations have been engaged in membership drives on a much greater scale than constituency Labour parties, partly because Conservative associations, being richer, have been able to afford paid canvassers on a bigger scale, partly because the Labour party as a whole has a large membership coming from the unions. Conservative associations must therefore have gradually come to enlist many lukewarm supporters or, at any rate, people who are not very interested in politics. Conversely, the constituency Labour parties require a larger proportion of active members simply because they are smaller. The number of jobs which have to be done is not related only to the number of members, but to other factors as well: if general elections are to be fought with any degree of organization, a certain minimum of active party supporters is required. In Newcastle-under-Lyme, where the membership of both parties was smaller than the average for the whole nation, the proportion of active members was larger, on both sides, than in the other constituencies which have been investigated.

Constituency leaders

By what seems to be a process of selection by apathy, 36 million electors thin out into 3.5 to 4 million members. These 3.5 to 4 million members thin out into perhaps 1.5 million of semi-active voluntary workers of whom probably only half or a third are really active. These more active members have definitely a greater say in the decisions which are taken by the local parties. They elect the local leaders and these local leaders emerge from among their group. Who are the local leaders and do they have the same characteristics as ordinary members and electors?

There are two main difficulties when one comes to consider the local leadership. The first is that the word 'leader' is ambiguous and embraces at least two circles of people, at any rate if the constituency organization is at all active. A few top leaders hold *constituency* offices and 'N.C.O.s' hold offices in the *component bodies* of the local associations and local parties. Local organizations normally have ward branches and branches open to women members and young members: these 'primary cells' all elect their own officers. If one includes these officers elected by the branches, the group of leaders becomes relatively large. Each of the Greenwich local parties was found in 1950 to have about a hundred officers of all types. If these figures were repeated all over the country, each of the two main parties would thus have over 60,000 officers of all types at a given time. This is clearly an overestimate. In many constituencies, large areas are not covered by branches. But the Greenwich figures give an idea of the total number of people who are involved, at various levels, in the 'leadership' of constituency organizations.

The consequence is that local parties have a hierarchy of leaders: it is the same kind of hierarchy as the one which is found on local councils, where the average member, like the average officer of a ward branch, allows himself to be led, to some extent at least, by more influential councillors and aldermen. In a local party organization, with forty, fifty, or more elected officers, only a fraction of these officers has much power at constituency level. When the constituency organization has to choose its parliamentary candidate, the group which draws the crucial short list rarely numbers more than half-a-dozen to a dozen members, even if the final decision on the candidates who have been short-listed is taken by a larger body.

The structure of local parties on both sides makes this distinction between two types of leaders both possible and normal. Each party is run locally by two sets of committees, one which is large and formally takes the decisions and another which is smaller and theoretically only prepares and implements the decisions of the other. The large committee, which is named

General Management Committee on the Labour side and Executive Committee on the Conservative side, has representatives of the wards, women's branches, and young people's branches, if there are any. The Conservative executive also includes representatives of the Conservative clubs and some co-opted people. The Labour G.M.C. naturally has representatives of the trade unions and other affiliated organizations. However, although in theory the Labour G.M.C. and the Conservative executive have more powers, they are too large (fifty or more people are customarily members of these bodies) to do much more than ratify the decisions 'prepared' by the smaller bodies.* These are the Executive Committee on the Labour side and the General Purposes Committee on the Conservative side and they are composed of members elected by the large bodies. On these smaller committees sit the really influential constituency leaders. Since these leaders are only indirectly (at least for the most part) elected by the rank-and-file, they are more independent of its whims and they may constitute a relatively closed group of leaders.

Indeed, it can even be argued that distinctions should not stop here and that one ought to consider, within the smaller committees, an even smaller group of people who are most influential of all, either because they have been members for a long time or because of their social position. One should perhaps also examine whether there are outsiders who wield some influence although they do not (or no longer) sit on any committee. One should examine the role of the agent, who attends committee meetings because he is the secretary of all the committees but does not technically belong to them. Agents can be influential because they know more about what happens in the constituency than many committee members and because they are in relation with central office and know what happens in the 'outside

---

* On the Conservative side there is also an Annual General Meeting, which, among other things, elects the officers of the Association, but this A.G.M. does not attract many members outside those who are members of the executive. It is rare for more than 150 members to come to these gatherings (out of usually around 5,000). The attendance is often much smaller. Candidates are also adopted by this body, but this adoption is purely formal.

world'. They carry perhaps more weight in the Labour party than in the Conservative party because the Conservative agent does not belong to the local 'establishment' and often seems to have the status of employee of the association rather than that of partner. The real situation varies, however, from place to place, which leads to the second difficulty in the analysis of the leadership.

When one considers the electorate or the whole membership, or even the whole group of leaders, one can perhaps generalize from the examination of the life of a few constituencies. Britain is fairly homogeneous: provided one is careful not to consider the details, but only the main trends, generalizations are probably valid. When, however, one considers the top leaders, their social characteristics, their relationships, these generalizations are simply not possible. Most probably there is no general pattern. Variations from area to area are likely to be considerable. The social groups and the history are different from one constituency to the next. Through accidental causes, one strong individual or a few strong individuals can play a considerable part. Until one or two *hundred* constituencies are studied in great detail, which is not likely to happen soon, any generalization at this level is entirely precluded. What we can do is, in the first place, to consider some characteristics, not of the top leaders only, but of all the leaders taken together, and, in the second place, to note some general contrasts between the local Labour leadership and the local Conservative leadership.

Social structure of the local leadership

One thing seems certain: the local leadership of both parties (taken in the widest sense and including 'N.C.O.s' as well as top leaders) is more middle class than the membership. Conservative local leaders are, therefore, two degrees remote from Conservative electors. This has been found to be the case in all the associations which have been studied. The manual workers seem to be almost entirely absent from the Conservative leadership, even from its outer circle. In Glossop, manual workers formed 50 per cent of the voters, but only 8 per cent of the leaders. In Greenwich, the lower income categories formed 60 per cent of the voters and 9 per cent of the leaders. In Newcastle-under-Lyme, only 6 per cent of the non-Labour councillors had been drawn, in the course of a long period, from manual workers.

Figure 5. *Officers, members, and electors in Greenwich (1950)*

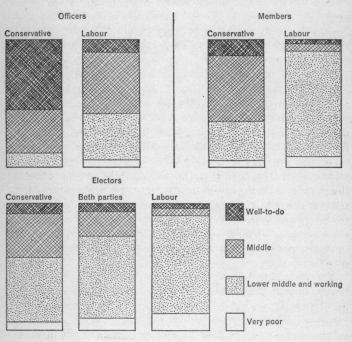

(constructed from data appearing in *How People Vote*, by Benney, Gray, and Pear, Routledge and Kegan Paul, 1956, pp. 47, 51, and 103)

This movement within Conservative associations is mainly to the disadvantage of manual workers; it does not seem to benefit the white-collar workers either. The main beneficiaries seem to be higher up in the social hierarchy, although the precise groups which are at an advantage seem to vary from place to place. They were mainly professional men, managers, businessmen in

Greenwich: these groups form 3 or 4 per cent of the electorate of the country, they formed 15 per cent of the Greenwich Conservative rank-and-file members and 56 per cent of the Conservative leaders. The leaders were mainly shopkeepers in Glossop, but leaders in other parts of the High Peak division were upper middle class. Local candidates were drawn from among shopkeepers and from among businessmen and professional men in Newcastle-under-Lyme, but the businessmen and the professional men managed, on the whole, to be selected for the safest seats.

There is one purely technical reason why the middle class, and even perhaps the solid middle class, is almost bound to be over-represented in the leadership of a Conservative association. Conservatives are more numerous in middle-class areas: as a result, unless the association is very well organized, branches will flourish in middle-class areas and remain half asleep in working-class districts. Consequently, there will be more officers in middle-class areas than in working-class areas, in proportion to the population and even to the Conservative electorate. Since, not surprisingly, working-class areas are more likely to throw up working-class leaders than middle-class areas, the leadership of a Conservative association will naturally show a tendency to be more middle class than a cross-section of the electorate and membership.

Yet this accident is not the only cause of the over-representation of the middle classes among local Conservative leaders. The general conditions in which local associations grew, the general values which are usually prevalent, the sense of leadership which is expected from the middle class also are important elements of explanation. The national headquarters of the party deplore this over-representation; in many cases – indeed perhaps in most cases – it does not come about out of a conscious desire to exclude manual workers. This exclusion or quasi-exclusion seems, however, to develop naturally within Conservative associations.

It must be remembered that Conservative associations are perhaps primarily social organizations. They are rightly called 'associations' and not 'parties'. These social organizations have a definite middle-class atmosphere. Whoever comes and acquires the tastes and values of these middle-class clubs is certainly welcome: the associations are not closed societies. On the other hand, those who do not have these tastes and values are barred, not by any conscious decision taken against them, but simply because these individuals are unlikely to feel at home in a society which behaves in a manner which is somewhat foreign to them. Moreover, many members of the middle-class groups consider that the participation in the activities of the local Conservative association is a kind of duty or that it goes without saying. This may no longer be the case for some of the members of the new managerial groups, as was pointed out for Glossop. We do not know whether the situation in Glossop is, in this respect, representative of the situation over the whole country. The members of the new managerial classes may have stood aloof from the local association in Glossop because Glossop is a small industrial town. It would be interesting to know whether one finds the same aloofness in large centres or in residential areas. In any case, even if the *new* managerial classes do stand aloof from the local associations, many businessmen and professional men do still consider that membership of, and leadership in, the local Conservative association is as natural as is the membership of the local golf club. 'Everybody' is not a member of the golf club; some people temperamentally object to the club or dislike the game. The same probably applies to Conservative associations, which are therefore likely to recruit many members of the solid middle class but not all of them. Eventually many of these members 'naturally emerge' as leaders. Not surprisingly, manual workers and even white-collar workers somehow do not seem equally qualified to enter the race for leadership.

Whatever distinctions must be introduced from constituency to constituency, it seems generally true to say that the local leadership of Conservative associations is not a representative cross-section of the membership and of the electorate of the party. Inner circles are not photographic images of outer circles. The structure of the party is more like a pyramid. Most probably the top posts of the pyramid are filled, in many cases, by members of the highest ranks of the social hierarchy. Admittedly, some of these posts do not carry much power, but some do.

Admittedly, one has to differentiate between rural and semi-rural constituencies, where traditional 'ruling' families probably still often form the apex of the pyramid, and industrial areas where the middle class is present, but not the upper class. The pyramid is often truncated, but the association is a social pyramid if one compares the bottom to the top.

Leaders of constituency Labour parties are not a photographic image of the whole of the membership either. Among them, as well as among local Conservative leaders, the middle class is over-represented. Manual workers are overwhelmingly strong among Labour members and electors, but they only formed one-third of the leaders in Glossop, half the leaders in Greenwich, rather more in Newcastle-under-Lyme. The result may not be, as in Conservative associations, the virtual disappearance of the manual workers from among the local leaders; manual workers remain prominent in local Labour parties. But they are not represented in proportion to their numbers lower down the structure of the party. As in the Conservative associations, middle-class groups manage to obtain more than their share of the seats in the leadership of local Labour parties.

There are probably general reasons which explain why they obtain more than their share, in the Labour party as in any other 'working-class' party. We shall see in the next chapter that, when one comes to consider M.P.s, the administrative skill and the training acquired at school or in the job automatically help potential politicians. At local level as well, manual workers are probably handicapped, unless they are union leaders, if they want to move up to the leadership. Yet the situation which obtains in the local Labour parties remains very different from the situation which prevails in Conservative associations. It is not only that the Labour party is generally based on principles of 'equality' and 'solidarity' which make it difficult for notions of social hierarchy to develop easily at the roots of the party structure. It is also that the non-manual groups from which the local Labour leaders come are usually very different from the groups which come to the fore in Conservative associations. The gap between manual and non-manual workers is probably very small in almost all cases.

There are, in the first place, many white-collar workers. As we argued in Chapter Two, the distinction between white-collar workers and manual workers is much less clear-cut than one might be inclined to think, at least in many cases. Many clerks, insurance agents, foremen, shop assistants, etc., come from working-class families and do not distinguish themselves, either by their manners, or by their income, from manual workers. White-collar workers are not just one large category. They may be class-conscious or come from middle-class homes. They may also, in almost exactly the same jobs and at any rate in the same social categories, feel that they belong to the working class, have many relations in the working class, and continue to live in working-class districts. One cannot say in advance that non-manual workers engaged in clerical or distributive jobs will feel different from manual workers. Some do, but others do not. Those who are in the Labour party often do not feel different. The white-collar workers who do feel different are more likely to join the Conservative party.

As for the middle-class groups who belong to the local Labour leadership, they seem to be almost exclusively composed of a few shopkeepers, a certain number of managers, and a large number of teachers. Businessmen, lawyers, and doctors are usually absent. Teaching was the only profession which was represented among Labour candidates and councillors in Reading and New-castle-under-Lyme in contests spreading over a quarter of a century. There are doubtless cases where the other professions are represented, but these would seem to be the exception rather than the norm. Lawyers and doctors may be more numerous in local Labour parties in large industrial centres. In medium-sized and small towns, the members of the medical and legal professions seem to be commonly found among the ranks of the Conservative leadership or, when they are not Conservatives, among the ranks of the Liberal leadership.

Although the local Labour leadership is thus not entirely 'representative' of the electorate and membership of the local Labour parties, its middle-class and lower-middle-class elements are not a cross-section of the non-manual jobs which exist in the country. With its trade union manual workers, its white-collar workers, and a number of teachers, the local Labour leadership does follow the traditional pattern of the leadership of Socialist parties: this pattern is that of the old alliance between the 'proletariat' and the 'intelligentsia'. White-collar workers form a link between manual workers and middle-class teachers.

There are clearly many variations around this model. A local Labour party in Norfolk is unlikely to have the same type of leadership as the Hampstead Labour Party or the Colne Valley Labour Party. However, the three main groups are probably often the working-class trade unionists, the white-collar workers, and the 'intelligentsia'. This is why class differences are not normally going to be felt. The centre of gravity lies towards the middle of the social scale. Politically active trade unionists are likely to be interested in and aware of the theory of socialism, and many teachers in many countries have been anxious to be involved in practical politics on the left. Moreover, the income differences between the members of these groups are not very large; the way of life of all these leaders is probably not very different. If the leaders of local Labour parties are, therefore, slightly more 'bourgeois' than the members and electors of the party, the gap is not sufficiently large to produce a break on social grounds alone between members and leaders or among the leaders.

Views of local leaders

Until a survey of party membership is undertaken all over the country, we will not know with precision the views of local leaders: we can collect some scanty information about the views of some of them in some constituencies, but since there is only a small number of leaders in each constituency, we cannot say whether their views are representative of the views of local leaders throughout the country.

One has, therefore, to rely on the Conference, which is, for the time being, the only source of information which the observer has. At the Conference, each year, a large number of resolutions are sent in by the local parties, and a small number of these are debated and voted upon. The resolutions on the agenda and the way voting goes are therefore two clues which can give an idea of the views of local leaders, although these clues are, unfortunately, very imperfect.

Large numbers of resolutions – four to six hundred – are placed on the agenda of the Conference of the two main parties by the local constituency parties (as well as by certain other bodies). This gives an indication of the state of mind of the leaders of the local parties, although one must treat this information with caution, for two reasons. In the first place, resolutions have to be placed within the context of the year in which they are proposed: resolutions on a subject may grow like mushrooms one year and scarcely be proposed the next. In the second place, the resolutions which are proposed by a local party are the result of a selection. This is particularly so in the Labour party, where each constituency can send only one resolution and one amendment. Two things happen: in the first place, leaders have to choose between several resolutions in which they are equally interested; we will have only a partial idea of their views. In the second place, the choice is not entirely without political afterthoughts: those who oppose a certain resolution may prefer to circumvent their opponents by suggesting another, equally popular, but innocuous. We may therefore have a distorted idea of the local leaders' views.

Given these reservations, resolutions do constitute a rough guide. They give a broad idea of the general views and of the support which these views have. They give a broad idea of the proportion of 'extremists'. A systematic analysis of the resolutions of the two parties in the second half of the 1950s thus showed that the proportion of extremist resolutions was markedly smaller than is generally thought. The author of this analysis, R. Rose, noted two points. Firstly, 'exactly half the resolutions pressed by Conservative parties were non-partisan, though, of course, not necessarily non-political'; 'the figures were not much different for the Labour party' (42 per cent in fact) (*Crossbow*, Autumn 1961, p. 36). Secondly, not all partisan resolutions were extremist. In the Conservative party, right-wing extremist resolutions formed just over a fourth of the total number of resolutions, left-wing resolutions constituted 3 per cent, and middle-of-the-road resolutions 21 per cent. Right-wing resolutions may greatly outnumber left-wing resolutions in the Conservative party; they do not much outnumber the resolutions which simply support the leadership line.

Extremism is concentrated each year on two or three topics, and these topics naturally attract the attention of political commentators because they concern the main questions of the day (nuclear disarmament, nationalization, crime and punishment, immigration, etc.). One places the relevant resolutions in the perspective of all the others which are on the agenda, they come to be seen as a minority. Furthermore, they are even more of a minority if we note that many local parties do not bother to send any resolutions, despite the fact that they have markedly grown in number in the course of the 1960s. Yet less than half the constituency associations sent a resolution in 1965. Conservative associations may send as many resolutions as they want while Labour parties can send only one: but only one Conservative association in eight (sixty-nine) sent more than one resolution between 1955 and 1961 and less than one in four did so in 1965 (143). The 'deluge' of extremist resolutions may not be a deluge after all. In 1968, eighty Conservative associations sent a resolution on immigration, which was an explosive and highly topical issue: this is less than one in seven of all the associations. The maximum number of resolutions sent in any one year on nuclear disarmament was 125 at the 1960 Labour Conference: this is less than a fourth of the total number of constituency parties.

However, because a constituency party or association does not send a resolution on an issue, or even because it never sends any resolutions at all, it does not follow that the party is moderate or politically uncommitted. There are more grounds for making such a deduction in the Conservative party, since associations can send as many resolutions as they wish, than in the Labour party, where local parties are limited to one. This is why it would be very useful to know details of voting at the Conference, a situation which unfortunately does not obtain. One is reduced to guesses and rough calculations.

On the Labour side, one knows how large unions vote: one

can deduct from the total figures those which correspond to the large unions and be left with the more manageable totals of the smaller unions and the constituency parties. The outcome of such calculations, made by M. Harrison for the period before 1960, was that local Labour parties were not as extreme in their views as is sometimes thought. They seem to have often been fairly evenly spread between right and left, and the most clear-cut case of ideological clash, when the party leadership only received a small minority of the votes of the constituencies, was German rearmament in 1954. An analysis made by P. M. Williams and K. Hindell of the 1960 and 1961 votes on unilateral nuclear disarmament showed that in both cases the majority of the constituency votes supported the leadership, although the left gained some ground between the first Conference and the second. This might suggest that the right has on the whole been gaining ground since the middle 1950s. It is more probable that the boundary between 'right' and 'left' is much more flexible than one is often led to believe. 'Right' and 'left' on detailed issues cannot be strictly defined among constituency leaders any more than they can be defined among electors and among rank-and-file members. In their general attitudes, the constituency leaders are probably left-wing: as we shall see later, this is reflected in the election of constituency representatives on the National Executive Committee, although one should not interpret these elections in strict political terms. There is a large middle-of-the-road section and both 'right' and 'left' are usually prepared to give in to the party leadership – at least when the party is in power.

In the Conservative party, votes at the Conference may very well be a good indication of the attitudes of local leaders in the constituency associations. Admittedly the 'representatives' of the associations who go to the Conference are not pledged to follow a line dictated to them by the constituency leaders or the rank-and-file. But these 'representatives' are often themselves officers and leaders of the associations. The difficulty comes rather from the fact that we do not know how these 'representatives' voted because figures of voting are rarely given; no attempt has ever been made even to guess. Yet the outcome of debates on matters such as corporal punishment or race shows that extremism may be rampant in some quarters, but that it could easily be tamed, to say the least, by a determined leadership.

Thus the views of local leaders of both main parties seem representative of the rank-and-file members, if not necessarily of all the electors. Local Conservative leaders hold views which are probably very similar to those of Conservative voters. Local Labour leaders are somewhat to the left of Labour electors. They are, like Labour rank-and-file members, almost evenly divided between left-wing Socialists and moderate Socialists and it will be remembered that, on the contrary, left-wing Socialists seem to be a small minority among Labour voters. There is not, on the other hand, such a difference inside the Conservative party between the views of the voters and those of the local leaders. In the last resort, this is probably because few Conservatives, be they leaders, members, or electors, hold, in this country at least, views which amount to a comprehensive 'reactionary' doctrine. One must avoid falling into the trap of wanting to balance, at any rate with precision, the extremism of the left by the extremism of the right. Socialism in the marxian or near-marxian sense can probably be fairly called 'extremism' since it wants to transform in a radical fashion the social and economic bases of British society. It is, therefore, probably right to call 'extremists' the Labour supporters who hold views of this kind. On the Conservative side, on the contrary, one finds very few people who should, if words are to keep their meaning, be called 'extremists'. Some people want a return to past policies on some specific questions; many simply do not like the pace at which Conservative governments have succumbed to the 'wind of change'. These people should not be labelled extremists. Only those who hold a comprehensive body of doctrine which purports either to put the block back or to constitute society on a completely different basis should be qualified in that way. There are few holders of such doctrines in Conservative associations.

One should not, on the other hand, exaggerate the differences between the two parties at local level by misunderstanding the impact which this 'extremism' may have on local Labour leaders. It is often noted that the polarization which appears at national level does not occur so much at local level. In constituency parties, many leaders seem to sit on the fence, and they do not manifest their opinions with great militancy. Many may be left-wing Socialists, but their extremism is tempered in day-to-day life. Indeed, personal differences are perhaps more widespread than purely ideological disputes. Moreover, extremism is tempered because the views of these local leaders are less intellectualized than those of national leaders. It is tempered because local government affairs often play an important part in their political life. In their own community, these less outspoken leaders may often be more prominent than more militant leaders. They are often better known outside the circle of the party membership. Admittedly, their zeal for local government may blunt their more general zeal for reform; 'militants' play an important part in providing them with a constant challenge. None the less, the less outspoken leaders, who are numerous in local Labour parties, fulfil two important functions. They help to keep together the more militant groups, of the right and of the left, which might otherwise fall apart. They help to keep the constituency Labour parties in contact with the outside world and prevent them from being political sects without profound roots in the community.

Region and area leaders

The eleven regions of the Labour party and the twelve areas of the Conservative party are rarely examined. According to the party constitutions, they are not really autonomous. They were created later than both the national and constituency organizations, after 1886 in the Conservative party, after 1938 in the Labour party. In both cases, they were meant to be mainly decentralized offices of the national organization. Unlike the constituency agent, the regional or area organizer is appointed by head office and he is entrusted with the task of stimulating the efficiency of the constituency organizations. He is a kind of regional commissioner, not a county clerk. None the less, representative bodies exist in the regions and areas, in the form of councils representing the constituencies and of executives and officers carrying out the administration between the meetings of the councils. Moreover, whatever the constitutions of the parties may say, these areas and regions constitute a link between the national and local leaderships. Party headquarters will know, by name and personally, the regional leaders. They may even to some extent – they certainly do so in the Conservative party – ask for the views and take note of the warnings of the regional leaders.

Among the elective offices of the area and of the region, the most important are those of chairman, vice-chairman, and treasurer (the secretary is the region or area organizer), although there are a host of other elective posts. The holders of these posts are prominent leaders in the constituency organizations and, in the Labour party, in the trade unions as well. The social differences which we noted between the local leadership of the two parties are therefore naturally reflected at regional level. Conservative chairmen of areas are predominantly recruited from the top groups of the middle classes, although rarely from the aristocracy. Of the 43 persons who held a post of chairman in one of the twelve areas during the period 1952–62, 29 appear in *Who's Who*, twelve perhaps because they were M.P.s, but seventeen on account of their social prestige only. This never happens for the respective holders of the office on the Labour side.

We can examine the background of these Conservative chairmen with somewhat more precision. Of the 27 whose education could be traced, 22 had been to a public school and 20 had been to universities or equivalent places of higher education; 9 had been to Oxbridge and 5 to one of the service colleges. Even if all the chairmen whose education had not been traced had gone to a grammar school, just over half the total would still have been to a public school, a figure completely out of proportion with the situation in the country, in the Conservative electorate, and even, it seems, in the local leadership. Of the 28 chairmen whose occupation could be traced, 13 were in business, in most cases big business; 7 had been in the professions, 5 in the services, and 3 in the civil service or another public body. Again, even if none of the 15 other chairmen were in any of these occupations but were all in lower-ranking ones, two-thirds of the total number would have come from the top sections of the middle classes. This is an even higher proportion than the one found for local leaders in Greenwich where the local leadership was found to be predominantly middle class. The pyramidal structure of the Conservative party does not stop at constituency level: one can trace its development at area level as well.

This situation does not obtain for all the members of the Conservative area executives. The 'parallel' groups within the party, women's branches, Young Conservatives, Divisional Councils of Trade Unionists, send representatives to the area executive, in the form of the chairman of their own area council. These representatives do not come from the same exclusive social groups as the chairmen of areas do. Trade union representatives come from the working class: Mr Mawby was chairman of a trade union area before becoming an M.P. and indeed was for a period the only Tory working class M.P. Chairmen of Young Conservative areas did not uniformly go to public schools and to Oxbridge. Chairmen of women's area organizations probably come from more mixed social groups than chairmen of areas, although many do come from the upper ranges of the middle classes. It may indeed be that as a result social groups are more mixed at area level than at constituency level. The parallel organizations, except the women's branches, are not equally lively in the constituencies; despite the efforts of national headquarters, Divisional Councils of Trade Unionists are sometimes constituted only on paper at constituency level while there is always a trade union representative at area level. None the less, the area chairman is the most important figure on the executive and he is usually drawn from exclusive social groups. This is in marked contrast with the proletarian or lower-middle-class background of Labour regional officers.

Posts of officers in regions or areas carry some influence and give a certain status. Whether people rotate in these offices may or may not affect their status, but it does probably affect their influence. Admittedly, areas are more important in the life of the Conservative party than regions are in that of the Labour party. Yet this very importance is perhaps both underlined and increased by the regular manner in which chairmen rotate in office in the Conservative party, while the practice is much more haphazard in the Labour party. The tenure of office of Labour chairmen is either very short (one or two years) or almost indefinite. The first type of system does not give the chairman much time to come to grips with the affairs of the region; the second method, which is in use in Lancashire and the Northern and Eastern regions, may indicate that the office is considered to be totally unimportant or that some individuals gained a strong influence on the life of their regions. Treasurers of the Labour regions also usually stay in office for very long periods. In the Conservative areas, the tenure of office is neither so short nor so long; it does vary slightly, but it always stays very near the average of three years for chairmen and of about four years for treasurers. This is probably a sign that these offices are both burdensome and thought to be rather important.

Areas and regions are the links between the national and the local leaders. Of course, M.P.s do provide this link individually, but many questions, mainly administrative questions, have to go through the regional machines. In this respect too, the situation in the Conservative party suggests that the area is taken more seriously than the region is in the Labour party. The Conservatives seem anxious to turn the area into a political as well as an administrative channel. Over a fourth of the chairmen of areas were M.P.s during the 1950s; one area, Yorkshire, has had only M.P.s as chairmen during that period. Labour, on the other hand, had only four M.P.s among its seventy-six regional chairmen and vice-chairmen. The attempt to link the Conservative parliamentary party with the life of the area has no equivalent on the Labour side. Labour has as many local councillors among its regional office-holders as the Conservatives: the Labour region is thus fairly and squarely in the hands of the local leaderships, while in the Conservative area a balance is struck between local people with local interests and local people with parliamentary interests. Moreover, the Conservatives have also found seats in Parliament for many of their area workers.

The real structure of the parties discloses many differences behind the similarities of the constitutions. The Conservative party is a pyramid; it is a social pyramid and it is a political pyramid in the way in which its component parts are integrated in the hierarchy of the party. The ward branches, the women's branches, the Young Conservatives, and the Conservative clubs federate into the associations. In the areas, the local associations, but also the women's organizations, the Young Conservatives, and the trade union organizations merge once more. In the Labour party, most 'parallel' organizations exist mainly on paper. The party structure is almost entirely based on the constituency parties. Wards constitute the only other really lively level of the party, because it is at the level of the wards only that the rank-and-file members are present and that they can speak and vote. Regions are administrative machines more set to satisfy the desires of Transport House than to ensure a closer *political* link between the constituencies and the national party. Of course, this is partly because Labour regions are much more recent than Conservative areas; but this is also because the nature of the two parties is different. The Labour party structure under the national level is focused on the constituency party which is represented by its delegates at the Conference. The Conservative party structure integrates each level into the next. This integration has probably had a part to play in the success of the Tory party.

National leadership

When we examined the local leadership, we considered mainly party workers. This is partly because local parties are small and manned by people who usually know each other, often see each other, and can informally influence each other. In fact the rank-and-file or their representatives are only one of several forces which strive or lead or, as some would say, to 'dominate' the parties. There are at least three other forces which are equally intent on 'dominating' political parties. One of these is the parliamentary group (and its leaders). Another is constituted by the pressure groups: in the Labour party, they act in the open, since trade unions and socialist societies are affiliated; in the Conservative party, the informal connexions with business are well-known, but more difficult to measure. Although we shall examine in later chapters the way in which these pressure groups are informally linked with parties, it is always worth remembering they they are likely to be present in some form in or near the national leadership. This is not a situation which need cause concern: only parties which are small sects will not attract the attention of the pressure groups. The last of these forces is the party organization, the party bureaucracy, its 'civil service'. At local or even at regional level, this force is represented by one man or at best by a small group: the influence is real, but purely based on personal skill. At national level, organizations are large; they are composed of administrative departments and research bureaux. Admittedly these permanent officials cannot, any more than State officials can, 'impose' policy, but, like State civil servants too, they can 'advise'. They prepare the drafts, they take the routine decisions, as a result of which bigger decisions may automatically follow. When one considers the top organs of a party, one must not forget the possible influence of the 'bureaucrats' any more than the possible influence of members of the three other groups.

It would be too simple if one could just glance at the formal structure of the bodies which run the national parties, isolate the representatives of the three or four forces which have been listed, and draw conclusions about the respective strength of each of them. Politicians have more subtle ways and one cannot be certain that a 'constituency' representative is necessarily going to be a constituency worker. Since the national organs are complex, on the Conservative side in particular, one must first start by examining them formally; since things are not always what they are supposed to be, one must look at who, in reality, sits on these bodies. One must consider especially the way in which M.P.s often infiltrate all the national organs of the parties.

Formal structure of the national leadership

Decision-making in the Labour party is based, in theory, on the principle of one man, one vote. In fact, the constitution of the party tempers this principle with a certain dose of federalism. The one man, one vote principle leads to the supremacy of the Conference. Although this body has declined in strength in recent years, partly because this is always the case when the party is in power, it would be exaggerated to define it as a mere sounding board. The federal principle is at work in the composition of the governing body of the party, the National Executive Committee. 20 of its 28 members are elected every year, during the Conference, by each section of the party separately. The trade unions (5·5 million members) elect 12 members, the constituency parties (800,000 members) elect 7 and the socialist societies (21,000 members) elect one. Moreover, at the beginning of each parliamentary session, the parliamentary Labour party elects its leader and deputy leader: they both have a seat on the Executive. The six other members, 5 women and the treasurer, are elected by the whole Conference. Finally, the bureaucracy of the party is not represented among the 'members' of the N.E.C. but the general secretary, who is appointed by the N.E.C., attends its meetings without a vote. The N.E.C. elects its chairman and its deputy chairman every year, normally on a seniority basis: the chairman of the N.E.C. is the chairman of the party.

Figure 6. *General Structure of the Labour Party.*

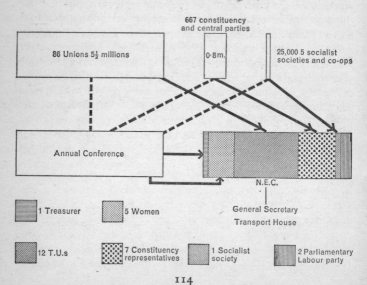

The four forces at work within any political party are there-fore represented on the Labour executive, but their representa-tion is not equal. The bureaucracy is there only on sufferance: if the general secretary wants to have his way, he will have to exer-cise skill, he cannot use force. The parliamentary party is scarcely better-off: its voice is one of prestige, since the leader and deputy leader are its representatives, but not of numbers. Party workers, with 7 members, and supporting organizations, with 13 members, are in a much stronger position. In theory, since the trade unions could stampede the Conference with their votes, they could ensure that the five women and the treasurer were acceptable to them and thus control an overall majority of 18. On the face of it, the Labour party executive appears to be controlled by supporting organizations, with party workers in the minority and parliamentarians and bureaucracy counting points on the sidelines.

Things are different in the Conservative party. In the first place, the 'democratic principle' of one man, one vote does not obtain. This is not, however, because the rank-and-file party workers are not represented in the national organs, but because the organization is split into two almost completely autonomous halves. On the one hand, there is a perfectly 'democratic' organ-ization of the rank-and-file, the National Union of Conservative and Unionist Associations, which is the federation of the con-stituency and area organizations. On the other, there is an 'auto-cratic' organization, the Conservative party proper, which runs the Central Office and therefore controls the officials of the party: that organization is an 'autocratic' one in the sense that decisions are taken by the leader of the party and by the leader of the party alone, at least in theory. Since the leader and his immediate associates on the front bench are to some extent con-trolled by the parliamentary party, however, the 'autocracy' is somewhat tempered in practice.

The National Union is as 'democratically' organized as is the Labour party. This is not only because of the Annual Confer-ence, which is a kind of rally of the party workers more concerned with politics than with the administration of the National Union. It is also because the top-decision-making organ of the Union, its Annual General Meeting, so to speak, the Central Council, is composed of 3,000 representatives mainly coming from the constituency associations. The governing body of the National Union is an Executive Committee, but it is so large (150–170 members) that the real work is done by a smaller General Purposes Committee (about fifty to sixty members) of that Executive. The members of these two committees, and particularly the members of the General Purposes Committee, are the national leaders of the National Union and they are elected by the lower ranks of the National Union; they are not the leaders of the Conservative party proper, however, and, in principle, the two halves of the organization have an entirely distinct leadership.

In practice, there are links between the National Union and the Conservative party proper. Admittedly, the party organization, its 'civil service', does not come at all under the National Union; it is headed by a chairman appointed by the leader (this Chairman of the Party Organization is the chairman of the party). The leader also appoints the officers (deputy-chairman, vice-chairmen, treasurers) and the head of the 'bureaucracy', the General Director. All these office-holders have in theory nothing to do with the National Union, just as the parliamentary party has nothing to do either with the National Union or the party organization. However, there are points of contact, and not only informal ones. In the first place, some seats are reserved on the two governing bodies of the National Union for the parliamentary party and for the party organization. In the second place, although the leader is officially all-powerful in matters of policy, he has come to be advised by an Advisory Committee on Policy of twenty-four members. This committee technically falls under the Party half, not under the National Union half of the Conservative structure. It is none the less composed of representatives of the National Union, the parliamentary party, and the party organization. The real power of this committee is not well known: it could very well become large and it may be that in practice the leader is not as 'autocratic' as he is often alleged to be and as the organization chart suggests that he is. In any case, it cannot be said that there are no representative organs in

Figure 7. *General structure of the Conservative party*

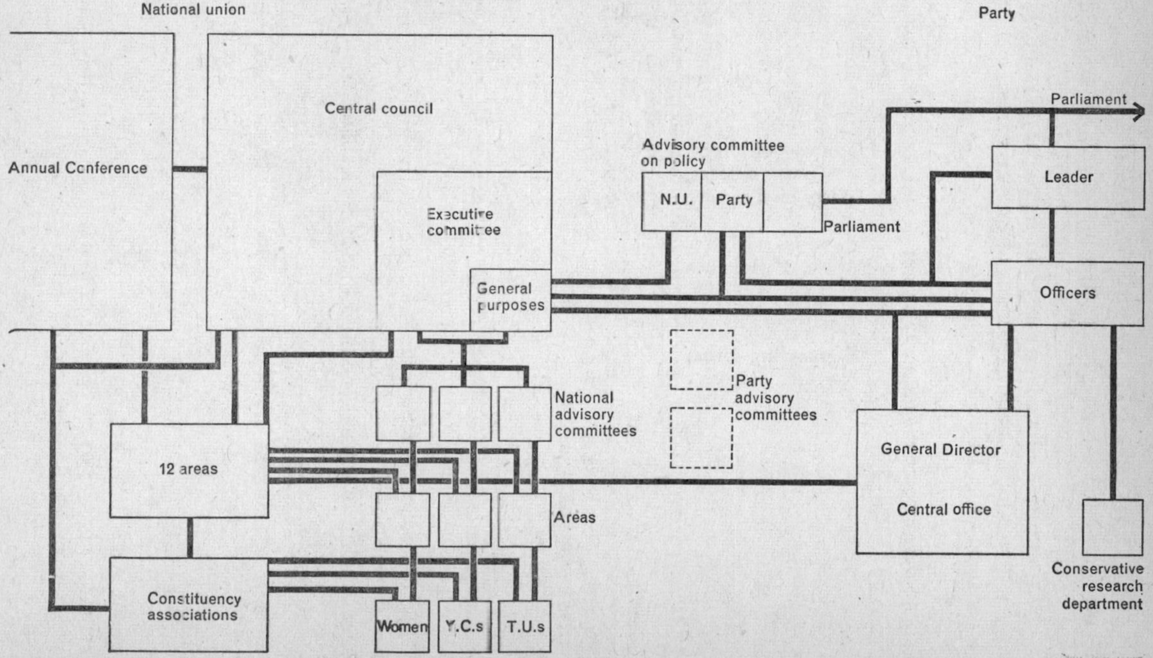

the party and that these representative organs do not have sections reserved to the various forces in the party.

The proportion of seats reserved to representatives of the various forces in the national organs of the two parties can be summarized as in Table 20.

Table 20. *Seats on national party organs*

	Party workers		Supporting forces		Parliament		Nominees of leader, party officers, party civil service		Co-opted		TOTAL
	No.	%	No.	%	No.	%	No.	%	No.	%	No.
LABOUR: N.E.C.	7	25	13	68 +6	2	7	(1 with no vote)		–	–	28 (+ 1)
CONSERVATIVES											
Adv. Cttee on policy (1968)	8	33	–	–	9	37	3	13	4	17	24
G.P. Cttee (1961)	36	67	–	–	3	6	10	18	5	9	54
Ex. Cttee (1961)	121	80	–	–	9	6	10	7	10	7	150

The differences between the Labour executive and the Conservative national organs are numerous. Firstly, supporting organizations, so apparent in the fabric of the Labour party, are conspicuously absent from the Conservative organs: representation of interests is done from the inside. In the second place, the higher the organ, the smaller the proportion of party workers in the Conservative party, but in all cases they have a larger proportion of the seats than they have in the Labour party. Thirdly, the parliamentary party is not proportionately more represented in the National Union committees than on the N.E.C. of the Labour party, but it has a much greater strength on the Advisory Committee on Policy of the Conservative party. Fourthly, the party bureaucracy is present on all the Conservative organs while it has only a back seat on the Labour N.E.C. Fifthly, some freedom is left to Conservative organs to add to their membership by means of co-option; the Labour N.E.C. has its membership fixed by the party constitution. Overall, if one can talk of federalism in the Labour executive, one must equally consider the Conservative organs as being subjected to a considerable dose of it.

Actual structure

The formal structure is misleading in many ways. It suggests that M.P.s play a minor part on these various organs, while they are, in practice, very numerous. It does not indicate who the co-opted members are in the Conservative party. It gives only an imperfect idea of the kind of 'federalism' which exists in both parties: the types of appointment within each group are as important as the number of seats reserved to each group.

Co-opted members reinforce the strength of the party bureaucracy on the Advisory Committee on Policy and the strength of the party workers on the two National Union committees. They also seem to enable supporting organizations to make a timid appearance on the scene of the Conservative party. The Advisory Committee on Policy has included a co-opted member who had no connexion with the party workers, the parliamentary party, or the party 'civil service' and happened to be vice-chairman of Aims of Industry, an organization which promotes the cause of private enterprise in the public.

Supporting interests are not otherwise represented as such on the Conservative organs. The trade unions are conspicuous, on the contrary, on the Labour executive. They generally elect their representatives as a result of a gentleman's agreement by which the twelve seats which are allocated to them are divided between the large unions and a certain number of medium-sized ones. The election is, in practice, the result of this carving-up. On paper, there is a single trade union division of twelve members; in reality, the biggest unions have a seat almost by right. Whether Mr Cousins is a supporter or not of the majority view among the unions, his union has a seat on the executive. Political considerations play a part in extreme cases only (the E.T.U. when Communist-controlled) and personal considerations for small unions only.* The 'federal' character of the executive is thereby increased: the unions, more than the trade unionists, are represented.

The union seats are given to unions more than to men. Individual unions usually decide who will represent the union. Once it is decided that a certain union will have a seat, the other unions accept whomever that union has decided to nominate. In some unions the general secretary is allowed to be a member of the Labour executive; in most large unions he is not, and the second-in-command is put forward. In all cases, the chosen delegate is among the top officials of the union. The trade union division is thus filled with national organizers who are not elected after having competed against each other but who are elected because they happen to hold the right kind of post in the right kind of union.

Some union posts carry, so to speak, a seat on the Labour N.E.C. Some posts in the parliamentary parties also carry seats on the national organs of the two parties. The leader and deputy leader sit *ex-officio* on the N.E.C. of the Labour party. The leader and chief whip sit *ex-officio* on the two committees of the National union; moreover, the leader appoints, as his representatives, the chairman and deputy chairman of the Advisory Committee on Policy. The Conservatives also give some seats to backbenchers as well as to frontbenchers, but these backbenchers are normally office-holders too: they are office-holders in the 1922 Committee of Backbenchers or in one of its sub-committees. The Chairman of the 1922 Committee, for instance, sits on all three national organs of the Conservative party.

Many members are thus elected because they hold an office in one of the organizations which are represented on the national committees. This is not always the case, however, particularly for the party bureaucracy in the Conservative party and for the representatives of the constituencies in the Labour party. The Labour bureaucracy does not raise any problems: its only 'representative' is the general secretary of the party, who does not

---

* However, it must be remembered that union officials can be nominated and elected on the Labour N.E.C. only if they are individual members of the Labour party.

even have a vote. The Conservative party bureaucracy is represented by some genuine party 'civil servants', *ex-officio*; it is also represented by a certain number of M.P.s who happen to have posts in the party organization: the officers of the party are usually M.P.s and some purely administrative jobs are also held by M.P.s. In all, half of those who may put the party organization point of view are also M.P.s. This is clearly not a mere coincidence: the leader of the party may 'own' the organization; he cannot govern it alone, and he entrusts to some M.P.s the job of running it with him.

Constituency representation also differs very much in the two main parties. One might have assumed that constituency representatives would be a cross-section of local and regional leaders. If this were the case, they would mainly be drawn, in the Labour party, from manual workers and white-collar workers; Conservative representatives should come from the upper middle class and middle class, although one might also expect to find some lower-middle-class representatives among Young Conservatives and some working-class representatives among trade unionists. Since Labour regional leaders include few M.P.s while Conservative areas have more, one might expect to find few M.P.s in the constituency section of the Labour N.E.C. and many more M.P.s representing constituencies on the Conservative organs. In fact, the situation fits expectations in the Conservative party only, with the reservation that one of the Conservative committees, the Advisory Committee on Policy, had so many M.P.s before 1953 that M.P.s have no longer been allowed to stand for its National Union section since that date. On the Labour side, expectations are not at all fulfilled: constituency representatives (and women representatives as well) are generally middle class, and M.P.s flood the representation.

Members of Parliament and the representation of the constituencies
On the Conservative committees, the constituency representatives come from the social groups from which local and area leaders have been found to come. In the Labour party, the constituency and women representatives mainly come from the middle class. Out of nineteen persons who were constituency or

women representatives during the decade 1952–62, only three were manual workers and one was a white-collar worker. There were three school teachers and two university teachers. The rest were five journalists, one doctor, one accountant, one consultant, and two civil servants. Business proper remains absent, as it is in the local Labour parties, but the range of the professions has become wider and journalism has come to be the single most common occupation. As was expected of such a group, the majority (twelve out of nineteen) had received a university education.

The social background of these Labour representatives contrasts with the social background of local Labour leaders. Yet a more striking fact is perhaps that eighteen out of nineteen were or had been M.P.s, and had usually been M.P.s for very long periods. This high proportion indicates a complete break with the type of representation which one finds at regional level. This break also contrasts with the continuity which one finds from one level to the next of the Conservative organization. In this Conservative continuum, M.P.s are neither as numerous as they are among constituency representatives of the Labour party nor as few as they are among Labour regional officers.

This situation partly arises out of the method of election of constituency representatives, which is different in the Labour party from what it is in the Conservative party. It is different in two ways. Labour chooses its constituency representatives on the N.E.C. on the basis of one single national roll; the Conservatives divide their representation into sections corresponding to the areas and to the component organizations of the National Union, such as the women, the Young Conservatives, or the trade unionists. Labour elects its constituency and women representatives *ad hoc* during the Conference; the Conservatives give the posts, in the majority of cases, to persons who hold offices in the areas or in the component organizations. In other words, on the Conservative side, representatives of the constituencies are selected to a considerable extent *ex officio*, by virtue of the fact that they are chairmen of areas or chairmen of National Advisory Committees, for instance; the principle is the same as the one which we described earlier for the representation of

M.P.s on these committees. Labour uses, roughly speaking, the same principle to elect its trade union and parliamentary representatives on the N.E.C., but it opens its constituency and women's sections to any member who is willing to test his or her popularity.

What prevents M.P.s from flooding the two committees of the National Union is the fact that representatives are elected because they hold an office in an area or in a component organization of the party. These posts are elective and the method is not undemocratic; but these posts are not sinecures. Area chairmen have to spend much of their time at area headquarters conferring with the organizer, seeing party workers, preparing executive and council meetings. The same applies to a lesser extent to other office-holders, like the chairmen of the National Advisory Committees in which the component organizations of the party are federated at national level. It is quite understandable that only a small proportion of M.P.s should volunteer or agree to be drafted. Yet, if they do not hold these posts, they cannot become constituency representatives on the two committees of the National Union, except for a few co-opted members on the Conservative committees. Before 1953, they could become constituency representatives on the Advisory Committee on Policy, and this is why, most probably, they did flood the National Union section of that body; since they can no longer stand for that section, it has become the entire preserve of the party workers.

On the contrary, the electoral system is particularly favourable to a certain category of M.P.s on the Labour side. Members sit on the General Purposes or the Executive Committee of the National Union because they represent an area, as M.P.s sit in Parliament because they represent a County or Borough division. But a member is not elected in the constituency or women's sections of the Labour N.E.C. on the basis of an area at all. There is only one division in each case, and that is the whole nation. Not unnaturally, no one is elected unless he is nationally well-known. Who is the delegate from Essex or Surrey who is going to vote for some regional office-holder in Lancashire or some woman delegate who is only prominent in her locality in the West country? Delegates will vote for national figures and not for obscure, if worthy, party workers. This is precisely why it does help to be an M.P. Someone who is well known otherwise might, like Laski, be elected. Someone who has become well known as an M.P. might be elected even when no longer in Parliament, like Mr Mikardo. Moreover, it is not sufficient to be an M.P. Backbench M.P.s who are only good constituency workers and who do not care to speak very often in Parliament, to write articles in the newspapers, and to travel up and down the country to address political meetings, do not have much chance of attracting the votes of the constituency delegates. This is why journalists, more perhaps than the members of any other profession, have a good chance of being elected.

Political considerations are well known to play a part in the election of the constituency representatives to the N.E.C. But we have already seen that attitudes on issues could not be too rigidly defined in terms of 'right' and 'left'. The very large majorities obtained by some left-wing constituency representatives do not necessarily coincide with a left-wing stand on detailed issues either. Indeed, there are nuances in the left, and a moderate left-winger like Mr Wilson or Mr Crossman has a better chance of being elected than an extreme left-winger like Mr Mikardo. These political considerations have to be associated, however, with the other more technical prerequisites of being a national figure of the party. Even in the women's section, for which the whole Conference votes, it is important to be well known. Political considerations may be different, since trade unions have tended, up to the late 1960s, to back centre rather than left-wing candidates; technical considerations are also different, since the very large unions are not numerous and good lobbying in the right kind of headquarters might be just as useful as any other form of canvassing. Yet it certainly helps to be well known and it is certainly not sufficient to be well known in only one part of the country.

If one adds the eleven or twelve M.P.s annually elected for the constituency and women's divisions to the two representatives of the parliamentary party and to the four or five M.P.s who are usually elected among the representatives of the trade unions and of the socialist societies, one finds that M.P.s always are in a majority on the Labour executive and indeed that they have generally two-thirds of the seats (eighteen out of twenty-eight in 1968). This is a higher proportion than the one realized on the Conservative national organs, even on the Advisory Committee on Policy where M.P.s and peers normally muster a smaller majority (fourteen out of twenty-four in 1968). The real position is thus different from the formal position which appeared in the previous table.

Table 21. *M.P.s and peers on the national organs of the parties (1968)*

	Party workers		Supporting forces		Parliament	Party Bureaucracy		Total M.P.s and peers	
	M.P.s and peers	not M.P.s	M.P.s and peers	not M.P.s		M.P.s and peers	not M.P.s	No.	%
LABOUR N.E.C	7	–	4	8	2	–	(1, with no vote)	18	64
CONSERVATIVE A.C.P.	–	8	–	–	9	5	2	14	58

However, the preponderance of M.P.s on the Labour executive does not mean that the parliamentary party as such is represented and that the constituency workers are somehow disfranchised. What happens is that, in the Labour party, constituency workers choose to be represented by Members of Parliament. It is no use being a good constituency chairman, or a regional chairman: one cannot, in that way, become a member of the N.E.C. of the Labour party, while one can become a member of the Executive Committee, of the General Purposes Committee, and even of the Advisory Committee on Policy in the Conservative party. Yet the seven constituency members of the Labour executive do not cease to 'represent' constituency workers because they are M.P.s: these M.P.s would not be elected by the parliamentary Labour party if that body was given seven seats to fill on the executive.

The fact that these M.P.s, and not others, are elected to 'represent' the constituencies epitomizes the difference between two concepts of representation. In the Conservative party, members are selected to sit on one of the national organs because they hold a post somewhere in the hierarchy of the National Union, the parliamentary party, or Central Office. The Conservative party aims at representing groups or bodies, the interests of which deserve to be defended or put forward. Similarly, in the Labour party, the distinction between a trade union section, a constituency section, and parliamentary representatives aims at representing different groups. Moreover, within the trade union section, as we saw, various groups are represented because they are important component units of the trade union movement.

In the constituency and women's divisions of the Labour executive, on the contrary, one is elected because one is known, and known to have broad attitudes and because these attitudes correspond to those of the 'electorate' of the group in question. Since constituencies are somewhat to the left, they elect left-wing candidates. The bond which links these representatives with their 'electors' is the bond of the attitudes which they have in common. The Conservative national organs are based on a kind of two-tier federalism. Groups are represented; within these groups, sub-groups – frontbenchers and backbenchers, different areas, women, Young Conservatives, trade unionists – are also represented. The Labour Party practises this two-tier federalism in the unions only; in the constituencies, in the women section, even the parliamentary party to some extent, the representation of political attitudes is substituted for the representation of sub-groups.

A consequence follows which is of some importance. As long as these representatives of the constituencies and of the women have the same attitudes as their electors, they are re-elected. There is no rotation in office. For the whole of the twelve posts, only nineteen different persons were elected during the decade 1952–62; four of the constituency members and one of the women members have been in office for the whole period. A seat on the constituency or women divisions is safer than a seat on the trade union section and is much safer than a seat on the national organs of the Conservative party.

This distinction between men who 'represent' attitudes and men who 'represent' groups has become more and more clear-cut on the Labour executive – particularly after 1952 through the influence of Bevanism. But, within the category of the men who 'represent' groups, one must also distinguish between the *permanent officials* and the *officers* who are elected by a component body. As a result, one finds really three types of representatives on the national organs of the parties. Constituency and parliamentary seats on the Conservative national organs are given to elective officers; so are the two parliamentary seats on the Labour executive. The trade union seats on the Labour executive and some of the seats of the party bureaucracy on the Conservative national organs are given to officials. Finally, the constituency and women seats on the Labour executive are given without reference to any post. In the first category, that of elective officers, the length of tenure is short, except for the frontbench representatives; all the other officers rotate in their office in the component bodies and, therefore, have to relinquish their seat on the national committee of the party. In the second category, that of officials of the unions or of the party 'civil service', the length of tenure is a little longer, because such officials do not rotate in office as officers do. However, these posts are fairly high in the administrative hierarchy of the party bureaucracy or of the unions, and their holders are fairly old when they are appointed to them; retirement comes sufficiently quickly after appointment to make the turnover, on the average, fairly high. For the third category, who are elected without reference to any post, the turnover can be very low. Only when attitudes change – as at the beginning of the 'Bevanite' period – do many seats come to change hands. It may commonly be thought that the representation of 'groups' leads to complete security of tenure and to perpetuation in office. In fact, it is the one who represents 'attitudes' who has the best chance of staying in office for rather long periods.

*

Are these parties oligarchies and do they perpetuate in office a certain class or a certain group? The answer is surely that neither is as open as one might have hoped and as their very large membership might have suggested that they could be. The 'class' barrier exists in the Conservative party and all that can be said is that this does not happen because 'common people' are consciously prevented from rising to the top. This barrier exists: not only, as we shall see, are candidates mainly selected from the middle class, and from the solid middle class at that, but, as we have seen, members and local leaders are recruited from a much more exclusive group than the electorate of the party as a whole. The barrier in the Labour party is a more subtle one; it is not one of 'class'; it is more the result of the development of a certain kind of professionalism, which tends to operate, admittedly, in favour of different groups of people, at two distinct levels. One feels its existence at local level; one notices it even more at national level.

These defects are real, but it must be remembered at the same time that British parties have avoided other kinds of defects which are very common in other countries, and that the 'closed' character of the parties must not be exaggerated. If some 'professionalism' exists in the Labour party, that party has avoided, and the Conservative party likewise, the very common danger of bureaucratization. On the Continent, large parties are often not only professionalized, but bureaucratized: the influence of the party 'civil service' on British parties is, by comparison, very limited indeed. Transport House has never dominated the Labour party, despite the fact that Transport House could claim that it has the knowledge of the skill of organization. In a left-wing party, where the proportion of manual workers who are not accustomed to administer is very large, there is a normal tendency for administrative machines to have – or to want to have – a large influence. On the Conservative side, the constant fusion between M.P.s and party 'civil servants' has prevented the rise of a bureaucratic élite. Other factors also play a large part. The party is such an old one, it has such a traditional implantation in the country, the political hierarchy is so closely modelled on the social hierarchy, that a successful domination by the London bureaucracy can never be much more than a distant threat. The 'class' structure of the Conservative party does contribute to prevent the party from being either a federation of 'machines' of professional politicians or an oligarchy of bureaucrats.

As for the class barrier and the future danger of professionalization, the first is perhaps in the process of being slowly, but probably surely, dismantled in the Conservative party, and the second is very difficult indeed to avoid. The Conservatives have, in a typical British fashion, added new groups to their existing local oligarchies; with the transformation of the class structure in the country, these groups are likely to gain more and more influence. A good index of the transformation of the party lies in the great care which has been taken, in recent years, to ensure rotation in office. Like other British institutions, the Conservative party may take decades to achieve its complete transformation, but it is a living organism and it has shown that it was capable of so many transformations in the past that it is difficult to believe that it will not carry its transformation further.

The problem of professionalization is graver for the Labour party, and it might even arise in the Conservative party with the ending of the class barrier. Professionalization has not come about as a result of some sinister conspiracy. It has come about because, when a party is predominantly formed of manual workers, the only middle-class groups which it is likely to attract are those who have 'ideas' rather than 'interests' in common with the manual workers; moreover, when workers cease to be workers as a result of their success in the trade unions or in politics, their only bond with other workers is a bond of 'ideas', of 'attitudes', of past recollections: it is not one of common interests. As a result, most of the non-working-class elements and some of the working-class ones are likely to become, when they are successful, full-time politicians. This is not only true because they do not have 'any other job'; it is also true from a psychological point of view. On the whole, most Conservatives probably consider politics as a hobby; Labour politicians or would-be politicians do not. Their main attraction in life, their real life, is the political life. Few enter politics as a matter of tradition: they enter politics because they like it. Professionalization stems, therefore, directly from the conditions in which working-class parties come to emerge and develop.

Professionalization, class barriers, machines, bureaucratization, all these dangers have to be taken into account when one tries to pass judgement on the social structure of the British parties. It is difficult to imagine that all these dangers can be avoided, particularly since it is often by avoiding one trap that one falls into the next. On balance, the traps into which British political parties have fallen are not too numerous. The atmosphere which one breathes is not always as pure as one would want, but many parties, in other countries, have a stuffier atmosphere. As long as this is the case, there is, at any rate, much hope for transformation.

CHAPTER FIVE

The Politicians

IT may seem arbitrary to draw a line between parties and politicians, particularly in a country like Britain. Independents
seem to have disappeared for good from the scene of the House
of Commons. They may remain numerous in the House of
Lords, but these independents rarely attend the sittings and
have little influence in political matters. The peers who become
members of a government have to be committed to a party.

One must, nevertheless, distinguish between parties and politicians, for the obvious reason that politicians play a more
direct part in the conduct of the affairs of the nation. One must
also distinguish between parties and politicians because politicians are not, and cannot be, drawn at random from party
members. A politician may have to be a party member, all party
members do not have equal chances of becoming politicians.
One must possess a certain number of talents and abilities, have
had a certain training and benefit from a certain number of
advantages if one can hope to have a sporting chance of success.

It is easy to poke fun at politicians. They are Jacks-of-all-
trades, knowing a little of everything, but really nothing in particular. However, even if that definition were adequate, it would
suggest that politicians must have a talent which all do not
possess. They must be able to grasp quickly the main points of
a question with which they are not familiar. Moreover, they
must have other talents: they must be able to speak reasonably
fluently in public, they must be able to argue a case in a debate
with some cogency, they must be able to retort quickly and see
the flaw in the other man's argument. In other words, they must
have an agile mind, as well as a flair for understanding administrative problems, not only if they want to become successful
ministers, but even if they want only to be able to criticize
ministers from the back benches. They must also have a strong
will-power and a rather thick skin. They must be able to sustain

public criticism without being plunged into defeatism, or anger, or both. These abilities may not amount to a readily definable technique; they are none the less abilities which a random selection of citizens, or of party members, is not likely to possess.

Some of these abilities are probably innate, whatever 'innate abilities' may be thought to mean. Unquestionably, 'innate abilities' gain by being cultivated and lose by remaining undeveloped. Nobody would deny that there are conditions under which these abilities are likely to develop. A certain selection occurs, as a result of which, even if the raw material of politicians were distributed at random among all social classes, the actual politicians are not likely to be distributed at random.

Let us consider only three of these conditions among many: the milieu from which a man comes, the education which he has received, the job which he exercises. A man who comes from a family where politics are never discussed is at a disadvantage compared to a man who comes from a milieu where politics matter. If this family has friends or relatives among politicians, there will be an added incentive to enter politics and entrance in the job will be facilitated. Milieu does not, moreover, mean only family; it also means contacts, outside the family: for instance, in the trade union movement. Some of these contacts occur almost naturally, some of them may happen by chance.

Education adds to the influence of the environment. It does so in two ways at least. It does so, more perhaps in Britain than elsewhere, by providing contacts and character-training as well as intellectual training. Contacts come through the better public schools, through the older universities. Character-training also comes through the public schools: they tend to inculcate a certain philosophy of the public service, as a result of which politics and the Civil Service come to be considered as worthwhile careers. Most important of all, the intellectual training of the best public schools, of the older universities, as well as, to a lesser extent, of grammar schools and other universities, is a preparation for the job of politician. A B.A. degree may not be required to enter Parliament, but university education does help.

Thirdly, the occupation which one exercises before entering Parliament is also important. It is important because it can supplement training or be a substitute for it. An administrator, a secretary, an organizer is more likely to become political material than a person engaged in a routine job: this is why the trade union movement is an almost essential channel for manual workers who want to enter politics. The type of occupation is also important because it may or may not give spare time before entering politics. White-collar jobs, and even more professional jobs, such as journalism, teaching, law, are great assets in this respect; they are also assets because some of them at least can be combined with a political life, supplement the relatively low income which can be derived from politics, and even sometimes be resumed full-time if the political career comes unexpectedly to an end.

These conditions, original milieu, education, and occupation are obviously not prerequisites. They need not all be present; one may be the substitute for another, although one is often the consequence of another. A middle-class milieu means a greater chance of a university education, and a university education means almost always at least a white-collar job. Because of the existence of these conditions, an unskilled manual worker, working in a trade where employees are not organized in strong unions, starts with a great handicap against a non-manual worker with a university degree or against a professional worker with a middle-class social background. Whether one likes it or not, politics is a middle-class job and the training appropriate for middle-class jobs is also a training for politics. The dice are loaded by the present structure of society as well as by the natural conditions which govern the job of politics in any society.

Since the dice are loaded in favour of some social categories in the case of all types of politicians, they are likely to be even more loaded when one considers ministers and other successful politicians. A minister must possess administrative talent, while the average M.P. may need only a more superficial skill. The line under which M.P.s are unlikely to be found is already pretty high in the social structure: that under which ministers are unlikely to be found is higher still.

These general conditions help some to enter politics and prevent others from doing so, irrespective of the parties. The structure of the political parties introduces at least two other sets of conditions. In the first place, selection committees of the parties regulate the *demand* for certain types of candidates; this demand is greatly influenced by the social composition and the views of these committees, as well as the notions which they have of what the ideal M.P. should be. Conservative associations are likely to choose candidates with more solid middle-class backgrounds than constituency Labour parties. The selection also depends on the *supply* of candidates. The supply varies from party to party: the Liberals had, at least in the 1950s, great difficulty in finding candidates. It also varies from constituency to constituency and particularly from safe seats to marginal and hopeless seats. Those who have great political ambitions and high opinions of their merit will flock to the safe seats and not turn an eye to consider the hopeless seats. The Conservatives may have a hundred or more applicants for a seat like Bournemouth East and Christchurch and practically no one for some mining constituency in Yorkshire or South Wales. In the first type of case, local selection committees will really have an opportunity to 'select'; in the second, they may have to get out of their way to ask some local man if he might be prepared to stand, almost regardless of his abilities and social background.

Three types of conditions thus enter the picture. Social background and/or intellectual ability form the first type. They depend both on the general social structure of the country and on the job of politics itself. Politicians are never going to constitute a microcosm of the nation, although different considerations may apply to different countries. On the whole, politicians will come from the middle class. Another condition is set by the social characteristics and views of the selection bodies, which in Britain consist of the local leaders of the constituency associations and parties. The third condition works almost mechanically within each party: it leads to a distinction between good and bad seats. The type of politicians which a country produces at any given moment depends, to a variable extent, on the way in which these three factors operate in conjunction.

Candidates

Let us first consider candidates, of whom there are usually about 1,500. Of these, over 1,200 belong to the two main parties, since they now contest almost all the 630 seats. The figure for the other parties varies, particularly in the case of the Liberals: they had as many as 475 candidates in 1950, as few as 109 in 1951. Communists and nationalists contest few seats and, since 1950 at least, Independents have almost completely disappeared.

Of these 1,500 candidates, only about 200 or so are manual workers and about the same number – in fact mostly the same ones – have had only an elementary education. In a nation in which two-thirds of the population are manual workers, manual workers produce only one-seventh or one-eighth of all the candidates. At the other end of the scale, 600 or so candidates are likely to be in one of the professions and another 350 in business. 750 will possess a university degree and 550 will have gone through a public school. In the nation 5 per cent of each age group goes to university, 3 per cent of each age group goes to public schools, but a third of the candidates has been to a public school and nearly half to university. To add to this disparity, women, who won complete political equality in the 1920s, form only about 5 per cent of all the candidates. The conclusion is clear: parliamentary candidates are not a cross-section of the population; all the sections may be present, but the proportions are widely different and men from the middle classes take the lion's share.

Within this general framework there are variations from party to party. Conservatives and Liberals have almost no manual workers at all (1 or 2 per cent of their total) and, correspondingly, very few of their candidates have only an elementary education. The Conservatives have the candidates with the most exclusive backgrounds. Professional men and businessmen are predominant, and their contingent of public schools men is the largest of all parties. They have as many old Etonians as Labour has candidates from all the public schools together (about ninety). In the Labour party, the advantages enjoyed by the non-manual workers are less marked: the bulk of the 200 or so manual workers comes from that party. However, even in the Labour party three-quarters of the candidates come from the middle class, and the professions alone contribute more candidates than the manual working groups. Correspondingly, university graduates are more numerous than candidates with an elementary education only, although the latter greatly outnumber public school men. While Labour in the nation is overwhelmingly a working-class party, Labour candidates are mainly drawn from the middle and lower middle classes. The general trend is subjected only to some variations from party to party.

Members of Parliament

The background of successful candidates is also different from the background of unsuccessful ones. There are so few Liberal M.P.s that any comparison is impossible within the Liberal party, but in both the Conservative and Labour parties M.P.s are drawn from rather more exclusive backgrounds than unsuccessful candidates, although trade-union-sponsored candidates introduce an important exception in the Labour party.

Among the Conservatives, the trend can be followed in great detail. It applies to broad categories: two workers out of eight were elected in 1966, but two professional men out of five were elected. It also applies to sub-groups within each social category: barristers are more successful than solicitors, directors of large businesses than small businessmen. The same trend can be found in the educational background: two-thirds of the candidates, but three-quarters of the M.P.s, have been to a public school; less than 60 per cent of candidates, but two-thirds of M.P.s, have been to university. The higher one is in the educational and occupational scale, the more one is likely to get selected for a safe seat in the Conservative party.

The converse can be found for unsuccessful candidates. Many candidates stand only once in all their life, either because they do not appeal to selection committees or because they are not eager to enter politics and have to be dragged into the arena. Eighty-odd Conservative candidates of 1951 – 15 per cent of the total – had never stood before and never stood afterwards: there were fewer public school men (and only two Etonians), fewer university graduates, fewer professional men, fewer big businessmen among them than even among other *unsuccessful* candidates. Most of them were local men, drawn from the lower ranges of the middle classes. The probable scarcity of supply led to selection committees being less 'selective'.

In the Labour party, the picture is not so simple. A general tendency in favour of the upper groups of the middle class is noticeable, but this operates against the lower middle class, not against the working class. In 1966, barristers had a four to one chance of being elected, university teachers a three to one chance, but only one out of three school teachers were elected.

Figure 8. *School background of M.P.s and candidates* (*1966*)

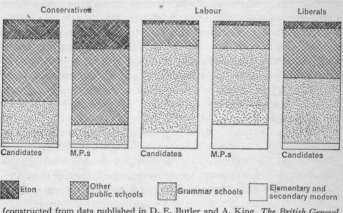

(constructed from data published in D. E. Butler and A. King, *The British General Election of 1966*, Macmillan, 1966, p. 208)

Businessmen and journalists had safer constituencies than clerical workers. Similarly, public school men were more successful than non-public school men and Oxford graduates (not Cambridge graduates in 1959) were more successful than graduates of Redbrick and Scottish universities. However, manual workers – and candidates with only an elementary education – also had a better chance of being elected than clerical workers or school teachers. Workers, who constitute just over a fourth of the Labour candidates, form a third of the parliamentary party. The manual working class remains underrepresented in relation to its strength in the Labour electorate and even in the whole electorate. But the trend which favours the middle class against the lower middle class and working class in other parties and which favours the solid middle class against the lower middle class in the Labour party does not extend to the working class as well in the Labour party.

This relative advantage enjoyed by manual workers in the Labour party is due to the special position which some unions enjoy in the selection of some Labour candidates. In all selection committees of the constituency Labour parties unions play a part, but in some cases a union declares itself ready to contribute a large part of the electoral and other expenses of the local party if the candidate of the union is chosen by the selection committee. About one-fifth of the Labour candidates are 'sponsored' in this way. In some cases, the union puts forward a candidate who does not come from the union; in most cases, however, it ensures the selection of one of its own members. Since the trade unions which sponsor seats are mostly manual workers' unions, the result is that most sponsored candidates are manual workers.

This explains why a large proportion of the manual workers is concentrated in the fifth or so of the seats which the trade unions sponsor. Moreover, these seats are not selected at random; many unions are reluctant to sponsor hopeless seats and even marginal seats. This is partly because they do not want to waste their members' money and partly because their aim is not to help the Labour party but to have representatives in Parliament. Since they can promise fairly large sums, they can usually obtain safe seats: only a third or a fourth of their candidates are defeated, against over half of the other Labour candidates. One union, the National Union of Mineworkers, succeeds in placing almost all of its thirty-five or so candidates in safe seats. The proportion of manual workers is thus substantially increased and the general trend in favour of the middle classes, which is quite noticeable in the other seats, is partly offset.

This correction introduced by some of the unions is, however, limited to a small number of working-class groups. Firstly, these M.P.s are classified as 'manual workers' because this is what they originally *were*; in most cases, this is no longer what they are at the time of their selection. They have become trade union organizers, i.e., in reality, white-collar workers or even managers. Secondly, these manual workers are not drawn at random from all the trades within the manual working class. They are selected from a number of unions, and principally from the miners' union, which takes one-fourth of all the sponsored seats. A worker employed in a trade where the union does

Table 22. *Sponsorship, 1966*

	Candidates	M.P.s	Percentage of candidates elected
Constituency parties	456	214	47·0
Trade Unions	138	132	95·8
Co-operative party	24	18	59·0
	618	364	59·0

(from the *Annual Report* of the Conference of the Labour Party, 1967. These figures do not include Northern Ireland)

not bother to sponsor seats is at a definite disadvantage against a railwayman or a miner. The sponsorship system redresses the overall bias against the manual workers, but it does so by creating other disparities among the manual workers. Apart from railwaymen and miners, manual workers are in no better position than most lower-middle-class candidates are.

The Conservative and Labour parliamentary parties

Some manual groups may be represented in the parliamentary Labour party, but the middle class as a whole is over-represented in both parliamentary parties. The higher one is in the social scale, the better chance one has of finding a good seat, unless, in the Labour party, one happens to be in a union which customarily sponsors many seats. There is thus a superficial similarity between the Conservative and Labour parliamentary parties. Labour may find place for one hundred workers and the Conservatives for only two; but Labour has many more manual workers among its electors and among its members than among its M.P.s.

The middle-class components of the two parties are very different, however. The Labour middle class is mainly composed of three groups, the teachers, the journalists, and the lawyers; other middle-class occupations are represented only by a few members each. The Conservative parliamentary party, on the other hand, has scarcely any teachers. Farmers and regular soldiers are more numerous than journalists and publicists. Lawyers and businessmen are more numerous than any two of these groups together. In the Labour party, the middle class is primarily a middle class of intellectuals or, at any rate, a middle class which can be distinguished from the manual working class and the white-collar workers because it discusses ideas, not because it makes money. In the Conservative party, the intellectual middle class exists, but it is in a small minority. The business middle class is even more numerous than figures of *original* occupations usually suggest.

Many professional men, lawyers, accountants, regular soldiers, become businessmen at some stage in their career: the difference between the occupations which Conservative M.P.s originally entered and those in which they eventually land is large. About one-third of Conservative M.P.s start in business, about three-fifths eventually have some connexion with business. In the Labour party, a fairly strict definition of business would cover only about 10 per cent of the parliamentary party and 20 per cent of the middle-class Labour M.P.s; a wide definition (including trustees, people on boards of charitable organizations, etc.) could raise the proportion to 20 per cent of the total parliamentary party, but it would be unrealistic to consider these men as 'businessmen' in the normal sense.*

It follows that one should not equate the middle-class groups of the Labour party with those of the Conservative party. It also follows that one should look at the difference between the two parties with other criteria besides simply the distinction between middle, lower middle, and working class. The Conservative parliamentary party may be thought to be homogeneous

* See p. 220.

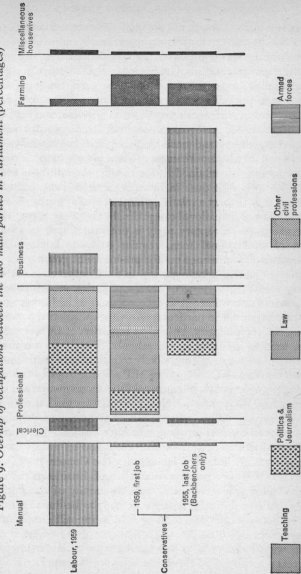

Figure 9. *Overlap of occupations between the two main parties in Parliament (percentages)*

(constructed from data appearing in D. E. Butler and R. Rose, *The British General Election of 1959*, Macmillan, 1960, p. 127, and in S. E. Finer, H. B. Berrington, and D. J. Bartholomew, *Backbench Opinion in the House of Commons, 1955–1959*, Pergamon Press, 1962, p. 80) because it is almost wholly middle class and even almost wholly composed of members of the professional and managerial classes. This is not the only cause of its homogeneity. It is also due to the intermixing between business and the other groups; it is due to the fact that the distinction between business and the professions is probably not very sharp. Since soldiers, lawyers, and chartered accountants often become businessmen, each of these occupational categories does not really constitute a 'group'. Oppositions and tensions are not likely to arise between them. For an occupational category to become a 'group', it must be reasonably self-contained; if the membership of these categories overlaps, as it does in the Conservative parliamentary party, one must expect a relatively large degree of cohesion, not only within the occupational categories, but between them. The Conservative parliamentary party is not subdivided into sub-groups of professional men, regular soldiers, intellectuals, businessmen. Businessmen are the predominant group.

There are more distinctions, within the Conservative parliamentary party, from the point of view of education. Moreover, differences in education reflect differences in social background as well as in training, in particular when one considers the public schools. A large minority, but only a minority, of Conservative M.P.s, went to exclusive public schools. However, even these differences in education are unlikely to cause more than superficial friction among Conservative M.P.s because of two factors. Firstly, public school men in general form three-quarters of the parliamentary party; non-public school men are too few to form an independent 'group'. Those who have been to a public school are likely to respect those who have been to an exclusive one. Secondly, Conservative values are based on a respect for tradition and for those who embody it. The Conservative parliamentary party is mainly composed of businessmen; its hierarchy is largely produced by the hierarchy of the public schools. Non-conformist views are unlikely to be due to differences in occupations; hierarchical values are still sufficiently strong to prevent those who have non-conformist views from getting widely out of step and from having many followers. The great part played by the public schools, not only in the upbringing of Conservative M.P.s, but also in the maintenance of general values within the club, explains why clashes on doctrinal standpoints are rare and are unlikely to last and why respect for the team of leaders will normally prevail. The parliamentary party is an organic union of all the groups composing the middle classes, not a juxtaposition of separate elements. This is a result which few parties of the right have been able to achieve in other countries.

The nature of the divisions inside the Labour party in Parliament cannot be reduced to an opposition between middle class and working class either. One has to examine more carefully the nature of the Labour middle class before one can analyse what these divisions are. The Labour middle class is, in the first place, an intelligentsia, and it resembles, therefore, to some extent, the middle class of the local Labour parties. The party in Parliament, like the leadership of a local Labour party, is an alliance between the proletariat, the lower middle class, and the intelligentsia. This makes the parliamentary Labour party very different from the Conservative party in Parliament. This, by itself, does not explain the tensions which exist within the parliamentary Labour party, since we noticed that local Labour élites could, in many cases, be socially united.

One source of tension inside the Labour party in Parliament – to the extent that tensions come from social and not ideological causes – is the gap between the working class and the top of the intelligentsia, which is much larger at parliamentary level than it is at local level. More specifically, the top groups of the intelligentsia are much more numerous in Parliament than locally. Unlike local Labour parties, the parliamentary party does not have only white-collar workers and a small band of teachers and managers. It has a large body of members of the 'old' and 'new' professions. The lower middle class as such is, in reality, rather small: we saw that it gets more of the bad constituencies and fewer of the safe seats. The lower middle class acts as a link between the groups at local level, primarily because it is a large section of the leadership of any local party. It is not sufficiently large in Parliament to play a similar part. In becoming larger, the middle class ceases to be an appendage of the manual and white-collar groups. It becomes a group in itself.

Nor is this the only source of tension. The intelligentsia is sufficiently large to be of two kinds. One resembles the local intelligentsia, the other has almost no counterpart locally. The two differ by their education and their occupations. There are those who exercise one of the more established 'old' professions, like law or medicine, who often went to a public school and to one of the older universities; there are those who exercise one of the 'newer' or less established professions, like journalism or school teaching, who often went to a grammar school and to a Redbrick university. There are exceptions, obviously; some of the public school men who went to Oxford and Cambridge went into journalism or school teaching; conversely, some of the grammar-school-educated, particularly if they went to Oxford or Cambridge, went into the 'older' professions. University teachers seem to be at the borderline: they are recruited from both groups and their occupation is half-way between the 'older' and 'newer' professions. Generally, however, men who come from the solid middle class and who have had the traditional English middle class education went to the more established professions, while those who come from lower-middle-class backgrounds went usually into school teaching or journalism.

The parliamentary Labour party thus has three different centres. Manual workers coming through the trade union movement form the first group. The established professions, with a traditional education and a solid middle-class background, form the second. In between the less established professions, with a more 'democratic' education, form the third. The divisions between these three groups are much more marked than divisions between groups at local level. The differences in background, occupation, education, and standard of living are sometimes vast, and never insignificant.

The Conservative party in Parliament succeeds in being homogeneous, while the Labour party, so often united locally, has three centres at parliamentary level. In the Conservative party, divisions and tensions are reduced, when they occur, because there is an underlying social unity, a common sense of hierarchy. In the parliamentary Labour party, the only source of unity is political, not social: it is the common adherence to a set of ideals. A successful Q.C., a school teacher, a miner have really only in common their acceptance of an ideology or their zeal for reform. This is why it is unrealistic to expect the parliamentary Labour party to be united in the way the Conservative party in Parliament can so easily be. As soon as the ideological bond begins to crack, difficulties emerge. Clearly, in many cases, it is possible to call on Labour M.P.s generally to rally behind a Labour government in difficulty, even when that government's policy is unpalatable to many of them. But ideological appeal and defence of the government are the only possible bonds: there is no way of healing the wounds by appealing, as in the Conservative party, to a fundamental social unity.

Attitudes of M.P.s

This common ideal exists in the Labour party, but it is periodically submitted to the test of the fight which has been going on, ever since the party was formed, between moderate and left-wing Socialists. Such a situation rarely arises in the Conservative party where differences, which are not at all uncommon, are of a minor character. The Conservative party in Parliament is thus, so to speak, doubly protected. The parliamentary Labour party is, on the contrary, open to two dangers. The fundamental doctrinal unity of all Conservatives constitutes a first shield. Of course, Conservative M.P.'s have differing views on many subjects: like members of local Conservative associations and Conservative electors, they oppose each other on practical aspects of foreign and home policy. These differences are, however, differences of degree rather than of kind; they are more often differences over administration than over policy. Moreover, and this is the second shield, these oppositions are not underlined by oppositions between social groups. On matters of detail, some businessmen may be in favour of a measure which other businessmen oppose, farmers may be opposed to some of the policies which industrialists propose. On matters of principle, however, one is rarely likely to find a 'group' opposing another 'group', for the simple reason that there are no very clearly marked 'groups' in the social sense of the word in the Conservative parliamentary party. This is why the divisions which may occur in the party on one issue are unlikely to turn themselves into battles of social, as well as political or economic, interests. This is also why battles are likely to be waged on one terrain at a time. This is at any rate why, if several battles are waged at the same time, they are unlikely to produce the same opponents fighting each other on all the fronts. One or two dozen backbenchers, at the very most, may be said to be right-wing on a large number of questions. Because the issues are rarely issues of principle, oppositions are likely to be transient; because the parliamentary party is socially homogeneous, they are unlikely to leave traces of bitterness which could become the emotional raw material of the next battle.

For exactly the opposite reasons, the parliamentary Labour party is in a position which is doubly difficult to hold. The social divisions which exist within the party serve to emphasize, at least to some extent, the political and ideological divisions of the party. One does not need to uphold an entirely marxian interpretation of the structure of politics to see that social and ideological divisions have some connexion. Broadly speaking, as might have been expected, the members who belong to the more established professions and who are also members of the solid middle class are, on most issues, if not on all, on the right or at any rate at the centre of the parliamentary party. These members are unlikely to be great partisans of nationalization, they are unlikely to be in favour of a radical change in the foreign policy of the country, and they are likely to be moderates in social matters. Some might say that they are 'liberals' rather than 'socialists'. The alternative is oversimplified, because these members are generally in favour of a measure of governmental intervention in economic affairs and of a measure of social equality which Liberals, on the whole, do not support. The only issues on which these members can be said to be 'liberals' – together with the other members of the middle-class groups of the parliamentary party – are the issues of civil liberties and humanitarian questions.

Members of the newer professions, such as journalism or

school teaching, are often to the left of the members of the older professions. Not only are they concerned with civil liberties, but many are neutralists in foreign affairs and outspoken socialists in home affairs. Since the internal party conflict has been centred mainly on foreign affairs in the course of the 1950s, the left-wing views of these M.P.s on neutralism and more recently on unilateralism have more often come to the fore. However, they are left-wing socialists on the home front as well: in 1959–60, many of them opposed the move for the revision of Clause Four of the party constitution, which states Labour's general policy of public ownership, as much as manual workers did. Indeed, they are probably the section of the parliamentary party which is most firmly committed to the *principle* of public ownership.

Manual workers, who form the third important part of the parliamentary party, are probably often more concerned with the detailed implementation of social reforms. They probably do not view the political struggle in such sharp ideological terms as many members of the newer professions do. This is why they often side with the members of the older professions and appear less 'doctrinaire' and more moderate. Yet they were certainly less ready to abandon Clause Four than some of the members of the older professions. On the other hand, they are usually neither left-wing in foreign affairs nor libertarians on matters concerning civil liberties. They are even perhaps to the right of the older professions on both these types of issues.

These conflicts are not class conflicts. They are not conflicts over which 'class' within the party should dominate the others or even conflicts about how the national cake should be divided. They are conflicts about political attitudes. But those who hold one set of attitudes are more likely to come from one of the social groups which compose the parliamentary party. The conflicts must not be exaggerated because, in the normal way, only questions of foreign policy threaten to disrupt the unity of the party and conflicts on internal matters occur less often and are much less acute. One cannot, however, dismiss them in the way one might dismiss the conflicts inside the Conservative parliamentary party, on the grounds that they are only conflicts over administration and superficial differences between the members of the same social club. They are, in reality, conflicts of principle. It is certainly to the credit of the British Labour party that it has been able to sustain these conflicts without splitting or without falling into a rigid orthodoxy: few Socialist parties abroad have avoided one or the other of these dangers.

Parliamentary leaders and ministers

These social and political characteristics do not help to distinguish the two parliamentary parties only. They also help to distinguish backbenchers from leaders and ministers. The Conservative parliamentary party is, like the party in the country, based on a social pyramid: it is not surprising that its parliamentary leaders and its ministers should be drawn from the apex of this social pyramid. This is not so apparent if one looks at occupations, partly because our distinctions are not sufficiently refined. Most Conservative M.P.s are businessmen, as we saw; the distinction between small, medium-sized, and big business is not always clear-cut and cannot be deduced from looking at rather dry records. Education provides perhaps a better clue, largely because education does often closely correspond to 'breeding' as well as to training.

The large majority of the Conservative senior ministers went to a public school and three-quarters of them went to Oxford and Cambridge. The Labour party often publicizes the fact that Old Etonians are present in large numbers in Conservative Cabinets; indeed, the Conservative party does not try to conceal this fact and it does appear to be rather proud of the situation. Of course, all Conservative Cabinet ministers are not Old Etonians, but about one-third are, while they form only a fifth of the total parliamentary party. If one considers all the exclusive public schools, one finds a definite hierarchy between back-benchers and junior ministers, some of whom have been to grammar school, and senior ministers who almost always went to a public school and often to one of the best. Clearly this does not mean that there is a conscious or systematic discrimination against non-public school men and non-graduates. It just happens that the choice comes to be narrowed down, the more one reaches the top, to M.P.s with the best background. It is probably a consequence of general attitudes in the Conservative party as well as a consequence of the requirements of the job which have been mentioned early in this chapter. It is certainly not an overt decision. Since the proportion of public school men has

Figure 10. *School background of M.P.s and of ministers*

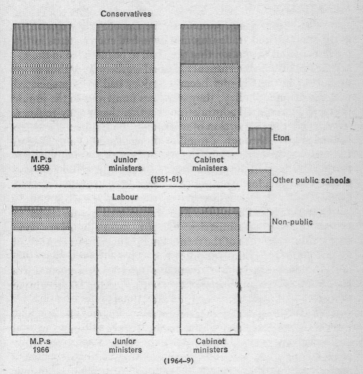

not decreased in the parliamentary party in recent years, however, the situation is not likely to change markedly in the near future.

In the Labour party, the situation is more complex. Education plays a part, but so do occupational and doctrinal differences. In the first place, ministers (and frontbenchers) need to have a better administrative training than the average M.P., and this requirement works to some extent against manual workers. Admittedly manual workers often become M.P.s after having gained administrative training in the trade unions. It might also be at times unwise for the leadership not to integrate trade unionists in the decision-making process when the party is in power. This explains why, in 1945, workers had more than their share of Cabinet posts. Moreover, the Labour party contained at the time various trade unionists who had such a status in the movement and the nation that they had to be included in the inner circles of the government. Manual workers were thus more numerous in the Cabinet because unions had to be associated with government policy; they were less numerous in the junior posts which required administrators rather than policy-makers. After 1950, the proportion of workers in the Cabinet started to decline, partly through a number of accidental causes. When Labour was in opposition, the proportion of manual workers further declined in the parliamentary leadership: this happened both in the Shadow Cabinet (the committee of twelve elected every year by the parliamentary party) and on the front bench, which is composed of all the M.P.s appointed by the leader to cover the range of ministries: in 1961, manual workers constituted only one fifth of the front bench. Since Labour returned to power in 1964, the proportion of manual workers among office-holders remained low: workers were nearly a third of the parliamentary party, but slightly over a quarter of the junior ministers and less than a fifth of the ministers.

Lack of administrative training may explain why manual workers often do not obtain as many seats in the inner circles of the parliamentary Labour party as their numbers in the whole parliamentary group would warrant. Members of the newer professions are also at a disadvantage, but not for the same reason: differences over policy are a more probable explanation. We noticed earlier that left-wing Labour M.P.s tended to come from these professions. But in opposition the parliamentary party as a whole does not elect left-wing members to the Shadow Cabinet in proportion to their numbers; in opposition or in office leaders rarely appoint left-wing members to the front bench or the Cabinet in proportion to their numbers. As a result, the groups which are most likely to be penalized are the newer professions. The situation which obtains within the parliamentary party is thus the reverse of the situation which obtains in the constituency section of the whole party.

As we saw, M.P.s who are elected as constituency representatives often come from journalism or school teaching. No lawyer was elected in the decade 1952–62. On the contrary, M.P.s who are elected to the parliamentary committee are more likely to be lawyers. In both cases, one of the reasons, if not the only reason, is the ideological conflict. Since the constituencies are left of centre, they are likely to choose their representatives among the social groups where there are many left-wing M.P.s. The majority of the parliamentary party, on the other hand, is more to the right: it is to some extent the result of the alliance between the manual workers and the members who come from the older professions. In recent years, this alliance has often been cemented over foreign affairs and it must be remembered that foreign affairs are one of the fields of policy where manual workers and members of the older professions tend to be in agreement. As a result, even though members of the newer professions may be technically well-qualified for administrative jobs, they normally do not succeed in being elected to the parliamentary committee in proportion to their numbers in the whole parliamentary party; the same type of reason probably accounts for the fact that the leader does not choose to appoint on the front bench many members who come from these social groups.

The older professions thus benefit from both these trends. A majority of the 1961 front bench were graduates; a third had been to a public school – almost twice the proportion among Labour M.P.s as a whole. School teachers were well represented, but other newer professions were somewhat under-represented, while lawyers and members of other older professions were at a considerable advantage.

The main causes of this situation are thus fairly clear: they are technical and political. Members of the older professions have both the administrative talent required and the political views which correspond to those of the majority of the parliamentary party. Whether there is, deep down, a more obscure and purely social influence at work is difficult to tell. One might be tempted to believe that, as in the Conservative party, there is in the Labour party an exclusive social circle which has a kind of 'manifest destiny' to rule the parliamentary party – in order for instance to make the Labour party appear more respectable in the country. By and large, however, this theory is difficult to substantiate. Manual workers are not entirely absent; nor are the members of the newer professions. The snobbery which might exist in some quarters cannot be allowed to go to extremes. There may be a pyramid in both parties: it is not the same pyramid and it does not come about for the same reasons.

It would be even more exaggerated to conclude that the leadership of both parties forms part of the same 'establishment'. The movement towards the middle class which one can trace when one analyses the composition of the parliamentary rank-and-file and leadership benefits social groups which are more exclusive; but these groups are not the same in both parties. The notion of 'establishment' is bound to be vague, since it attempts to embrace a social reality which cannot be reduced to distinctions of a legal or statistical character. Even so, it does not seem realistic to consider that the two middle-class groups which 'run' the two parliamentary parties belong to the same large social circle. One might perhaps say, at least at this stage, that the leadership of the Conservative party has the characteristics of an 'establishment'; even this proposition is a doubtful one. It is surely exaggerated to say the same about the Labour party. One cannot easily single out, within the Labour party, a group which could constitute, in the true sense of the word, an 'establishment'. The trade unions are a self-contained world of their own; the two middle-class groups are profoundly distinct in many ways. Members of the older professions, who usually run the affairs of the parliamentary party – with the consent of the trade union members – have to accept the fact that the newer professions are customarily preponderant in the constituency section of the National Executive and are also influential in various sectors of left-wing opinion in the country, particularly in some sections of the left-wing press. The newer professions have perhaps as much a claim to be considered as an 'establishment' as the older professions. Many of them are influential in the rank-and-file of the party and indirectly on the parliamentary leadership. The parliamentary leadership saw, at the time of the Clause Four controversy, that the limits of its influence were more circumscribed than it perhaps thought.

The members of these older professions who lead the parliamentary party belong to a very different circle from the circle which 'runs' the Conservative parliamentary party. Many Labour leaders may have, broadly speaking, the same kind of education as many Conservative leaders. But one should not push the comparison too far: Eton and Harrow do not sell many ties to Labour frontbenchers. The occupations and milieux are usually very dissimilar. The leading circles of the parliamentary Labour party do not come from the same kind of intelligentsia as the middle-class intelligentsia of local Labour parties; but they do not have the business background and connexions of the Conservative leadership either. Even if it were conceded that 'oligarchical tendencies' flourish in both parties, one would have to add that these tendencies do not produce the same oligarchies on each side.

The cursus honorum *in Britain*

Complaints about the 'passing of Parliament' are numerous. The discipline is tight, the pay, by middle-class standards, is comparatively low. At the same time, with the end of the 'leisure class', professionalization is said either to be coming or to have already come. Is the House of Commons, far from being a representative image of the nation (which socially speaking, at any rate, it never was) in the process of falling into the hands of career politicians anxious to move up the ladder as would professional men, businessmen, or civil servants?

In fact, the career of a politician is neither long nor secure. One enters the Commons rather late in life and one usually leaves before retiring age. On the average, an M.P. is in his early fifties, a little younger on the Conservative side, a little older on the Labour side. On the average also, an M.P. enters Parliament at the age of forty and he is unlikely to stay in the House after reaching sixty.

One sometimes assumes that M.P.s enter Parliament late because they have to contest several bad constituencies before they are given a safe or marginal seat. This is the case sometimes, but not usually so. Indeed, even the bad seats are rarely contested by men in their twenties. One imagines the young graduate picked by a constituency to contest the next general election, but one finds that even in the Conservative party, where candidates (both successful and unsuccessful) are rather younger, only 10 per cent of the candidates are under the age of thirty. If age groups were to be respected, there should be twice as many candidates under thirty among Conservatives, and four times as many in the Labour party. People who expect, early in life, to become prominent in politics, may be numerous; people who can transform this dream into reality – even if this reality means only the grim prospect of contesting a completely hopeless seat – are much less numerous.

This new M.P. approaching forty (and sometimes much older) can scarcely be said to be, in most cases, a 'professional politician'. Of course, he has been involved in politics; of course, he might have written political articles or, if he was a trade union organizer, he might have played a prominent part in the politics of his union or of his local Labour party. But he cannot be described as being, in the strict sense of the word, a 'professional politician'. Very few British M.P.s have never experienced the life of 'ordinary' British people, even if that 'ordinary' life is, more often than not, an 'ordinary' middle-class life. The career of politics, in mid-twentieth-century Britain at least, is a second career and, in many cases, a promotion.

This second career is often followed by a third, because many politicians retire from politics before retiring from all activity. At the end of each Parliament, large numbers of M.P.s retire, and many retire between elections. They retire not only because they are old, not so much because they fear electoral defeat, but presumably because they do not want to continue with their political career and prefer to go back to their original occupation or to start a third life. Defeat and death do not account for even half the changes which take place from one Parliament to the next. Early retirement is, in fact, quite common. It is more common in the Conservative party than in the Labour party, and this was to be expected. Labour M.P.s are older when they enter Parliament, partly because trade unions 'offer' safe seats to middle-aged trade unionists: the disillusionment with the parliamentary career is clearly connected with the number of years spent at Westminster. Moreover, Labour M.P.s have fewer outside contacts, and in particular fewer business contacts. Conservative M.P.s can return to their family business, or enter some new firm. Some professional M.P.s, some of the lawyers for instance, can return to their professions, but only provided they did not abandon all contacts with it when they were in Parliament; Civil Servants and teachers have even more difficulty in returning. This may have little impact on Conservatives who are professional men since they might well be able to enter some business, but it is likely to affect Labour members who are in the professions. Journalists are in a better position to return to their old career, but only provided they have made a sufficient name in Parliament and in the outside world. As for manual workers, to abandon Parliament is nearly always out of the question: trade union organizers have relinquished their job and will rarely find a substitute. They can, if they are lucky, find a post in journalism or earn their living by their publications. But, for the great majority, Parliament constitutes such a promotion – while it is only a transfer for many Conservative M.P.s – that they are unlikely to abandon politics before they are old.

Conservative M.P.s leave Parliament rather earlier than Labour M.P.s, but, since Labour M.P.s come later, the amount of time spent in the Commons is about the same on both sides. M.P.s make place for new blood. The career of an M.P. is not long enough to substantiate the view that British politicians are divorced from the life of the community. Despite safe seats and despite (or because of?) the rigid party system, the turnover is quick. At the beginning of each Parliament, M.P.s who come back to the House of Commons have spent, on the average, eight years at Westminster; by the time that Parliament draws to its

close, they will have spent about twelve years. Through resigna-
tions and defeats, the average will fall, once more, to eight years.
An M.P. who comes to Westminster for the first time is about
forty; the chances are more than four to one that this average
M.P. will have left the House before he is fifty-five.

Ministers and junior ministers are luckier than average M.P.s.
They stay in the Commons, on the average, longer than the
others (presumably because ministers, unlike backbenchers,
can claim to have been successful). Yet the prospects of staying
in office for very long periods are very remote indeed. The ministerial career is likely to start fairly late: one often becomes a
junior minister at forty-five only, a minister of Cabinet rank at
fifty, and a Cabinet minister at fifty-five. But all these successful
politicians have only a taste of glory, even though their party
may regularly be returned to power, as the Conservative party
was in the 1950s.

Consider the fate of that 'average' junior minister, who at
the age of forty to forty-five is called for the first time to join the
government. He is lucky to be a British politician, because the
British government, with over ninety posts, is much larger than
governments on the Continent. He joins the band of fifty
junior ministers who aspire to become one of the forty full
ministers and indeed one of the top twenty ministers who are in
the Cabinet. But, if he looks back at the fate of those who were
junior ministers before him, he will see that he has only four or
five years in front of him to enjoy this post of relative glory.
After that he must – unless he becomes a 'case' – climb or fall.
If he falls, he will have had five years of life marked by destiny.
If he climbs and becomes one of the ministers (always assuming
that the party is returned), he has in front of him two, three, or
four years before retirement. Only nine of the twenty-five persons who were promoted to ministerial jobs between 1952 and
1957 and who began their career as junior ministers in almost
all cases in 1951, were still in office in 1961. Most junior ministers
never become ministers, but, of those who do, two-thirds
retire (or are retired) before ten years have passed since they
left the backbenches.

Even when the same party is continuously in power, Cabinet

posts are not much more secure. During the decade 1951–61, Britain had one party in power, but she had three prime ministers, and almost a new Cabinet and a new Government. It happened by repeated reshuffles, and the pace was quick. Seventy-five persons were given posts by Sir Winston Churchill in the 1951 government: only sixteen of these persons were still in office ten years later. The bulk of the junior ministers had disappeared: only six of them – all but one in a ministerial post – had politically survived. Ministers of Cabinet rank and Cabinet ministers did a little better, but only ten of them, or about a quarter, had remained ministers for the whole of the period; and four of these ten saw their career finish abruptly in the summer of 1962. Many retired because of old age, some because of political disagreement, but many also abandoned their posts for no other reason than their ill-luck, their disappointment, or the displeasure of their prime minister.

One may find that the honour and advantages of a ministerial life are rewarding, but these honours and rewards are transient for those who belong to the party in power, and simply non-existent for the opposition party. A political career is one which begins late and is unlikely to lead to office. If it does, it is unlikely to leave a man in office, even when the pendulum does not swing, for more than five or ten years. The political career, whether on the backbenches or in ministerial office, ends early except for a few stars whose fortune may be such that, for a whole decade, they may remain in the councils of the government and expect that the greatest prize of all, that of the prime ministership, will eventually come their way for perhaps five, six, or seven years. For the others, and even for the very lucky, complete security of office is never attained and, as in Ancient Rome, the Tarpeian Rock remains in present-day Britain very near the Capitol, although in civilized Britain the Rock usually takes the form of a seat in the House of Lords. The career of politician may seem to have been straightforward in an age of small and uniform swings. As soon as one comes to draw the lucky number of a safe seat, one can hope to have, once and for all, the confidence of the electorate. Yet the politician has still to face real dangers, even though he may not have to fear the censure of the electorate.

The real dangers lie in the loss of confidence of his colleagues, in the loss of his own self-confidence, and most probably in the sheer exhaustion and the disillusionment which the job creates. The British electorate can rest in peace: if the two-party system remains, the age of safe seats will probably remain, but the seats will only be safe for the parties, not for the men. The age of a calm, easy, and long career has not yet come.

CHAPTER SIX

The Representation of Interests

THE centre of gravity of the study of British politics has slowly
moved from parties to interests and to interest groups. Interests
seem to work more in the open. Interest groups have greatly
developed their action in the post-war period. Admittedly most
interest groups were created before 1939: trade unions were
already powerful before 1914; professional associations and
trade associations had become active in the later part of the inter-
war period. Yet, before 1939, the open action of many associations was not as common or as readily accepted as it has been
since the war. Traditional theories of politics still prevailed, and
they usually ignored interest groups either because they were
too small or because they did not fit with the principles of representation on which British democracy was said to be founded.

Views have changed and a new theory of politics has emerged
and indeed been widely accepted. Under the influence of
American studies, interest groups have been analysed; they
have been justified, instead of being criticized. The theory of
representation has been enlarged to include them. Democratic
government is now established on two columns, parties and
interest groups, while it was, before the war, founded on the
single column of the parties. Most theorists now consider that
the representative system of government would neither be
efficient nor really democratic without interest groups. An
'economic and social chamber' may not ultimately be created,
although the National Economic Development Council leads
the way and although the House of Lords has come to include a
wider range of the interests of the nation than in the past. Yet,
if that economic chamber is not formally created, it may simply
be because interest groups will have found other and better
channels through which to exercise their influence.

The importance of interest groups in the representative
process is undeniable. We must examine them. But we cannot

examine them in the same detail as political parties. Their numbers are vast; their structure, their size their objects vary enormously. In the course of one chapter we can hope only to consider the one aspect of the life of interests which is most important for the political process, the problem of representation: it is in many ways different from the representation which is effected by political parties. Interest groups differ from political parties by their aim, which is not to take power but only to exert pressure. They differ from parties by their objects, which are usually limited in scope. They differ from parties by the nature of their membership, which is often limited to one section in society. There are so many difficulties in the field of the representation of interests that one can expect only to tackle even this problem alone in a general fashion.

Interests and the notion of representation

Interest groups must be divided according to their aims. The most important – at any rate the most effective ones – are the *protective* groups, which defend a section in society: trade unions defend the workers, professional associations defend members of the professions, trade associations and trade federations such as the Chambers of Commerce, the Chambers of Trade, and the Confederation of British Industry created by amalgamation of the National Union of Manufacturers and the Federation of British Industries, defend the interests of business. Local authorities or motorists are defended in the same way. The list is huge. All these associations, unions, federations, etc., have one thing in common: they each defend a certain group, a certain number of hundreds or thousands or hundreds of thousands of people who think that their interests, as a group, must be defended.

The other type of groups are the *promotional* ones. These are the ones which want to promote a cause by appealing, not to a section, to a special group, but to everybody. The Campaign for Nuclear Disarmament wanted to promote nuclear disarmament, the Royal Society for the Prevention of Cruelty to Animals wants animals to be better protected, the Council for the Preservation of Rural England wants rural England to be better preserved.

Some of these societies may want to protect a special group, like the National Society for the Prevention of Cruelty to Children, but they do not do so by appealing to members of this group only. They appeal to the whole public: anyone in the British Isles can be a member of the N.S.P.C.C.

We already encounter one way in which the notion of representation varies among interest groups. Groups of the protective type represent each a section of society: one can find out the section which is covered by the group – or at any rate which the group aims to cover. If there are 10,000 university teachers in Britain, an Association of University Teachers can expect to have only 10,000 members, but, if it has 10,000 members, it will 'represent' the university teachers, at least from the point of view of their professional interests. Promotional groups do not have a predetermined sphere of representation. Their aim is, presumably, to have as many members as possible among the whole population of the British Isles. The maximum membership of the Association of University Teachers may be 10,000, the maximum membership of the R.S.P.C.A. could be, if not 50 million, at least 30 or 35 million. If one used the word 'representative' in the same sense, these should be the figures which the R.S.P.C.A., and C.N.D., etc., should aim at in order to become 'representative'. This is why it is, in practice, difficult to measure, and indeed even to examine, the 'representative' character of promotional groups. Admittedly, parties, like promotional groups, hope to obtain the support of the whole population and do not; however, we know through elections which proportion of the population supports each party. There are no elections enabling promotional groups to show their real strength. If we consider only the figures of membership, we probably underestimate the scope of their influence; yet there is usually no other criterion. In some cases, Gallup polls can be a guide: we have an idea of the proportion of the population which has the same aims as those of the R.S.P.C.A. In most cases, we just do not know. This difficulty limits the study of interest groups. When the 'representative' character of groups is considered, generalizations and comparisons can be made for protective groups, but they cannot easily be made for promotional

Table 23. *Some examples of interest groups*

Business	Number of members (approx.)
Federation of British Industries	8,607 firms and 280 trade associations
National Union of Manufacturers (the above two organizations are now united in the Confederation of British Industry)	5,110 firms and 53 trade associations
Association of British Chambers of Commerce	60,000 members
National Farmers' Union	approx. 200,000 members

Labour and professions

Trade unions affiliated to the Trades Union Congress:
170 and 8,867,522 members (1965)
of which the largest are:

Transport and General Workers' Union	1,443,738
Amalgamated Engineering Union	1,048,955
National Union of General and Municipal Workers	795,767
National Union of Mineworkers	446,453
Union of Shop, Distributive and Allied Workers	349,230
National and Local Government Officers' Association	348,528
Electrical Trades Union	292,741
National Union of Railwaymen	254,687

Non-affiliated:

National Union of Teachers	about 230,000

Professional associations:

British Medical Association	about 70,000
Institute of Directors	about 40,000

Local authority associations

Association of Municipal Corporations	County Boroughs and Boroughs
County Councils' Association	Counties (except G.L.C.)

Other

Automobile Association	approx. 3,000,000 members

Promotional groups

National Federation of Old Age Pensioners	about 400,000
British Legion	about 850,000

(from Trades Union Congress Report, 1966; S. E. Finer, *Anonymous Empire*, Pall Mall Press, 1965, *passim;* H. Eckstein, *Pressure Group Politics* (the B.M.A.), Allen and Unwin, 1960; P. Self and H. Storing, *The State and the Farmer*, Allen and Unwin, 1962) groups. Since, on the whole, promotional groups are less influential and less successful, it may not matter so much that we should not be able to compare both types of groups. But the problem does exist.

There are other difficulties which concern protective groups as well. One comes from the difference in size between the social groups which protective organizations cater for. We have mentioned the Association of University Teachers. It has to be examined together with other groups, like the National Union of Mineworkers which has over 400,000 members, and the Association of Town Clerks which has a few hundreds. Generalizations are difficult to draw because the size of the membership has important repercussions on the structure of the organization, on the relationship between the leadership and the rank-and-file, and on the 'bureaucratic' character of the machine of the organization.

Yet this difficulty is perhaps dwarfed by two others which strike at the root of the nature of the 'representative' character of interest groups. In the first place, it is very difficult to compare the representative character of associations which are composed of individual members with that of associations composed, wholly or in part, of other associations or companies. Bodies like the Association of University Teachers or the National Union of Mineworkers have a certain number of members, each of whom is a single individual. One can count heads. Presumably, the views of the Association or of the Union are the views of the majority of its members. If one wants to examine the 'representative' principle at work, one examines, as for the parties, the local branches, the regional organizations, if there are any, and the national leadership. One can conclude from this analysis whether the organization is democratic or oligarchical, whether the oligarchy is one of 'bosses', of 'natural social leaders', or of 'bureaucrats'.

One cannot as easily use these criteria when one considers associations which are partly or wholly composed of other associations or companies. A trade association is composed of member-firms. These firms are unequal in size, in assets, in staff. One cannot expect a straightforward majority rule to prevail: it is not clear whether such a majority would be a majority of firms, of assets, or of both. In fact these criteria are difficult to use: small firms will not easily submit to the domination of the few large firms which have big assets, and the few large ones cannot be expected to agree with the verdict of a majority made up of a host of insignificant firms. Neither of these systems would be 'democratic'. What 'democracy' might mean is therefore unclear and, as a result, what 'representation' would mean is equally unclear. It becomes difficult to define the notion of 'oligarchical' rule in such associations.

This situation would not be serious if one could decide, as we did earlier for promotional groups, that associations composed of companies or societies are not sufficiently influential to deserve being examined in detail. This is obviously not the case. Firstly, business associations and local authority associations are built on this model: they have to be and always will be. Secondly, associations of wage and salary earners also fall in this category when primary organizations come to be grouped into 'federations'. The T.U.C. is only partly an association of individual members, it is also – and indeed formally only – an association of trade unions. Admittedly, decisions are taken at the Congress on the basis of the total number of members of the T.U.C. In practice, however, the decisions are taken through the means of the block vote, which gives to the leaders of the large unions a greater weight than to the leaders of the small ones. Even in the General Council, unions do not receive seats in precise relation to the number of members of each union. A precise apportionment would clearly be impractical and too rigid. The result is that the organization is not just composed of some millions of members, expressing themselves through delegates, but of a number of groups, the individual unions. The analogy with federal countries, which is sometimes used – and used in the very name of many organizations – is, in reality, misleading. Federations are based on a compromise between the representation of populations and the representation of territories; the compromise is effected by the existence of two chambers, neither of which, usually, can impose its will on the other. There are no such distinctions in interest groups. In business or local authority associations, the basis of representation is usually left unclear, probably because no one ever found a satisfactory criterion. In organizations such as the T.U.C., the 'federal' principle is superimposed on to the representation of individual members in the primary units, the unions. The result is more like a 'confederation', or the United Nations, despite the maintenance of the majority principle at the Congress. Decisions are based on the relative power and prestige of some of the groups rather than on the sheer weight of the numbers of the individual members.

This difficulty is not the only one: another drawback comes from the fact that interest *groups* do not cover the whole field of interests. Earlier in this chapter, we divided interest groups into protective and promotional. We made this distinction as if we assumed that in our society the organizations devoted to the defence of certain sections were the only ones which fulfilled either of these functions. This is clearly not the case. One must sharply distinguish between wage and salary earners who have to constitute protective organizations in order to defend their interests, and other sections which can protect their interests without having to set up an organization solely for the purpose of defence. Admittedly, unions and professional associations were not created to put pressure on the State; they were created to put pressure on private employers. Only later did they also come to be used in order to obtain certain concessions from the State, chiefly because the government became a large employer and because it began to regulate conditions of employment in many branches of the private sector. But both to put pressure on private employers and to put pressure on the State, wage and salary earners needed these organizations. For them, there was no defence possible except through these unions and associations, and these have remained the only bodies which can ensure the protection of the interests of people in these categories of employment.

Other interests also formed protective groups: trade associations have proliferated, local authority associations are powerful. But these organizations are not the only means by which business or local authorities can defend their interests. In contrast with wage and salary earners, individual firms or individual local authorities are often large enough to be able to present their case by themselves. Employees may have to congregate into groups to be able to lobby, but Unilever or the Lancashire County Council do not need to do so. Indeed, these powerful bodies sometimes prefer to negotiate with the government and its representatives directly.

Nor is this all. It is not only that the big firms are large enough to lobby by themselves, it is also that the very structure of business is often an adequate substitute for a formally organized interest group. What is required for interests to defend themselves is not an interest group as such, solely designed for this effect and, as it were, 'registered' as an interest group. What is required is a set of contacts through which a common policy can be defined. Small business has often remained unorganized, and it is largely subjected to the conditions of individual capitalism. Big business, on the contrary, has become more and more integrated. Personal connexions link many companies. These connexions are underlined, or caused, by large capital participations of firms in assets of others. Large industrial and financial companies do not need to create *ad hoc* interest groups: they are already organized into holdings or associated through participations in order to achieve industrial efficiency or to obtain financial support. They can use their own network to exercise pressure on the political and administrative worlds.

The purpose of these remarks is not to overemphasize the influence of business. We will examine later what can be said about that influence. Moreover, business is not alone in being able to use pre-existing organizations for the purpose of exercising influence. Some cultural organizations, such as the churches or the universities, do exercise pressure in a similar way. They use pre-existing channels and they do not have to create an interest group before being able to lobby the State or its representatives.

The distinction between formally organized groups and informally constituted groupings is very important in practice: it circumscribes the sphere in which the representative principle plays a part and the sphere where there is pressure, but no representative principle, at work. We said at the beginning of this chapter that interest groups are a means by which the views of the citizens come to be represented. This is why one can and one must, admittedly with the reservations already made, examine whether the views of the rank-and-file are adequately transmitted to the top within interest groups. But among informally organized groupings, in companies, churches, universities, it becomes pointless to start discussing the 'representation' of a rank-and-file. Clearly, even in an organization as hierarchical as the Roman Catholic Church, there are channels through which the views of the rank-and-file are communicated to the top, at any rate if these views are strongly held. This happens even more in a network of companies, despite the principle that those who own or control the majority of the capital can dictate their policy to the whole of the network. Yet this is not representation.

If we want to see, as we do here, whether the representative principle works well in the field of interests, we can therefore look at formally constituted interest groups only. We must not forget, however, that, while looking at representation, we are looking only at a certain number of interests and not at all of them. We must always remember that interest groups are the only means of pressure which wage and salary earners possess, while, on the other hand, business, the churches, some other cultural groups, possess other means of influence. Conclusions which are reached about wage and salary earners' organizations should always be put in perspective with the conclusions which can be reached when one examines all the channels by which business can exercise pressure. The realistic comparison is not the one which compares the T.U.C. with the C.B.I. alone, but the one which compares the T.U.C. on the one hand with, on the other hand, the C.B.I., the City, and other major business organizations.

The membership of interest groups and its characteristics

Let us examine briefly, in the first place, the membership of interest groups. The question of course arises only in formally constituted interest groups, but, even among these groups, we already noticed that protective groups differ from promotional groups in this respect. In promotional groups, it may be of some general interest to know the absolute figures of membership, but we cannot relate them to any wider circle of potential membership. If we know that the C.N.D. has had up to 40 or 50,000 members or that the R.S.P.C.A. has perhaps 10,000 members, we have only a rough guide to the extent of the support for these organizations in the nation. A better guide – although still a crude one – is sometimes the comparative strength of two diametrically opposed organizations.

For protective organizations, on the contrary, we can compare the actual membership of the group with the number of people (or of firms) which the organization endeavours to cover. An organization with a '100 per cent' membership is clearly more 'representative' than an organization which has only a 5 per cent membership, even if the latter has a large absolute number of members. Absolute figures are totally misleading for protective associations, at any rate if one is concerned with the 'representative' character of the organization.

Despite their great numerical strength, trade unions come out as being much less 'representative' than many professional and trade associations. The ten million or so trade unionists constitute less than half the potential membership of the unions. The British Medical Association, on the contrary, contains over 80 per cent of the doctors; the Institute of Directors, which had a very rapid growth in post-war years, has 40,000 members and about four-fifths of the total number of directors in the country.

The differences from trade to trade can be very large. Some groups of manual workers, such as the miners, are more organized than doctors or teachers. Traditional jobs, skilled jobs, jobs where the members are concentrated in large firms have a high percentage of organized members. Unions composed of unskilled workers, of workers scattered in very small firms, as in catering or in the distributive trades, enrol a low percentage of their potential membership. In many of these firms, membership of a union is still frowned upon. In many of these occupations, there is a high proportion of women, and women are more reluctant than men to join a union. The reasons are not much clearer than the reasons why women are more right-wing than men, but they are certainly connected. It is also because there is a smaller proportion of trade unionists in small firms that it seems reasonable to assume that the Labour vote is also smaller, in proportion, in these firms. One does not know which phenomenon is the 'cause' of the other or even whether there is in this matter a 'cause' and an 'effect', but the two points are surely linked.

Table 24. *Some examples of the proportion of organized workers and professional people*

	Approximate percentage of organized members (1958)
Non-manual:	
teachers (mainly N.U.T.)	80
local government (N.A.L.G.O.)	84
doctors (B.M.A.)	80
directors (Institute of Directors)	80
Manual:	
coal miners	90
transport	74
printing	58
building	38
clothing	28
distribution	15

(from S. E. Finer, *Anonymous Empire*, Pall Mall Press, 1958, *passim*, and Political and Economic Planning, 'Trade Union Membership', *Planning*, broadsheet vol. XXVIII, no. 463, July 1962, p. 156)

It is important to notice the percentage of the total group which belongs to a protective organization, be it union, professional association, or trade association. It is also important to notice that there are very few cases where more than one protective organization competes for the membership of the same group, although, when it arises, the competition may be bitter, as is the rivalry between established and breakaway unions. Promotional groups compete for the same members, as political parties do; of course, most promotional groups are relatively small, and the extent of the competition is often limited. Yet it is often true to say that a promotional group – if it aims at promoting a controversial cause, as many do – comes to be opposed by another group aiming at mobilizing opinion in the opposite direction. This does not happen so much with protective groups. Business groups oppose workers' organizations, but this is an opposition between two camps which have each a predetermined sphere of influence. Businessmen cannot join trade unions and workers cannot join employers' organizations. The party conflict, as we know it in the political world, rarely occurs, at least in Britain, among protective organizations: the main conflict is more akin to the international conflicts where nationals of each side are drafted into fighting against each other and cannot choose to cross the line or wait on the sidelines.

Of course, one does find some examples of 'party' conflict within protective groups: these are the conflicts which occur when more than one organization tries to secure members within the same social category. In several countries the trade union movement is divided into competing organizations: in France, there are three equivalents of the T.U.C.: a Christian, a Communist, and a Socialist T.U.C. In Britain, outright competition in the trade union field does not exist, but some guerilla warfare, such as poaching and demarcation disputes, occurs in borderline cases both in organizations catering for manual workers and in organizations catering for non-manual workers, such as for instance among teachers. Outside the trade union world, one sometimes finds competition: the National Union of Manufacturers and the Federation of British Industries did to some extent cater, before being united into the C.B.I., for the same people, although the N.U.M. mainly organized small firms and the F.B.I. large firms. The clearest case of competition occurs in the motoring world, where the A.A. and the R.A.C. (and the Scottish R.A.C.) compete for the same group without appealing more particularly to one sub-group than to another.

It is worth noticing this difference between protective associations and promotional organizations, as it is worth noticing the difference between protective associations and political parties. It is also worth contrasting the situation in the trade union world in Britain and in France or some other Continental countries. The fact that disunity is the exception rather than the norm proves that the situation in the world of protective interest groups is very different from the situation which exists in the political world, where competition for the same electors is always considered to be one of the fundamentals of Western democracy. Such competition is regarded with disfavour among interest groups because, at the same time, these protective organizations fight their main battle, almost permanently, with 'the other side'. The situation is somewhat similar to the situation in a democratic country in wartime, when the parties agree to a political truce in order to fight a common enemy. Indeed, when there is competition among protective groups, or at any rate borderline guerilla warfare, there are often agreements which try to diminish the intensity of the conflict: unions know that their prestige is damaged by demarcation disputes and try to solve them by themselves. The T.U.C. has been given powers to regulate outright poaching. Business organizations often have joint committees, standing or *ad hoc*, enabling them to pursue a common interest or at least to face emergencies.

When conflicts remain, as between the French unions, the causes are not primarily industrial but political. Political conflicts overflow into the industrial field. Trade union disunity is often the consequence of deep-rooted ideological disputes which cannot be avoided at the industrial level. Yet even in these cases, the conflicts are not considered as being 'normal', in the way that the party conflict is considered as being 'normal' in the political field. Their occurrence is generally regretted even if, in fact, little is done to heal the wounds or gloss over the differences. At a different level, the same reasons perhaps account for the fact that one rarely finds permanently organized factions, within each trade union, in Britain or elsewhere, unless some *politically* determined minority, such as the Communists, perpetuates these conflicts. Many think that a permanent division between a majority and a minority works against the united front which trade unions (and also other interest groups) want to present against the common enemy.

Active and passive members; local leadership
Some interest groups recruit larger proportions of employees

than others; protective groups usually recruit much higher proportions of potential members than political parties. These proportions fall very markedly, however, when one comes to consider *active* members. Admittedly, in some cases, it is clearly difficult for members to take an active part. Some organizations do not have local branches and only hold Annual General Meetings in London. But in most protective associations, trade unions, professional associations, and trade associations, there are local branches, which hold frequent meetings at which the policy of the organization is discussed. These local branches elect their own officers and also elect delegates to the Annual Conferences. However, even then, attendances are low: trade unions complain about this passivity. Perhaps half a million people, out of ten million trade unionists, attend meetings of their branches, and not all of them do so regularly. Even though there may be a number of technical reasons for this poor attendance – branches hold meetings in the evenings, not necessarily very near the residence of each member – the main point is that the large majority of trade unionists are just too apathetic to come to the meetings of their union.

It is sometimes alleged that these low attendance rates make the local leadership of these organizations 'unrepresentative' of the rank-and-file and, consequently, that the decisions taken by these 'unrepresentative' leaders do not correspond to the views of the mass of the members? It is generally argued, in respect of trade unions, that active minorities, whether Communist or not, can, as a result, have an influence which their real support does not warrant. Even though this might not very often be the case in the branches, it is certainly true that, in the plants, many shop stewards are extremists, although extremist shop stewards are clearly not a majority. In other interest groups, extremism is also said to be rampant. Many local organizations are thought to be run by 'activists', deeply committed to the cause and prepared to undertake militant action.

There are certainly some extremists among local leaders, although there are also many sleeping local organizations, where the leaders' sin is apathy and inaction rather than militant extremism. What is probably true is that, quite logically, active local organizations are likely to be in the hands of people who are more 'excited' than the mass of the members. Otherwise they would not go to the trouble of being secretaries of branches or of other local organizations. These positions are usually cumbersome and bring little reward in terms of cash or power. Such an extremism is, however, limited in two ways. Firstly, the chores and the administrative burdens are bound to consume some of the extremist energies of the local leaders. Secondly, there is a clear limit to the amount of extremism which active leaders and local leaders can generate: they have to rely on the whole of the rank-and-file to follow their decisions. Interest groups are only successful in their campaigns if they can count on the active support of the whole body of members. Extremism is bound to be tempered by the knowledge that the members 'will not follow'. Active members may – or some of them may – be 'activists' in words; they are likely to be more careful in their deeds. In fact, many local leaders are 'unrepresentative', not because they are too extreme, but because they are too moderate. Many become cautious; trade union leaders know the difficulties and hazards of industrial action. Revolts of the rank-and-file are not, or no longer, revolts of the moderate common man against excited agitators: they are usually revolts of an excited rank-and-file. Some may, at the lowest levels, try to stir up trouble and succeed in doing so; in the normal way, the troubles are spontaneous and the local leadership is 'statesmanlike and responsible'.

One often blames the whole body of members for their inactivity, but it is sometimes forgotten that there is one form of 'activity' which members do not refuse: the support for industrial action asked for by the union leadership is usually widespread. The 'inactivity' of members is limited to the fact that they do not turn up at local meetings. This suggests that the notions of representation on which unions and other interest groups are based do not perhaps entirely correspond to the notions which are prevalent among the whole body of the rankand-file. The trade union movement is based on the assumption that the organizations are 'democratic'; this 'democracy' entails that each branch must discuss problems and that the representatives of the branch come together to form policy at national level. *Mutatis mutandis*, the same principles prevail in other organizations. However, in practice, the whole body of the rank-and-file probably does not understand 'democracy' in that way. Many people join an interest group for the same reasons as they take out an insurance policy. They expect a service, or, more specifically, they expect to be covered against a certain risk. They do not expect to be asked to form policy. There are, admittedly, large variations. The notion of representation is much more present in the minds of trade unionists than it is in the minds of the members of the A.A. Business and professional associations are intermediate types. Yet nowhere is the notion of representation sufficiently deep-rooted to be much more than *global*. Global representation suggests that the union as a whole represents the members; individual representation, on the other hand, would mean that each member would feel personally committed to shape the details of policy. Few members consider that they are personally 'represented' by the delegates whom 'they' send to the Annual Conference.

More people join protective groups than political parties or promotional associations: they do so because they expect, rightly or wrongly, that they can draw more immediate benefits from the membership of a protective organization than they can from that of a promotional association or a political party. They do so because there is more social pressure on the part of friends, neighbours, or colleagues. The net result is probably that *less* members, not more, expect the protective organization to 'represent' them in a detailed fashion. In political parties we saw that most members are 'apathetic'; they certainly do not join the party *in order* to form policy. The incentive to join a union or any other protective organization is greater than the incentive to join a party: the result is that most members think that the association is 'theirs' in the vaguest fashion. It is 'theirs' because it is the symbol of the whole of the group, not because they feel obliged to run it as they would run their house or their business.

Since such attitudes are prevalent, one should not be surprised to find that local leaders are of a rather peculiar 'type'. This is not so much because they are drawn from a certain social class. In some purely social organizations, such as the Women's Institutes, the local leaders are drawn from noticeably higher social backgrounds than the mass of the rank-and-file; but leaders of most protective organizations are not different in that way. They differ from the rank-and-file because they are more committed, because they are temperamentally more interested in the administration of the organization. Some of these people may be 'activists'; the belief in the value of 'active minorities' may develop among some of them. For practical purposes, the danger is more imagined than real, since, in the last resort, the whole of the membership – and even the non-members – must support the leaders when 'action' comes to be required. This is, in most protective organizations, the real test of 'representation'. Indeed it is probably because local leaders are temperamentally 'unrepresentative' that many organizations survive and prosper. This characteristic is more often to their credit and to the advantage of the large majority of members than their 'activism' is to the detriment of members and society alike.

National organizations

One encounters the problem of 'representation' at national as well as at local level, but the conditions in which the problem arises are different. Many organizations have large full-time establishments at national level, while they have only unpaid voluntary officers at local level. These national establishments are, in principle, almost everywhere based on the 'democratic' machinery of Annual Conference, elected executives, responsible officers, and general secretaries. Yet, in practice, is it well-known that annual or quarterly meetings of delegates do not 'control' the officers and that even the officers often do not 'control' the officials. In the process, the 'democratic' rule often appears modified by the influence of 'oligarchies': either oligarchies of 'top people', who might be big businessmen, leading members of the professions, skilled manual workers; or oligarchies of 'bureaucrats', permanently in charge of the association, while officers are transient and ill-informed. While 'activism' is often said to prevail at the grass-roots, the London circles are said to be the prey of 'responsible statesmen' who turn to their profit the potentially rebellious forces of the rank-and-file and their local leaders.

Rule by top people?

One form of oligarchical control is the control which 'top people' might exercise in the organizations. In business associations, large firms often are permanently represented on the executives, as large nations are on the Security Council of the United Nations. Officers are often recruited from the directors and managers of these large firms. The most obvious example was that of the F.B.I., which is now merged into the C.B.I.: the Federation had a 'democratic' Grand Council, on which all the interests were represented; but the Grand Council was only the 'Delegate Conference' of the Federation. The inner body which advised the President was an Advisory Committee whose members were recruited by co-option: very large firms had a considerable say in the selection process. In professional associations, leading specialists sometimes sit on executive committees. In some trade unions, craftsmen and skilled workers seem to play a larger part than their members would warrant. In the T.U.C., the leaders of very large unions are often considered to be 'bosses', who combine their forces to 'dominate' the trade union movement.

This kind of model does not stand up to a more precise analysis of the workings of interest groups. In the first place, it is not because 'top people' are asked to stand on governing bodies that these top people are necessarily unrepresentative of the smaller groups. There may be very good reasons why a trade association will prefer to appoint leading businessmen to its executive. Jobs of officers or of committee members are time-consuming: the managers of a small firm may not be able to afford to take time off and run the risk of seeing their business decline. In order to achieve results, one needs contacts in the right places. Big businessmen are much more likely than small businessmen to have the right contacts and to exercise influence. The leader of a small business in the provinces naturally wants to be represented by the leader of a large London firm. Indeed, small businessmen often complain when they notice that the leaders of large businesses do not attend executive meetings or send only their second or third in command in their place. They feel that the leaders of the large businesses are letting the association – and the small businesses – down.

In the second place, it is just not true that trade associations, professional associations, let alone trade unions, include only representatives of such top organizations on their executives. An empirical investigation of the composition of the governing bodies of trade associations showed that they included many small businessmen: one in ten of all the firms employing less than 200 people had one of its members on a trade association executive. Since there are many more small firms than there are large firms, a 10 per cent representation of the small firms meant a considerable proportion of all the seats on the executives.

Moreover, a dry analysis of the powers of the governing bodies can be as legalistic as a dry analysis of the constitutional powers of delegate conferences or annual general meetings. We know that delegate conferences do not 'run' these organizations; we should not conclude that the governing bodies 'run' the organizations in a dictatorial fashion either. Business associations are not ruled by governing bodies taking decisions in isolation. Decisions are taken by the governing bodies and endorsed by the annual conferences, *after* they have been prepared by committees, standing or *ad hoc*, which have examined the question in detail and made recommendations. It is very rare for the executive committees to reject these recommendations and, if they reject them, the annual conference is likely to ask why. On these committees, great care is taken to see that all the interests concerned, whether large or small, are represented. Small firms may not be consulted on all the problems, but they are consulted when their direct interests are at stake. On top of the 10 per cent of the small firms which had one of their members on the governing bodies of a trade association, it was found that a further 16 per cent had one of their members who sat, permanently or temporarily, on committees dealing with specialized questions.

The situation in the F.B.I. illustrates this point. On the surface, the ruling group was oligarchical. In practice, consultation took place with all the members. It must be remembered that, in any case, the F.B.I. was an organization representing big business rather than the small firms, which, on the whole, preferred to join the National Union of Manufacturers. Yet, even in the F.B.I., questions were discussed through an elaborate system of committees formed, not of members of the 'governing' Advisory Committee, but of members of the trade associations and firms which composed the Federation. Selection was made on the basis of the degree to which the problem concerned the component bodies. These committees were, in fact, the policy-forming bodies, because the Advisory Committee and the Grand Council did not take a decision unless the relevant specialized committee had come to an agreement and produced a report. Moreover, the Federation rarely relied on majority votes and usually preferred unanimity. This practice favoured the small firms – or at any rate prevented the 'oligarchy' from being 'despotic'. Indeed, the Federation has been known not to take decisions on controversial issues, in order to avoid taking a line which would alienate a section of the industry concerned with the problem. It will be interesting to see what forms consultation and decision processes will take in the new C.B.I.

Interest groups representing business are 'representative' of – or at any rate attentive to – the views of the rank-and-file. Some businesses may none the less be more influential than others; they may exercise this influence within the interest groups, but they are more likely to exercise it outside the network of interest groups altogether. Large businesses have the means of exercising influence through the network of their companies and do not necessarily need to use the channel of the interest group. In many cases, they prefer to use that channel, because it gives to the views which they want to promote a more official and respectable outlook, but they do not confine their influence and pressure to interest groups. An 'oligarchical' rule of some leading business interests can prevail through the direct contacts which these interests have with the members of the political world. This is, however, outside the field of 'representation'. It does not entail a rule by 'top people' within interest groups. It means operating outside the field of interest groups altogether.

In associations of professional men and in trade unions, the conflicts between leading grades and 'small men' have often been acute and have sometimes produced a division of the members into two associations or trade unions, one of which is more specifically devoted to the defence of the leading grades. These leading grades have often been incensed by what they felt was the gradual deterioration of their status and of their 'differentials'. By keeping separate organizations alive, they have, in some cases, succeeded in preventing the fall from being too rapid, although they have probably to some extent diminished the strength of their combined organizations. This is scarcely, in any case, an instance of rule by 'top people'. While, at the beginning of the twentieth century, it was still very common for trade unions to be run by craftsmen and for the great mass of professional people to be unorganized and to accept the lead of the London specialists, the situation has been almost completely reversed in the inter-war and post-war periods. The rearguard battles of the leading grades are more common than the instances of rule by 'top people'.

Even in federations and confederations like the T.U.C., the rule by 'top people' is more a myth than a reality. The block vote system can, in theory, enable leaders of large unions to 'dominate' the Congress. Even if it were true that these leaders 'dominated' their own unions and therefore 'owned' the votes of their members, it would not be true that, at the Congress or in the General Council, these union leaders could act in a dictatorial fashion. One is always apt to overestimate, from the outside, the unity of these 'oligarchs': the recent instances of divisions between the leader of the T.G.W.U., Mr Cousins, and the other union 'bosses' indicate that this unity is probably a myth. On the General Council, in any case, the large unions do not have more, but less, of the share of seats which the numbers of their members would allow them to have.

At the Congress, political and general industrial questions

might be decided by the weight of numbers, but positive industrial action cannot be recommended in the same way. In fact, little practical action is ever recommended, formally because the T.U.C. does not have the necessary powers, in reality because practical action requires the active participation, not only of the leaders of small unions, but of the bulk of the trade unionists as well. As at the local level, the limits of the practical power of trade union leaders are such that leaders would simply never

Table 25. *T.U.C. General Council*

	Percentage of members	Number of seats	Percentage of seats
Eight large unions:			
T.G.W.U.	16·3	3	8·4
A.E.U.	11·8	3	8·4
N.U.G.M.W.	9·0	3	8·4
N.U.M.	5·0	2	5·6
U.S.D.A.W.	3·9	1	2·8
N.A.L.G.O.	3·9	1	2·8
E.T.U.	3·3	1	2·8
N.U.R.	2·9	1	2·8
TOTAL	56·1	15	42·0
9 other unions over 100,000	16·6	8	22·1
17 unions over 50,000	13·5	5	13·8
137 unions under 50,000	13·8	8	22·1
	100	36	100

think of bulldozing small unions and run the risk of not being followed.

Therefore, what distinguishes organization of workers or of other occupational groups from business, local authorities, or some cultural groups, is not that the latter are more likely to be dominated by 'top people' than the former. The leadership has to be 'representative' in the sense, at any rate, that it has to be responsive to the general desires of the rank-and-file. The difference lies rather, as we suggested at the outset, in the fact that trade unions and professional associations are the only means of exercising pressure for workers and professional people, while big business still seems to exercise part of its influence outside the channels of interest groups. 'Top people' do not seem to have tried to perpetuate their power through the means of interest groups or else they do not seem to have succeeded in doing so.

Rule by bureaucratic managers?

It seems difficult to substantiate the view that interest groups are 'dominated' by their wealthiest or most skilled elements. This may become irrelevant, however, if the greatest danger turns out to be that of bureaucratization. This danger has loomed in the background in many organizations; it is often said that it will happen everywhere, in professional associations and in trade unions, in wage and salary earners' organizations, and in business groups. The natural cause is the growth in size. The growth in size leads to an increase in the number of top managers, either research officers who do the home work, or ex-civil servants or professional men who have their entry in Whitehall and are skilled negotiators. These people cannot be expected to remain passive: they are bound to have views about the policy of the interest group and they are in a position to exercise power.

They can exercise power, in the first place, because, like civil servants faced with a minister, they have the advantage of permanence and technical knowledge. They are experts; this is why they are recruited. They are also permanent, while officers are not. In trade unions, officers and committee members rotate fairly quickly: every two years, half the executive of the T.G.W.U., for instance, is rejuvenated, not as a result of any hard-and-fast rule, but simply because it so happens. In business and professional associations, officers and committee members rotate, either because there is a rule, or because the burden of office is just too heavy: the President of the F.B.I. spent about half his time working for the Federation. After two or three years, an officer resigns his post in order to devote himself to his own business. The permanent officials of the associations are therefore in the same advantageous position as are the State civil servants confronted with transient ministers.

Indeed, the permanent official of an interest group is at a still greater advantage. He can influence his public – the members of the association – while the civil servant cannot. The civil servant operates in the darkness of Whitehall, screened from the nation by ministers and other politicians. Officials of interest groups can, on the contrary, influence the members through publications, pamphlets, and notes published by the organization. These are meant to inform the members on technical problems. The officials can use them, to some extent at least, to 'educate' as well as to 'inform'.

Moreover, the power of these officials also comes from the fact that they conduct negotiations and know their opposite numbers in other associations and in the civil service. Officials live in a world of their own. They know what is acceptable to their respective 'masters'; they also know how much room for manoeuvre they are likely to have. They can inform each other, have tentative arrangements, prepare the bargains. The broad framework of these bargains is determined by the governing bodies, but the details leave officials with opportunities to exercise their initiative. Members of the governing bodies depend on the loyalty of these officials and have, to some extent, to accept both their views and their appreciation of the situation.

The danger is real, but the picture can be overdramatized. Officials are unlikely to betray the confidence of their 'masters', since these 'masters' determine their career. Moreover, in Britain at least, bureaucracies of interest groups have not, as yet, grown large enough to be uncontrollable. Bureaucracies of individual firms are large, but the bureaucracies of the interest groups rarely exceed staffs of one or two hundred. American unions still have five or six times more staff per member than British unions.

Moreover, one should not, in Britain at least, overemphasize the divorce between the bureaucracies and the rank-and-file or the governing bodies. In some interest groups, ex-civil servants and other experts are brought in from outside the organization, but this is not yet the most common practice, not only in trade unions, but even in other associations. Bureaucracies are still mainly staffed with people coming from within the trade, either from rank-and-file members or from member firms or organizations. There may be some divergence of views, but not a divorce.

Fundamental misunderstandings are exceptional. Even in trade unions, where the psychological gap between workers and administrators is very large, the bureaucracy is still controlled, and often overcontrolled, by persons who have worked their way through the whole of the trade union hierarchy. General secretaries and their assistants are not 'managers' in the ordinary sense. They are normally permanent, whether they have to put up for re-election or not, since members usually re-elect their general secretary until he decides to retire; indeed, the permanence is even greater because, before spending ten or fifteen years at the top of the union, the general secretary has usually been assistant general secretary. Yet these general secretaries are not drawn from a different world from that of the members of the executive. They come from the rank-and-file, they have often been members of the executive themselves. The members of the executive are their friends rather than their 'masters'. They do not work behind closed doors, but in the eyes of their own public and, indeed, of the public at large. They are often said to be bosses: this is very much open to question. But if they tend to be strong leaders, it is not in the fashion of bureaucratic managers; it is in the fashion of elective, albeit 'charismatic' leaders.

It is fairly clear that, in most cases, the leadership of interest groups is, in a general way, representative of the rank-and-file. The notion of 'representation' varies, but one has to take into account the fact that members usually do not want to be bothered with details, and judge in bulk, from results, rather than from each aspect of policy. One may consider that these leaders constitute 'oligarchies', but this implies stretching the meaning rather further than is legitimate, given the desires of the rank-and-file not to participate. In promotional groups, which have usually a smaller audience and less influence, 'oligarchical' tendencies are probably more noticeable. In business and cultural circles which operate outside the field of interest *groups*, indeed perhaps more specifically in banking, the influence of small and rather closed networks is noticeable and it is often denounced. In protective groups, oligarchical tendencies are, on the whole, limited.

Coming as they do from the mass of ordinary members or, at any rate, from the mass of active members, leaders of interest groups, whether officers or managers, are unlikely to develop into a self-contained circle with too few contacts with the rank-and-file which they are elected or selected to defend, and too many contacts with leaders of other groups. Leaders of different groups have many contacts with their opposite numbers; they may be in agreement on details, even against their own rank-and-file. Yet they are not, in this, 'betraying' their rank-and-file. In particular, it is plainly untrue to think that leaders of trade unions and leaders of business groups can come to some fundamental agreement. One does not find an 'establishment' of interest group leaders, but simply trade union leaders, leaders of professional associations, leaders of business groups, all knowing the rules of the game, but aiming at using these rules to further the interests of those people with whom they remain, in a general fashion, temperamentally associated. Whether all of them have the same influence remains to be seen. But it is difficult to substantiate the view that they are divorced from their members.

CHAPTER SEVEN

The Bureaucracy

THERE are two extreme views about the role of the bureaucracy. The first is based on the traditional theory of democratic government. In this view, the bureaucracy does not and must not interfere in the determination of policy. Politics is the job of politicians. Pressure groups, which represent some segments of the population, may try to influence politicians. Civil servants ought not to do the same; they should confine themselves to the application of predetermined policy, to the giving of impartial advice, and to the suggestion of alternative lines of conduct. The second view, at the other extreme, holds that modern industrial societies have become so complex and so technical that only experts can manage them. Private corporations are more and more managed by experts; public bodies should follow suit and, some maintain, do in fact follow suit. The line between policy and administration is, in practice, impossible to draw: civil servants take the lion's share, simply because ministers and other politicians are incapable of forming policy when technicalities have become such an integral part of policy. In the most extreme form of that view, politicians have lost the initiative: they are used by civil servants, rather than the reverse.

There is no need to adopt an extreme form of the second theory to have to recognize that civil servants have become increasingly involved in the job of managing the State together with politicians. Civil servants, particularly higher civil servants, cannot be deemed merely to implement a predetermined policy. Their advice and suggestions are recognized by all to be essential; they prepare the ground by collecting written information and having informal conferences with the various interests concerned. Without them, ministers would be harassed – in fact they would be unable to judge the situation and to implement any kind of policy. As soon as it is recognized that policy formation is a lengthy process in which all administrators, whether politicians or civil servants, must play a part, the role of civil servants in the 'politics' of a country appears considerable.

If this is a correct description of the situation, however, the problems of the neutrality and reliability of the civil service are radically transformed. As long as the civil service is meant only to execute, the problem of its reliability consists in ensuring that the letter of the decisions of the ministers and other political 'masters' is carried out. This may be difficult in practice: traditions can be built over a period of time only; some countries may be more successful than others. Yet it is only a problem of administrative organization: it can be solved by recruitment requirements, by careful determination of the conditions of service, by well-planned training. When, however, it is recognized that civil servants are asked not only to implement but also to conceive, jointly with politicians, the question of their reliability acquires a different character. Moral integrity and even academic standards are no longer the only yardsticks by which a good civil service can be measured. We have to consider whether the civil service actively supports the policy of the politicians in power. We have to examine whether civil servants are likely to be prejudiced against the dominant party, against certain types of policies, against the feasibility of certain plans. 'Reliability' ceases to be mechanical; it can no longer be measured according to a pre-established code. It becomes a problem of group psychology.

Studies of the structure of the British civil service have therefore taken a different course in the twentieth century. In the original analysis, the British civil service was praised for its impartiality and integrity; the recruitment system was usually said to be one of the most advanced. More recently, criticisms have sprung up, not because these qualities have ceased to exist, but because observers have come to look at the concept of 'reliability' from a different and less formal angle. Nobody doubted that the service was ostensibly impartial, but some claimed that its members were selected from a rather restricted social group which had restricted social views. Some claimed also that higher civil servants came from one part of the country only, the Metropolis, and were unaware of the problems of the provinces. Some came to question the methods of recruitment on the grounds that they were biassed in favour of certain types of candidates, over and above – indeed perhaps despite – the academic qualifications which other candidates could show. Some came to criticize the service for an alleged lack of dynamism, an intrinsic reluctance to adopt new ideas, an exaggerated reliance on amateurism.

These criticisms, made on technical or social grounds, were criticisms on political grounds as well, since these alleged defects were likely to have political consequences. It was said that the civil service, particularly the higher civil service, was likely to be instinctively opposed to social change and to exaggerate the difficulties involved in carrying out any plan for radical reform. This point has mainly been made, admittedly, when the Conservatives were in power. But it has also been argued that Ernest Bevin was influenced in his Middle-East policy by foreign service officials who had diplomatic traditions fundamentally opposed to the views of the broad mass of the Labour movement. Although some had thought before 1945 that it might 'sabotage' any consistent Labour policy, the home civil service was never seriously criticized for having had an exaggerated influence on the minsters of the 1945–51 period; it was even praised by some of these Labour ministers for its neutrality and its impartiality. Yet this influence might have been so profound and so concealed that ministers might not have been aware of it and it has sometimes been suggested that a 'truly socialist' government would experience great difficulty from the higher civil service. It is often felt that the natural caution, and indeed timidity of British civil servants always bring them, spontaneously, on the side of conservatism and against reform.

The whole of this problem cannot be investigated here. It has increasingly concerned the government and the civil service itself and found a powerful expression in the Fulton Committee on the Civil Service which reported in 1968. Major reforms on structure are being implemented gradually: they relate both to the distinction between classes and to the distinction between general and specialist civil servants to which we are now coming. The investigations which led to the suggested reforms uncovered interesting elements of information, both on the attitudes and on the social background of civil servants. But it remains more difficult to draw general conclusions on patterns of attitudes than on the family and school background of civil servants and of higher civil servants in particular. More importantly, although these data enable us to have an idea of the origins of civil servants, they do not enable us to conclude that these origins automatically produce certain attitudes and a certain social or political philosophy. But we might be able to say as a result whether higher civil servants constitute a small, self-contained circle or whether they are a broad cross-section of the community.

The special role of the higher civil service

These difficulties mainly concern the higher civil service. For the bulk of the civil service, administration essentially remains a question of good execution. As long as these civil servants obey orders and show moral integrity, it becomes irrelevant to know whether they tend to come from the middle class or whether they constitute a representative cross-section of British society. As it happens, they are not a representative cross-section: their parents are more likely to have non-manual occupations than manual occupations. This may be partly a fault of the education system, but it may also be the natural consequence of the well-known fact that middle-class parents are more prepared to see their children stay at school longer and are better equipped to help them in their school work and in the choice of a career. The problem is a problem of general social mobility, and of general social mobility only. It does not really concern the influence of the civil service on the political life of the country.

These social characteristics of civil servants could affect the nature of politics in one way, however. Civil servants, higher and lower civil servants in the same manner, help to give to the average citizen a certain image of the civil service and of the State. If civil servants are aloof and distant, the man in the street will have the impression that the State is a bureaucratic machinery against which he is impotent; if civil servants are easy to approach, and if they do not constantly invoke the 'power' of the State, the ordinary citizen is likely to consider public bodies as organizations designed to help, rather than to dominate.

The social background of civil servants and the traditions of the service contribute to build this general image. In Britain, the image is by and large favourable, certainly more favourable than in many others countries. Jokes about the work and attitudes of civil servants are numerous, as they are everywhere, but the general public probably does not feel overwhelmed by a mass of bureaucratic red tape. The welfare State has not simplified matters, admittedly; the most immediate result of the development of welfare institutions is the increasing number of controls and the increased number of bureaucrats. The manual worker, who is not accustomed to deal with official correspondence, may be more at a loss than the middle-class employee. Civil servants may sometimes have different attitudes when they are confronted with people with 'right' and 'wrong' accents. By and large, however, the image which the civil service projects is not one of authoritarianism; the public has general confidence and even respect for it. If this situation was dramatically to alter, if the public were to feel more and more helpless in front of the administration, the question of the social background of *all* civil servants might become of crucial importance. In reality, feelings of inferiority *vis-à-vis* civil servants have probably decreased, and the average civil servant is probably more aware than before the war of the equality of all before the law.

The main problem concerns, therefore, the nature and characteristics of higher civil servants. The higher civil service is a small group and its structure is complex. The exact size of the group is difficult to define. One has to draw a somewhat arbitrary line at some level. This line could be drawn rather low, taking in all the group traditionally known as the *administrative* class, since this group is 'concerned with the formation of policy, the coordination of government machinery, and the general control of departments of the public service'. The line can be drawn higher, as official documents and academic observers usually do: administrative class civil servants who are responsible for decisions of a routine character only and who are not frequently called in by ministers to advise, explain, or suggest are usually excluded. In the first definition, one would include about 3,000 *administrative* class civil servants; in the second less than 1,000. In both cases the numbers are small, and most of the personnel is posted in London.

The structure of the service raises perhaps more problems. Despite the existence of a Civil Service Commission in charge of recruitment, the civil service is not homogeneous. It is, on the contrary, sharply divided traditionally between three types of officials. In the first place, there are the general classes, which one finds in almost all departments. Members of these classes are primarily administrators: administration is their technique, they have no other specialization; they might be today in the Ministry of Agriculture and tomorrow in the War Office. These include about 200,000 civil servants, half the total of non-industrial civil servants outside the Post Office. The highest class is the administrative class. We have already decided that we should probably consider only the highest ranks within that class.

The second category is composed of a number of *departmental* classes. These exist only in one department. They are administrators, but administrators with a certain specialization as well. The foreign service and the Inland Revenue are examples of these classes. Within them, one also finds a hierarchy: in the foreign service, for instance, higher civil servants are to be found in Branch A. Members of this branch have an equivalent (and indeed perhaps an even superior) status to higher civil servants of the general administrative class.

The third category has a very different type of function. It is composed of a different type of personnel. These are the specialist and *technical* classes. Scientists, doctors, lawyers belong to this category. Although they are not in the 'civil' service, regulars of the three armed forces who work in the service departments have a similar role. These technicians differ by their degree of specialization from general civil servants, but, unlike departmental civil servants, they can often be found in many departments: lawyers, for instance, have their place in the legal division or the legal branch of all government departments.

They also differ from the others by their function. British

central administration traditionally works on the principle that specialists advise and almost never administer directly. They are organized, in pools or individually, around the administrators, departmental or general. They help these administrators to administer when technical advice is needed. They are neither above, nor under, the administrators: they are alongside them, often concentrated in one division or one branch of the ministry. In many foreign countries, technicians are placed in charge of technical departments; in local government, departments are run by expects under the supervision of committees of the council. In central government departments, technicians are appointed only to advise.

This rather technical distinction is important because it may mean that experts do not have as much influence on the conduct of British central administration as they have in a country like France where they are the heads of branches and divisions. It follows that one has to decide whether to include them or not when one assesses the influence and nature of the British higher civil service. If they were in charge of departments, there would be no question: they would have to be included. Since they are somewhat on the side, it may be misleading to include them when one examines the background and attitudes of higher civil servants. The conclusions which might be drawn may be entirely different, since there are at least as many technical higher civil servants as there are higher civil servants in the general and departmental classes.

The consensus among students of administration seems to be to exclude the specialists: we shall follow suit, but mainly because data about specialists are almost entirely missing. We do not really know how much influence these specialist civil servants have; it varies probably from speciality to speciality and from department to department. Moreover, no comprehensive study exists of their family background, or of their school background. They cannot therefore be examined alongside the non-specialists. On balance, the laymen seem to have more influence in Britain than elsewhere, and the exclusion of specialists of the analysis can, therefore, be justified to some extent. But we must remember that they have been excluded. Some generalizations which can be made about *lay* civil servants might not be equally applicable to *all* civil servants, whether specialist or not. Certain attitudes of the lay civil servants are usually

Table 26. *Some examples of higher civil servants*

		Numbers (1955)
GENERAL:	administrative class	983
	top executive class	138
DEPARTMENTAL:	foreign service Branch **A**	656
TECHNICAL:	scientific	581
	works group	628
	legal class	120
	medical officer class	503
		3,609

(this list is not exhaustive; one should perhaps include some regular soldiers as well)

Higher civil servants and other civil servants	
Administrative class	2,596
'Treasury' classes	190,637
Non-industrial civil servants (including 247,000 from the G.P.O.)	635,436
Industrial civil servants	422,760
TOTAL	1,058,196

(from W. J. M. Mackenzie and J. W. Grove, *Central Administration in Britain*, Longmans, 1957, *passim*)

described as being typical of the British higher civil servants in general: they may in reality be the attitudes of the lay civil servants only. Indeed, perhaps it is because they are lay civil servants, in charge of departments which, by and large, deal with technical or semi-technical matters, that they have these attitudes.

Social background of higher civil servants in the administrative class

The British civil service is often characterized by certain attitudes. It is commonly considered to be unified. Its various elements appear integrated. Does this integration simply come from the fact that the men and women who are in the highest ranks of the service have a very similar social background? Or, if this is not the case, is it that one social group is so predominant that it forces other groups to adopt its attitudes and its values? We noted that the Conservative party was integrated and that this integration helped people with a more exclusive background to play a major part in the leadership of the party. Is the higher civil service integrated in the same way and, if it is, can it be said that those who have the most exclusive social background are more likely to shape its outlook and its main attitudes?

If we consider the higher civil servants who belong to the administrative class, one point is fairly clear: they are not a closed group limited to a rather restricted category of candidates. This might not be the case for other categories of higher civil servants; this will have to be qualified, as we shall see, for foreign service officials. But, in the administrative class, people with very different social backgrounds come to be integrated and no one category can be said to be predominant.

There are several routes of entry into the administrative class. Posts are not filled by competitive examination among university graduates only; they are also filled, in varying proportion, by transfers from other classes of the service and in particular by promotion from the executive class. R. K. Kelsall found that, in 1950, slightly over two-fifths of the higher civil servants had been recruited by competitive examination, while over a third had been promoted from the executive class and the rest had been transferred from posts of equivalent rank to the administrative grades.

Moreover, as can be seen from Table 27, these different routes of entry existed before the Second World War. Long before 1945, there were higher civil servants who were promoted from the executive class. The proportion of 'promotees' did increase between 1929 and 1950, but it might very well have decreased since; the Civil Service Commission has noted with concern the fact that the number of candidates from the executive class who had entered the bottom ranks of the administrative class was small in the late 1950s.

Table 27. *Routes of original entry of higher civil servants into the administrative class* (percentages)

	Open competition (direct entry)	Promotion	Transfers	Total
1929	56·4	16·9	26·7	100
1939	57·9	20·5	21·6	100
1950: all ranks	43·6	35·9	20·5	100
assistant secretaries (lowest rank in the higher civil service)	34·5	41·6	23·9	100

(from R. K. Kelsall, *Higher Civil Servants in Britain*, Routledge and Kegan Paul, 1955, p. 16)

Admittedly, there is a tendency for the 'promotees' to be more numerous at the bottom of the higher civil service and for 'direct entrants' to be more numerous at the top. In 1950, 'promotees' formed two-fifths of the assistant secretaries – the lowest rank in the higher civil service – and only a quarter of the officials above that rank. But 'promotees' enter the administrative class at a later age than 'direct entrants' and they are, therefore, less likely to reach the highest ranks. Moreover, at any given moment, the proportion of officials in the highest ranks reflects the proportion of 'promotees' to 'direct entrants' fifteen or twenty years before and not the proportion which exists at the bottom of the administrative class at the time. Some 'promotees' have perhaps also been prevented from moving up to the top steps of the ladder because they did not have the 'right kind of social background'; but this conclusion cannot be drawn from the sole consideration of the relative proportion of 'promotees' to 'direct entrants': more detailed information would be required to pass a definite judgement.

The higher civil service is thus not closed to 'promotees' of the executive class, and these 'promotees' were even found to be numerous in 1950. Moreover, the social background from which these civil servants come is far from being exclusive. In the administrative class, neither higher civil servants in general, nor 'direct entrants' in particular, come predominantly from the upper middle class. These higher civil servants are drawn from families belonging to a wide range of social groups. In 1950, they were found to come in large numbers from three of the five social 'classes' of the census. Two-fifths came from families belonging to the intermediate groups of the middle class (class 2 of the Census). About 30 per cent came from families belonging to the professional and proprietorial groups (class 1) and slightly under a quarter came from families belonging to class 3 which includes the white-collar employees and the skilled manual workers (Table 28).

Table 28. *Social background of higher civil servants in 1950* (percentages)

Social class (Census)	Percent-age in the nation (1951)	Open competition	Promo-tion	Other	Total
1. Professional, pro-prietorial	3	35·2	10·4	34·1	29·3
2. Intermediate (non-manual)	15	42·9	35·1	38·6	40·5
3. Skilled manual and routine white-collar	53	16·2	46·7	22·7	24·2
4 and 5. Semi-skilled and unskilled (manual)	29	1·4	7·8	2·3	3·0
Not given	–	4·3	–	2·3	3·0
	100	100	100	100	100

(from Kelsall, op. cit., p. 153)

The recruitment is predominantly middle class: only 3 per cent of these higher civil servants came from families of semi-skilled and unskilled manual workers, which constitute over a quarter of the total working population of the country. Yet it is not predominantly upper middle class. Classes 2 and 3 of the census are composed of the middle and bottom categories of the middle class and even of a wide section of the manual working class, while even class 1, which includes business proprietors as well as professional people, is partly composed of small proprietors who cannot in any way be described as upper middle class.

The figures which have been analysed in Table 28 cover the whole of the higher civil service included in the administrative class. They are therefore averages between the various categories of higher civil servants. But even among those who entered the administrative class directly by taking a competitive examination, the upper middle class is not predominent. Admittedly, among them, the proportion of sons of lower-middle-class and skilled working-class parents falls from a quarter to less than one-sixth and the proportion of sons of semi-skilled and un-skilled workers becomes minute (1 per cent). But the proportion of civil servants drawn from families belonging to the inter-mediate groups of the middle class slightly rises and it is larger than the proportion of civil servants coming from families belonging to the professional and proprietorial groups.

This situation is not the consequence of a recent 'democratic' development. The civil service is and has always been a profession which sons of lower-middle-class or ordinary middle-class parents want to enter. It gives status, and a reasonably good salary, while it does not entail the possession of any capital to buy a practice. If one looks at the family background of higher civil servants in the past – and even if one considers 'direct entrants' only – one does not find that the upper middle class is preponderant. The lower middle class and even the skilled working class started to produce a sizeable number of 'direct entrants' in the inter-war period.

The inclusion of 'promotees' does not, therefore, profoundly modify the character of the service. Without 'promotees', the centre of gravity of the higher civil service would be somewhere towards the top of the intermediate group of the middle class; with them, it tends to be somewhere towards the bottom of that group. In both cases, the centre of gravity is within that inter-mediate group. This makes the intermixing between 'direct entrants' and 'promotees' fairly easy, although it does mean that, whatever the route of entry, the manual working class is markedly under-represented. From the point of view of their family background, these various types of entrants do not constitute profoundly distinct groups, and nowhere the upper middle class is found to be predominant.

There are more differences if we consider education. One group has been to university and, almost exclusively, to Oxford or Cambridge; the other has not. One group is more likely to have been to a public school, the other to a State or private school.

Table 29. *Education of entrants into the administrative class in 1950 (percentages)*

	Open competition entrants	'Promotees'	All
20 best boarding schools	24·3	1·1	15·1
Other public schools	46·3	18·4	32·9
Private schools	11·8	26·7	17·7
Local authority secondary	16·2	34·1	25·1
Other (including elementary only)	1·3	19·8	9·1
	100	100	100
Eton alone	2·2	0·7	1·3
Oxford or Cambridge	82·2	20·1	47·3

(from Kelsall, op. cit., pp. 125 and 128)

University education provides us with the greatest contrast between 'direct entrants' and 'promotees'. 'Direct entrants' have to be graduates; 'promotees' do not need to be graduates and, in fact, the large majority are not. Moreover, among the graduates, few have been to provincial universities; even in recent years, Oxford and Cambridge continued to supply four-fifths or more of the graduates who enter the administrative class. However, since there are many 'promotees' who have no university education, one surely cannot claim that an Oxford or Cambridge outlook entirely dominates the higher civil service. One may deplore in principle the fact that the number of Redbrick graduates who enter the service is small. Government departments might gain if more of them were appointed. But the causes of the situation are varied: to attribute them to a deliberate or even unconscious bias in favour of Oxbridge would be either plainly wrong or at best misleading.

School background, moreover, has probably a greater impact on character and attitudes than university background. Yet, in this respect, the contrast between the two main types of recruits into the higher civil services is not as marked as one might have expected. Admittedly, there are more public school recruits among 'direct entrants' into the administrative class; but the vast majority of these recruits do not come from the major public schools and the proportion of grammar school entrants, which was already sizeable before 1939, has become larger since the Second World War. At the same time, recruits from the ranks are not wholly products of the grammar schools: it was found in 1950 that a fifth had been to Headmasters' Conference schools and over a quarter to private schools. Entrants from either route tend to be recruited from small public schools, from private schools and, increasingly, from grammar schools. This result closely parallels the family background of these candidates. The top ranks of the middle class are not represented in large numbers and unquestionably do not monopolize the higher posts in the higher ranks of the administrative class; higher civil servants who went to one of the more exclusive 'Clarendon' schools are in a small minority.*

Foreign service and home civil service

It is precisely in this respect that the difference between the home civil service and the foreign service is very marked. Although the Foreign Office has somewhat diversified its intake in recent years, candidates coming from major public schools are still very numerous. During the period 1945–53, about one-third of the successful candidates came from one of these schools. Eton produces only 2 per cent of the entrants to the administrative class, but it produces 10 per cent of the recruits of the Branch A of the foreign service, and 5 per cent of the Sandhurst cadets.

* For a definition of these schools, see p. 40.

Eton does not supply a smaller proportion of officials to the home civil service simply because the absolute numbers of posts are larger. It does not only produce a smaller proportion of successful candidates to the administrative class: it produces a relatively small number of candidates, both successful and unsuccessful. With its 1,200 boys, it has an output of about 200 a year. In twenty major boarding schools, about 2,000 boys from the upper middle class finish their education every year. Yet these twenty major boarding schools produced only fifty-three candidates in 1938 and forty-nine in 1950. Only about 2·5 per cent of the boys who went to these schools seem to care to compete, after having gone to university, for the home civil service examinations. It does seem that schoolboys from the best public schools are simply not attracted by the home civil service, but that they much prefer to compete for Foreign Office examinations. This distinction is not new: it is perhaps one of the most traditional differences between the home and foreign services.

Moreover, the school background seems to play a much greater part in the subsequent career of members of the foreign service than it does in the career of members of the administrative class. 'Direct entrants' into the administrative class may have a slight edge at the entrance examination, as R. K. Kelsall's analysis of the results of the open competitions which took place before the war showed. They gained this advantage at the oral part of the examination, largely because they could impress the interviewing board by their appearance and character. Some were appointed although their marks in the written papers were rather lower than those of other candidates who did not have the same exclusive public school background. In this limited sense, a candidate from one of the nine Clarendon schools had a better chance of entering the home civil service than someone who did not come from one of these schools. Yet, in the course of the career, this advantage seems to disappear. The civil servants who were successful because of their performance at the oral examination did not have a quicker promotion than the others; on the contrary, their promotion was rather slower. This finding unquestionably throws some doubt on the value of the oral examination, particularly in the form which it took before the Second World War. However, it does not allow for the conclusion that candidates from these exclusive Clarendon schools exercise an undue influence on the home civil service as a whole, since these candidates are no less likely than others to reach the top.

This contrasts with the situation in the foreign service, where recruits from Eton and other Clarendon schools do not only form a larger proportion of entrants than in the home civil service, but where they also occupy a large number of top posts both in London and in the embassies. In 1955, half the Foreign Office officials of the rank of counsellor and above and almost half the ambassadors had been to one of the Clarendon schools.

The foreign service may still have a definite upper-middle-class outlook, but the home civil service is clearly not the preserve of the upper middle class. It is not even the preserve of the solid middle class, although the middle class as a whole is favoured to some extent in comparison to the manual working class. Possibly because most children from upper-middle-class backgrounds do not care to compete for home civil service examinations, the bulk of the higher civil servants in the home departments comes from the intermediate grades of the middle class and many come from the lower middle class as well. Oxford and Cambridge may to some extent transform the character and values of these men; but if the background of childhood and adolescence leaves any mark at all, these civil servants are not likely to have the type of attitudes and reactions which are commonly associated with the upper middle class.

Attitudes and unity?

British home civil servants may form a 'class', they may constitute a self-contained group, with its own traditions and manners, but they do not belong to what is loosely considered as being the 'ruling class'. One often notices that the very senior civil servants have higher salaries than ministers, that most higher civil servants have higher salaries than junior ministers, and that all higher civil servants have higher salaries than Members of Parliament. This is of course true if one considers only the income which M.P.s draw from their membership of the House of Commons: we shall see in the next chapter that many politicians have connexions with interest groups and often supplement their income in that way. Moreover, business people often have larger incomes than civil servants: if civil servants were to despise politicians – in particular their ministers – because they earn more money than their 'masters', businessmen should equally despise civil servants. If it is suggested that civil servants are reluctant to obey ministers who earn less than they do, businessmen should equally be reluctant to follow the civil servants' advice and suggestions. In reality, income is only one of the considerations which explain the relative status of ministers and civil servants. Other considerations are the social background, the family connexions, the educational background: in this respect, home civil servants at any rate are not 'equal' to Conservative ministers. The parliamentary Conservative party, and *a fortiori* the Conservative ministers, do not come from the same social groups as higher civil servants, except in the Foreign Office. In fact, the background of higher civil servants is more often similar to the background of Labour ministers and M.P.s than it is to the background of Conservative ministers and M.P.s.

The background, education, training, and experience of higher civil servants perhaps leads to a certain lack of drive: these civil servants are administrators – pure administrators – and not technicians. Some have moved up the ladder from the executive class and they have learnt caution. Others have come from public schools and universities with no definite specialized training. They are all placed in the difficult situation of having to consider plans prepared and suggested by their departmental experts and to decide on them. Someone who read classics or modern languages at Oxford or Cambridge may have to advise his minister on the value of a water scheme or on the reorganization of the railways. The social background of civil servants may explain why they are cautious, but the organization of the British central government also plays its part in the explanation. When those who have to take the decisions – or to suggest them to ministers – are not experts themselves, they are unlikely to be as emphatic about the value of technical projects as they might have been if they had conceived the projects themselves. Road engineers are more likely to press for new road projects even if the cost is high and the need is not very urgent. This is why one would like to know the exact position of experts before any definite conclusion is drawn. If the experts gradually increase their influence in later years, the members of the administrative sections of the higher civil service will find themselves more and more subjected to pressures which they might not be able to resist. But since, as far as one can see, experts do not have this amount of power at present, caution and scepticism may be more common than wildly dynamic attitudes.

Caution does not necessarily mean favouring Conservative attitudes, however. It may perhaps mean conservatism with a small c; it may mean that civil servants, once they have adopted a certain line, are unlikely to change it unless some pressure is exercised. But that line is not necessarily right-wing. In fact, episodes such as Crichel Down seem to show that the line adopted can be left-wing as well as right-wing. Although a Conservative government was in power, the policy which was carried out by officials of the Ministry of Agriculture was a policy of experimentation on the land by a public body: this is not the type of policy which upholders of free enterprise are likely to adopt. In that particular case, the line might not have been specifically approved by lay civil servants, but the important point is that it was not specifically opposed either. If higher civil servants were definitely committed in favour of right-wing policies, incidents should have happened not because a left-wing type of policy was carried out under a Conservative government, but because a right-wing type of policy was carried out under a Labour government.

Caution has, moreover, two other aspects, which are somewhat contradictory. One is that the civil servants in the administrative class might be less likely to press for new schemes than they would do if they were specialists. Another is that they are less likely to present their views to the ministers in the form of demands than they might do if they were experts. The power of the ministers is thus probably greater than it is where experts are more influential. The service may not be as forward-looking as some would like it to be; there is, however, probably less systematic resistance when the minister does come out with a plan of his own. The civil servants are not so adamant to have their own plans adopted instead. Critics of the attitudes of the civil servants sometimes appear to want to have it both ways. If the civil service is not dynamic, enthusiastic for new plans, if it is, on the whole, more *blasé* than one would like it to be, it is probably also ill-prepared to fight desperately against a minister who has a new idea, or a party which has a programme. The minister must come along with some scheme; he may not be presented so readily with ideas of reform. His views are more likely to be accepted, however. Perhaps the net result is that the British system of government is not in many ways as efficient as it might be; but it is not as undemocratic or 'technocratic' as it could otherwise be. Under these conditions, it seems difficult to sustain the view that the civil servant is bound to oppose passive resistance, let alone more overt forms of obstruction, against a radical, but determined, government.

The recruitment of higher civil servants, at least in the home departments, seems to have too broad a basis to justify the view that civil servants lack experience of the conditions of the bulk of the British people. They do not come from a narrow exclusive class; they come from the middle class, on the whole, but the lower middle class is almost as well represented as the more solid elements of the middle class. Grammar schools and the provinces are represented. There are too many higher civil servants promoted from the ranks to make the service a preserve of Oxford and Cambridge. Higher civil servants may be a group because they live the same kind of life in Whitehall. But they are unlikely to be so moulded in their experiences as higher civil servants that they will entirely forget the conditions of life of 'ordinary' people. All groups have collective attitudes; all groups are somewhat self-centred. There is no reason to suppose that civil servants are more divorced from the community than any other professional people. As is well known and as we shall see in the next chapter, they have occasion to meet, in the course of their job, representatives of all kinds of interest groups.

They are not isolated in an ivory tower. They have contacts with the outside world and their past experience, if it is relevant, will not be forgotten and brushed aside.

Is the higher civil service a caste, or an 'establishment'? These are, for the most part, questions of semantics rather than of sociology. It is a united group, has to be, and should be. Otherwise, the civil service would present so many faces that the administration of the country would be forgotten while permanent battles were carried on between sub-groups of the service. It is not a caste since it is not closed to entrants coming from most groups in society; civil servants are not even recruited from among sons of civil servants more than it would be reasonable to expect (10 to 15 per cent for the higher civil service). Perhaps the economic situation of Britain requires more drive, more dynamism, at the expense of this unity. It would not necessarily follow from such a change, however, that the civil service would become more open to other social groups and more responsive to the politicians' views. Perhaps the social situation of Britain requires people who are more attentive to the social needs of many groups in society: it has to be demonstrated that if higher civil servants were *recruited* from these social groups, they would necessarily be more attentive to the needs of the sections of society from which they came.

CHAPTER EIGHT

The Web of Government

Now that we have sketched, however briefly, the component forces in British politics, we must try to see how these forces meet. We have often stressed the compact character of British society: it is integrated and even in parts hierarchical. Centralization has not been imposed on it from above, it has naturally grown within it. This means that the main social forces, those of the politicians, of the interests, of the public service, must have developed a rather elaborate system of connexions. The structure of British politics is shaped by the nature of these connexions as well as by the nature of the forces themselves. The actors are important, but also the stage on which they play.

Some of these connexions are the product of the British constitution. The cabinet system of government works on the principle that the cabinet constitutes the connecting link between politicians and civil servants, as well as the apex of the pyramid of power. Ministers and higher civil servants are in constant consultation: cabinet decisions are transmitted to the top civil servants for implementation; civil servants advise their respective ministers on the feasibility of plans, give information on detailed or technical points, and suggest possible alterations. Ministers are in constant contact with Members of Parliament and, through them, with the parties. They are naturally in closer contact with the members of their own party; they keep in touch with them not only on the floor of the House or in official committees, but also in the parliamentary committees of their backbenchers and in the party committees outside Parliament. Ministers also keep in fairly close touch with members of the opposition parties, because, when the House is in session, they have to answer questions, reply to debates, discuss points in committees. Admittedly, many exchanges are acid: ministers must permanently remain on their guard. None the less, there is a certain community of feeling between all Members of Parliament and there are possibilities – not always used, however – of informal contacts. In this way, a link is created by the constitution itself between the parties and the government and, through the government, between parties and civil service.

Nor are these the only links between M.P.s and civil servants. Admittedly, the relations between these two groups are not always excellent; they belong to two different worlds, and are often prone to criticize each other. The function of M.P.s is to scrutinize policy and administration: this naturally leads to reactions on the part of civil servants. Some of the criticisms made by M.P.s appear to the civil servants to be malicious or ill-founded. There is no doubt that this is, in some cases, and perhaps in many cases, a correct assessment of the situation. Conversely, M.P.s often find civil servants secretive, unduly caught in bureaucratic procedures, insufficiently concerned with public relations. This, too, is often probably true. However, especially in recent years, better and closer contacts have started to develop between M.P.s and civil servants. This is not so much because there are many ex-civil servants among M.P.s; there are not many of them and, in particular, not many higher civil servants. One finds a number of M.P.s who have served in the civil service on a temporary basis during the war, but the race is bound to become extinct in the more or less distant future. What is perhaps more important is the development of the role of a number of committees ('Select Committees') of the House to which higher civil servants are called to submit evidence. The investigations of the Public Accounts Committee, of the Committee on Estimates, of the Committee on Statutory Instruments, and of the Committee on Nationalized Industries are valuable not only because they enable M.P.s – and the public – to acquire information about the running of government departments and nationalized industries; they are valuable also because they constitute a permanent meeting-place between M.P.s and higher civil servants. Investigations do not, as in the United States, take a sharp inquisitorial turn, although they are usually quite searching. Questions are candid, designed only to obtain information and not to make political points. Answers are frank and very detailed. As a result, M.P.s and civil servants have gone a little way towards understanding each other, although they could still go much further. M.P.s begin to know the problems which the administrators have to face, and civil servants see the reasons for some of the criticisms and are less prone to dismiss them as part of a prejudiced anti-bureaucratic attitude. The indirect line of contact between M.P.s, the government, and the civil service, which is the permanent and constitutional link, is now supplemented by a direct means of exchanging ideas and understanding general points of view.

Such institutional and well-established links do not exist or have only recently started to exist as far as interests are concerned. Taken together, interest and interest groups represent all the sections of the community. Yet they have not been given the same status as parties. They do not have seats in the House of Commons. The only members of the House who represented a sectional interest, the university members, disappeared after the Second World War. In the House of Lords, only the Established Church is represented as such. Moreover, the Upper House clearly does not have sufficient political power to constitute an adequate platform for the bulging forces of the interests.

The links between interests and other political forces started, therefore, much more informally than the links between the politicians and the civil servants. They began on an *ad hoc* basis and developed piecemeal: in some cases these links quickly acquired a rather rigid structure, in others, contacts were purely informal. These links developed partly automatically, partly as a result of conscious efforts. They often grew on the initiative of the government, the parties, or the civil service. Often they were initiated by the interests. In one case, that of the Labour party, an interest – the trade unions – even took the initiative of creating a party. But appearances remained very much the same on the constitutional plane. Parties continued to dominate the political scene; the Labour party emerged more and more as a purely political force and not as the political wing of the trade unions. Consultation did grow between interests and government departments, but, since it remained on the level of advice, the traditional predominance of political parties did not seem affected.

However, the practice and reality of representative government was drastically modified. The advice given by interest groups became essential to the administrative machinery. Indeed, interests were, in some cases, associated with *executive* decisions and no longer relegated to advisory functions. In a sense, the House of Commons has always been an economic and social chamber; but, with the growth of formally constituted interest groups, the influence of the social and economic forces became more obvious. Even the House of Lords was affected. If that august body has recently regained some authority, it probably owes its rehabilitation to the fact that it is becoming more representative of all the interests of the nation. It is interesting to note that the reorganization of the House of Lords has been based on the idea, not of competition with the House of Commons or representation of local authorities, but on that of a better *de facto* representation of the various interests of the nation.

Since these developments took place almost without changing the surface of the institutions, the precise forms of the contacts between interests and institutions are sometimes difficult to discover. The relative importance of different types of contacts is also often difficult to assess: more can often be done by informal contacts than through formally constituted channels, but we are more likely to hear about the formal links than about the informal ties. Categories are sometimes misleading; lists are not comprehensive. Statistical data often cannot be produced. Yet, even if the exact colours are not always known, the general design of the landscape can be drawn and this design is, in some parts, quite revealing by itself.

Politicians and interests

The types of alignments between leaders of interests and politicians are almost as varied as are the interests. The nature of the links is often ill-defined, however. Only in the case of the trade unions is the situation fairly clear, at least on paper; but, even there, the practice does not always correspond to the theory. In the complex network of relations, one can perhaps note two prevailing patterns. In the first, the association between interests and politics is of a formal character; it is then (usually) materialized by the appointment of 'representatives' of an interest in a political party. In the second, the association is more likely to be due to the accidental – or at any rate apparently accidental – fact that some politicians are also closely connected with some interests. The first case mainly concerns interest *groups*; the second concerns more specifically organizations which are interests in their own right. Evidently, however, there are a number of cross-currents.

Politicians and groups

The most formal and also closest association is that of *affiliaton* to one political party. It is not very common, however. It is only possible in the Labour party (and in the large, but satellite, Co-operative party), because the other parties allow only individuals, and not corporate bodies, to join them. In the Labour party, sixty-six unions and six co-operative and socialist societies are thus affiliated. The latter constitute a tiny fraction of the Co-operative membership and of the total membership of the Labour party; the former constitute a small proportion of the unions (one in seven) but a very large proportion of the membership of the trade union movement and about five-sixths of the total membership of the Labour party.

Affiliation to the Labour party must be distinguished from pressure on the Labour party by outside bodies. The Campaign for Nuclear Disarmament, for instance, which tried to convert the majority of the Labour party to its policies, never was affiliated to the party and never wanted to be. It included Liberals, Communists, and even possibly Conservatives as well as Labour members. Broadly speaking, the Campaign lobbied the Labour party in the same way as others did, or could have done. However, the C.N.D. appeared sometimes to constitute more than just a lobby outside the party; it seemed to be a faction within the party. To that extent, it should perhaps be classified as a political wing of the Labour party as much as an 'interest' or a 'promotional' group.

Affiliation of corporate bodies cannot, according to their rules, take place in the Conservative and Liberal parties. In practice, however, some of the effects of affiliation are achieved indirectly. Everyone knew for a long time (and the law of 1967 which compelled firms to disclose donations showed) that *firms* (as distinct from individuals) financially support the Conservative party; as a result of the 1967 Act precise figures of sums given by individual firms have become known. In some cases, large sums may also be given by individuals but it is probable that, in the great majority of cases, donations are made by the directors on behalf of the firm as a corporate body. If this were the case, at least the financial effects of affiliation might be similar in the two main parties.

A much more common form of integration of interest groups with politics is the one which takes place, not with the parties in the country, but at parliamentary level. This type of association can, however, take several forms, some of which are very loose and even difficult to ascertain. At one extreme, some candidates are *sponsored* by an interest group and become the group's representative even before they have been elected. At the other extreme, some M.P.'s may be contacted by an interest group in one particular instance and have had no connexion with it before or afterwards. There are many intermediate types of alignment which vary according to the character of the link between the organization and the M.P. and according to the amount of loyalty which the group expects of the M.P.

Like affiliation, sponsorship is well known but not very common. A sponsored candidate may either be promoted or supported by an organization. If he is promoted, the organization chooses him freely and makes him contest the seat, either outside the main parties or after having secured his adoption by one of the parties. If he is supported, the organization merely picks one of the already selected candidates and gives him its official backing. In both cases, the organization is likely to cover at least part of the election expenses.

In practice, sponsorship has developed on a large scale in the Labour party only. About 130 candidates are usually promoted by the trade unions at each general election; a further twenty-odd candidates are candidates of the Co-operative party as well as of the Labour party, under a national agreement between the two parties. The distinction between the two situations is rather thin, but strictly speaking, these candidates are not 'sponsored' by the Co-operative party, which is not a pressure group, but 'adopted' both by the Co-operative and Labour parties. A large majority of the trade union candidates are elected, because, as we said in Chapter Five, trade unions usually sponsor candidates in safe or relatively safe seats. Yet the unions which sponsor seats are not numerous, and the number of sponsored seats is far from being proportional to the numerical strength of these unions. Slightly over two dozen unions (out of sixty-six which are affiliated) sponsor candidates. The miners' union, which is only the fourth largest, has by far the largest number of candidates and of elected M.P.s, a fifth and a quarter respectively. The reasons here, are tradition as well as the compact geographical character of mining communities. There are even larger inequalities: the Transport and Salaried Staffs Association, with less than 100,000 members, sponsors half as many candidates as the National Union of General and Municipal Workers, which has ten times more members.

Few other interest groups have tried, at least openly, to promote their own candidates, although the same results are perhaps sometimes obtained by behind-the-scenes action. The National Farmers' Union thought at one time to promote candidates in the Conservative party: since in agricultural constituencies members of the N.F.U. form a strong section inside the Conservative associations, they might perhaps have succeeded. But this technique was not used for very long. Some other bodies thought of promoting and occasionally did promote candidates outside the main parties, but the idea did not gain much ground. It is perhaps more common for interest groups to support candidates already nominated by one of the parties, but even this method has not been much followed. Some bodies firmly believe in the system; the National Union of Teachers has always tried to support an equal number of candidates from the three main parties. It seems to have encountered difficulties in finding candidates wanting to be supported. In general, as a result of these half-hearted and only half-successful experiments, several associations have rather large political funds lying dormant in the banks which in some cases have been there for several decades.

Table 30. *Trade unions and sponsorship, 1966* (Largest unions affiliated to the Labour party and sponsoring candidates only)

	Number of members	Number of candidates	Number of M.P.s
Transport and General Workers' Union	1,444	27	27
Amalgamated Engineering Union	1,049	17	17
National Union of General and Municipal Workers	796	10	10
National Union of Mineworkers	446	28	27
Union of Shop, Distributive and Allied Workers	349	8	8
Electrical Trades Union	293	2	1
National Union of Railwaymen	255	8	7
National Union of Public Employees	248	5	5
Amalgamated Society of Woodworkers	192	1	1
Union of Post Office Workers	175	4	4

More widespread is the converse system: instead of supporting a candidate and trying to see that he is elected, the organization looks for potential 'representatives' among already elected M.P.s. This system is the one which naturally comes to the mind when one refers to 'interest group representation', except for the case of trade union M.P.s. However, even there, there are considerable variations in the type of alignments between M.P.s and the organizations. At least three distinct methods are in common use. One is very near to sponsorship – in fact it is difficult to distinguish it entirely from sponsorship, or at any rate behind-the-scenes sponsorship. This is the system by which permanent officials of organizations become M.P.s or, vice versa, by which M.P.s become permanent officials of organizations. It is difficult to know whether the organization *wanted* to have an M.P., or whether the official simply divides his time between politics and interest group activities. Fortunately, the category is small and the question has little practical importance. There were only seven cases of this kind in the 1951–5 Parliament, which has been the object of a detailed analysis by J. D. Stewart. They were the cases of three Conservatives and four Labour members: two of the Labour members were union secretaries, one of an affiliated union and the other of a non-affiliated one.

Interest groups more often use another system. They give an honorary post of vice-president or hon. secretary to one or several M.P.s in the hope that the M.P. or M.P.s will, in return, defend the association. In the 1951–5 Parliament, 187 posts were thus distributed. Many associations distribute more than one post and several distribute an even larger number. The analysis of the posts given by associations during the 1951–5 Parliament gives an idea of the importance which should be attributed to this system of 'representation' of interest groups in Parliament.

Few unions use this system, but this does not come as a surprise: unions which want to be represented normally use the sponsorship method. What is more significant is that the other posts are not distributed in the way one might have expected them to be. Let us examine business first, which had in the 1951 Parliament just over half the total number of posts, with 87 M.P.s. If one judges in terms of the economic power of its members, the business organization which concentrated the greatest number of influential firms was the F.B.I. Whether the F.B.I. was the only medium through which big business exercised its influence is a different matter; but, if one compares the F.B.I. to other business associations, there is no doubt that it was the organization to which the most important firms and trade associations belonged. Yet it had only one known representative in the 1951–5 Parliament, while the National Union of Manufacturers, which represented smaller firms, had four.

If instead of considering industry we look at commerce, we find the Association of British Chambers of Commerce and the National Chamber of Trade represented in Parliament. The former represents the bigger trade firms: it had five M.P.s. The National Chamber of Trade federates the Chambers of Trade

Table 31. *Honorary posts given to M.P.s, 1951–5*

Interest groups		Number of posts distributed
BUSINESS GROUPS		87
among which:		
Federation of British Industries	1	
National Union of Manufacturers	4	
Association of British Chambers of Commerce	5	
National Chamber of Trade	40	
Motor Manufacturers Association	1	
Poultry Association	7	
LOCAL AUTHORITY ASSOCIATIONS		50
among which:		
Association of Municipal Corporations	8	
County Councils' Association	2	
Urban District Councils' Association	13	
Rural District Councils' Association	15	
PROFESSIONAL ASSOCIATIONS		3
TRADE UNIONS		3
RELIGIOUS BODIES		12
among which:		
Church of England	6	
OTHER VOLUNTARY BODIES		32
among which:		
Automobile Association	1	
Royal Society for the Prevention of Cruelty to Animals	5	
National Society for the Prevention of Cruelty to Children	2	
		187

(table composed from data appearing in J. D. Stewart, *British Pressure Groups*, O.U.P., 1958, Appendix)

and represents the small shopkeepers: it had forty M.P.s among its honorary officers, eight times more than the Association of British Chambers of Commerce, forty times more than the F.B.I.; it had almost half the total number of M.P.s who had such honorary posts. Only one conclusion is possible: the number of posts given to M.P.s by business associations is clearly not proportional to the strength of the business association concerned in the economic life of the country. It is *inversely* proportional to the influence of the association. In reality it seems that some interest groups want to have M.P.s on their executive committee or among their officers, not so much in order to be able to put pressure on Parliament, but in order to give added prestige to the association concerned.

A similar inverse relation exists in other fields. The most influential local authority associations are the Association of Municipal Corporations and the County Councils' Association; but they had only eight and two M.P.s respectively among their honorary officers. The Rural District Councils' Association and the Urban District Councils' Association are much less influential, but they had distributed posts to fifteen and thirteen M.P.s respectively in the 1951–5 Parliament. Important professional associations, such as the British Medical Association, had no representatives. Indeed, only two professional associations had representatives. About a fifth of the representation went to promotional groups of a non-controversial or at any rate non-political character. The churches had twelve representatives, the R.S.P.C.A., the N.S.P.C.C., the National Temperance Federation, respectively five, two, and two. The system does therefore enable non-party organizations, local authority associations, and small business groups to be represented. It does not enable all the social and economic forces to be represented in a way even broadly corresponding to their strength.

The third system is completely informal. Organizations contact M.P.s and ask them whether they would be prepared to take up cases when the occasion arises. One such system is that of the 'parliamentary panel' on which organizations place a number of M.P.s. We know very little about the extent of the practice and statistics would be entirely misleading. Since the ties are informal, they may leave no traces at all, particularly if, during the course of a Parliament, the spokesmen or some of the spokesmen do not have occasion to speak or act on behalf of the organization which they support. As a result one finds few M.P.s of whom one is certain that they are spokesmen of organizations: in his comprehensive analysis of the 1951–5 Parliament J. D. Stewart found only four groups 'represented' in that way. These were two voluntary organizations, a trade association, and the National and Local Government Officers' Association, which is said to believe firmly in the method. There are probably many more.

These are the main means by which interest groups come to be represented in the House of Commons. Even taken together, the sponsorship system and the more informal methods clearly do not ensure an adequate representation of the economic and social forces of the nation. We must mention, however, one last and rather different method which is commonly used. It is different because, unlike the previous systems, it is not based on the attempt to ensure individual ties between one or several M.P.s and an association. It is based on a collective approach of M.P.s through already existing or specially constituted committees. Some groups use the collective method exclusively, but many use both the individual and the collective methods. In reality, the collective method can be such a loose way of lobbying M.P.s that it might not indicate any genuine collaboration between the interest group and the committee.

One of the associations which believes in a collective approach is the National Farmers' Union which, as we saw, abandoned the idea of sponsorship and has turned to lobbying the backbenchers' agricultural committees of the two main parties. It claims that it gains a much better understanding of its problems in that way. Many organizations use variations of this system, either on a permanent or an *ad hoc* basis. When some major clash occurs between an association and the government, it is very common for groups of M.P.s to receive a delegation and hear its explanations. Some interest groups have to limit their lobbying to one side of the House: the Road Haulage Association has been mainly in contact with the Conservative backbenchers' committees. Other groups operate through all-party committees: the British Medical Association does so to some extent with the 'Medical Group', but the best examples of organizations which use this method are probably the R.S.P.C.A. and the British Legion.

However, even if we add these collective forms of representation to the representation which takes place through individual M.P.s, we still do not find that interest groups are represented in proportion to their strength in the economic and social structure of the nation. Trade unions and business groups as a whole have a good many representatives – between eighty and a hundred each – but the detailed distribution is rather haphazard. Among trade unions, the number of sponsored M.P.s bears only a loose relationship with the size of the union. It is often based on tradition, as with the miners. Some unions, for instance the railway unions, are definitely keener than others to sponsor M.P.s. Among trade associations, among local authority associations, among promotional groups, contacts are developed when the organization is not strong, or not highly politicized. This state of affairs is understandable. M.P.s are likely to defend a non-political cause which will not upset local politicians and constituents. A smaller or less influential body needs a correspondingly greater representation than a larger and more powerful organization. Yet it does seem that, at any rate for large business organizations, the House of Commons is no longer as necessary, nor indeed as useful, as its constitutional importance suggests that it should be.

Politicians and informally constituted groupings

We often noticed in Chapter Six that formally constituted interest groups did not cover all the range of interests: many interests are large enough to defend themselves outside interest groups; they can combine with other similar interests on an informal, purely personal, and *ad hoc* basis, which does not require the creation of an organization of defence. We noted that this situation often arises in the business world as well as to some extent in the cultural sphere.

The contacts between such interests and politicians may equally be informal. A firm may have a Member of Parliament among its directors and its interest may be represented in this way. If the firm is large, if it is a holding company, the Member of Parliament can in fact be as 'representative' of a whole sector of the economy as if he were given an honorary post in a trade association. Large firms often 'lead' a whole section of business: an M.P. who is a director of a large firm may not only 'represent' that firm, but may also 'represent' in a looser fashion the general interests of the sector of business with which he is associated.

Admittedly 'representation' cannot be taken here in a literal sense. The 'representation' of informally constituted groupings in Parliament is not as frank and direct as the 'representation' of interest groups. In the case of these groups, the term 'representation' can be used without too many reservations. A sponsored M.P. is meant to represent his union; an M.P. who is vice-president of a trade association is likely to be the spokesman – or at any rate to be regarded as the spokesman – of that association. But, when we consider the case of an M.P. who is the director of a firm, we notice only that the same man occupies two different posts at the same time: someone who happens to be chairman, vice-chairman, director, or senior executive of a firm may also be a Member of Parliament. Besides, the problem is further complicated by the fact that M.P.s who are directors of firms are not deemed to 'represent' these firms in Parliament and that it is common – although not done in all cases – for an M.P. to 'declare his interest' when his firm is involved in the subject which is being debated. Conversely, M.P.s are protected by parliamentary privilege if a firm (and indeed an association as well) should insist on denying political independence to him.

Yet we cannot leave the examination of the problem at this level. It is not sufficient to know that an M.P. is not deemed to 'represent' the firm to which he belongs; it is not even sufficient to know that he is not consciously acting as a 'representative' of the firm. He may unconsciously act in favour of the firm's interests; he is often likely to try consciously to further the general advantage of his firm. One famous case was that of the 'Katanga Lobby' in 1961: its power may have been more limited in reality, but defenders of the mining and other companies in the Congo and Rhodesia showed some activity. It is difficult to deny that the M.P.s who were associated with these interests did, in a general fashion, act in broadly the same way as 'representatives'.

There is thus a kind of 'representation', but it is unfortunately practically impossible to measure it in detail. We cannot know which Members of Parliament are *meant* to be the spokesmen of their firm if the occasion arises. Admittedly one could perhaps find out whether the M.P. entered the firm before he entered Parliament, or vice versa, but even that information would not necessarily be very useful. Even if he entered the firm after he entered Parliament – particularly if he had not been in business before – one should not conclude that the firm was interested in having an M.P. to defend it. The M.P. might have entered the firm because he had family or other connexions which had nothing to do with him being an M.P. He may simply have wanted to supplement his income and have found a part-time directorship which enabled him to achieve just, and only just, that aim. Conversely, a firm which employs somebody may or may not be involved when this person wants to enter Parliament. Other directors may sometimes be reluctant to see one of their colleagues spend part of his time in parliamentary and ancillary political activities. Some firms may believe, on the contrary, that great benefits will ensue. Conclusions cannot safely be arrived at in matters of this kind. Even if M.P.s who are directors can be assumed to be subjected to a certain number of cross-pressures, it cannot be established *a priori* that their aim is to 'represent' the firm to which they belong. They would certainly defend it in extreme circumstances, but 'representation' implies more than a last resort defence. It is probably true that such M.P.s 'represent' business in general; it becomes an entirely different matter to say that they represent a particular firm or a particular branch of the economy. The situation probably varies enormously from individual to individual, from period to period, and from firm to firm.

Moreover, it becomes very difficult indeed to hold the view that business M.P.s 'represent' their firm, rather than business in general, if we consider what sort of businesses have, in fact, 'representatives' in Westminster. We know that many M.P.s are businessmen. A large majority of Conservative M.P.s (about 80 to 90 per cent) and a small proportion of Labour M.P.s (between one in ten and one in five) occupy positions ranging from that of chairman to that of senior executive and the number of M.P.s holding such posts has increased gradually in the 1960s: only three-fifths of the Conservative M.P.s had connexions with business in 1959. The number of directorships per M.P. has also increased. It has been calculated by A. Roth that in 1961 the 330-odd M.P.s connected with business held an aggregate of about 800 posts, while a further 300 posts had been held in the past by M.P.s who used to be connected with firms: in some cases the severance of ties is due to a legal requirement, as in the case of ministers. By 1965, 347 M.P.s had 1,100 directorships.

These numbers are not significant by themselves, however, if one is concerned with the influence of large business interests. They show that there is a numerous business group; they do not show the extent of the influence of 'representation' of individual business interests. In fact, if the directorships and chairmanships are examined, as they were by A. Roth, they show that big business is, on the whole, under-represented. In the first place, a number of M.P.s are associated with businesses which are businesses with a difference: among the fifty or so Labour M.P.s who are connected with 'business', many are directors or chairmen (or hold equvalent posts) in trusts, charitable societies, co-operative societies. Others are associated with very small firms only. Perhaps only half a dozen to a dozen Labour M.P.s can be said to be associated with medium-sized business; very big business is almost entirely absent on the Labour side.

This is not very surprising. Yet, even in the Conservative party, a large proportion of M.P.'s is associated, not with big business, but with small and medium-sized business. In fact, few M.P.s are associated with very large firms, of the type which are sufficiently large to have, by themselves, an influence in the economy of the nation. I.C.I., Unilever, and English Electric have scarcely ever been represented in the House of Commons. The biggest ship-owning companies are not represented. The large insurance firms have few of their members in Parliament. The only large and well-established interests which are represented are the banks: some of them have or have had prominent Conservative members and ex-ministers among their directors, although some of the largest clearing banks and most of the merchant banks are not represented in the House of Commons. At the same time, the interests which are perhaps more represented and have tended to increase their representation in recent years are those which are less well-established or which need to develop a good system of public relations. Property companies, investment trusts, advertising companies, and some of the Colonial and Commonwealth interests (but not all) are 'represented' in Parliament. If one is justified in using, in this respect, the term 'representation', one can therefore perhaps say that it is not so much 'big business' as such which is represented, but those elements in the business and the financial world which are less secure, both politically and economically. It may be that the more well-established economically a firm is, and the less politically threatened it feels, the less it bothers to ensure representation in the House of Commons.

The examination of business interests, both from the angle of interest *groups* and from the point of view of individual interests, does suggest that there is a certain reluctance on the part of some of the very large economic groups to become involved with Parliament – unless it means that parties (in practice, for most intents and purposes, the Conservative party) are reluctant to select candidates who bear an obvious 'big business' label. There is probably a little of both. Conservative associations may not be altogether enthusiastic about 'big business' candidates, who may not be good constituency members and who may not appeal to the electors. Leaders of big businesses probably do not feel that they have the time or the inclination to contest seats and to be associated with the tedious intricacies of parliamentary work. Big businessmen have many directorships: each one may not require much of their time, but, taken together, all of them clearly do. The House of Commons is a world of its own, with its rules and its peculiar comradeship and equality in which a big businessman is unlikely to fit, at least at the present day. It is clear that big businessmen will not get money, or glory, out of being Members of Parliament. If they want glory, a peerage is more satisfactory, and many do, indeed, become peers. It can legitimately be asked whether, in fact, big business would acquire more power if it was better represented at the expense of, for instance, medium-sized and small business. The probable answer is that it would not; the facts seem to indicate that big businessmen do not think that it would.

Politicians and big businessmen do meet, as well as politicians and members of other interests. But much is done behind the scenes. It cannot – or it can no longer – be said that the House of Commons is a representative cross-section of the social and economic interests in the nation. While examining the Conservative party in Parliament, we found that business was its main component and its catalyst. Yet it is not, as far as one can see, big business. Big businessmen are the exception. Businesses do not fight each other to get their men in Parliament. They seem to be content with a general situation which gives to business as a whole a stake in Parliament: this suffices to frustrate attacks aimed at the whole of the business world. Big businessmen clearly do not use Parliament to achieve their more specific aims. Nor, it seems, do other large interests: despite their large representation, the trade unions themselves have probably ceased to see in Parliament more than a shield or a platform for the defence of their general interests. Parliament is left wide open to the small groups, the unorthodox, the unsuccessful: it is not monopolized by the 'inner circle'.

Civil servants and interests

Some would say that the reason why Parliament is not monopolized by the 'inner circle' is because relations with the higher civil service are entirely monopolized by it. Indeed, much consultation takes place between the civil service and private interests. There are, firstly, the formal advisory committees. One does not know exactly how many there are; depending on the definition, they seem to be between 450 and 850. Even if the lowest figure is adopted as realistic, the two dozen or so main departments of the government had an average of about twenty committees giving advice and exercising pressure at various points of the administrative machine. Several departments were found to have as many as thirty-five and even more.

Secondly, there is the informal advice, which goes on, in many quarters, almost permanently. It is sometimes said that one has reached the stage when the administrators do not even think of a plan, of a suggestion, without having first to go through a lengthy procedure of consultation, submission of drafts to all concerned, reconsideration of the plans, resubmission of the drafts, etc. For this to take place, administrators do not just listen to what committees have to say; they go out of their way to suggest meetings in Whitehall, they write and telephone to representatives of interests. They provoke advice from outside as much as they listen to grievances which have originated outside and which have to be heard in order to let steam blow off.

Thirdly, there is the perpetual process of reform by committee. Departmental committees are set up to investigate the merits of proposed plans; Royal Commissions are set up when the problem is too vast to be examined by a departmental body. On these committees and commissions outsiders collect evidence and write reports, with the hope that these will help the departments to mould public opinion, parliamentary opinion, ministerial opinion. At this stage, consultation becomes active participation in administration, as if the administrators were no longer able to bear alone the burden of the administrative State and had to pass it on to private individuals.

Fourthly, there is the development of the 'corporate' State. Britain is a capitalist country, but the form of 'neo-capitalism' under which she lives is in many ways reminiscent of the medieval system of guilds and very distant from the traditional model of free enterprise organization. This is not only because Britain enjoys a Welfare State, but because the administration of production, distribution, and social services has been farmed out, to a considerable extent, to men and women who do not belong to the civil service or, indeed, in many cases, to the public service, even defined in the widest sense. Universities are supervised by the University Grants Committee, which is mainly composed of academics: this committee was established in order to maintain academic freedom. Hospitals are run by boards to which the Minister appoints local government councillors and people engaged in the profession: this was in order to avoid 'remote control' and the excesses of bureaucratization.

In the economic fields, the encroachments are even more blatant. Agriculture is controlled to a considerable extent by marketing boards on which representatives of the profession play a large part. The nationalized industries are run by boards on which the Minister appoints, not civil servants, not even 'public' servants in the wider sense, but some trade unionists, a large number of managers and technicians, and an even larger number of directors and chairmen of private firms. All these men and women are associated with the civil service, not as advisers, but as agents, as partners, as equals.

The situation is quite clear: the intermixing between outsiders and the civil servants has now reached a point where the distinction between 'administrative decisions' and 'decisions taken by private individuals' is more and more difficult and more useless to make. In a first appraisal, this development cannot but be entirely approved of. The traditional theory which isolated the civil servants from the rest of the nation and considered them as servants of ministers without any contacts with the individuals whom they ruled was in reality undemocratic. It conceived the democratic process as being entirely limited to parliamentary and governmental circles. There was much to be said, both in theory and in practice, for a much closer integration between the civil service and the various sections of the public.

This development did not come about only in order to make the administrative system function more 'democratically'. It came about also because the administration needed the cooperation of interest groups in order to rule the country efficiently. Modern societies have become so complex that it would be impossible for the administration to rule from an ivory tower. Civil servants need the goodwill of those who are administered. Governments can impose policies on unwilling interests from time to time, but, in the normal way, they have to be willingly obeyed. The civil service has to develop contacts with the groups if the administration is to be run without unnecessary frictions and with some mutual understanding.

There is an even more imperative reason for such a cooperation. Administrators have to rely on interests to supply them with information about the state of their businesses, the problems which are encountered, and the new developments which are taking place. If firms and other interests were to starve the civil service of that information, the administration of the country would come to a halt. Decisions which would be taken would not meet the reality of the situation; forecasts would become impossible. The civil service knows that this is the case, and so do the interests. When steel was nationalized for the first time in 1950, the steel companies threatened non-cooperation and complete severance of the daily contacts between the industry and the civil service. This threat was considered in all quarters to be of the most serious kind. In theory, a country where the civil service could rely only on its own sources of information might be administered; but it would be administered at a price. Inspectors would have to be multiplied; the bureaucracy would be slow-moving and heavy-handed. In practice, consultation is the only way in which the civil service can solve many of the daily problems with which it is faced.

Yet it remains to be seen who, in that manner, comes to participate in the consultative and executive process. The civil servants have to listen to the interest groups but they cannot listen to everybody. They have to be selective, and the value of the system depends very much on the kind of selection which they operate. This selection seems to function on two principles. On the one hand, the large interest groups exercise considerable influence; on the other, 'leading' individuals are used, in different capacities, in order to fill some of the gaps which the interest groups could not fill alone.

As for interest groups, the larger they are, the wider the economic and social interests which they represent, the more influence they seem to have. In Parliament, there is a kind of free-for-all: anybody can try to convince an M.P. to defend his views. In the departments, one has, so to speak, to show one's 'assets'. The bigger these 'assets', the larger the consultative part one seems to be called on to play. In Parliament, the National Chamber of Trade has the largest representation of all the business federations; in the advisory committees of the administration, it is the C.B.I. Similarly, among the local authorities' associations, the County Councils' Association and the Association of Municipal Corporations are called to sit on many more committees than the other organizations.

Table 32. *Representation of some interest groups on advisory committees (1958)*

	Number of committees on which the group is represented
BUSINESS GROUPS	
Federation of British Industries	21
National Union of Manufacturers	11
Association of British Chambers of Commerce	13
British Employers' Confederation	13
National Farmers' Union	16
LABOUR AND PROFESSIONAL GROUPS	
Trades Union Congress	30
National Union of Teachers	5
LOCAL AUTHORITIES' ASSOCIATIONS	
Association of Municipal Corporations	16
County Councils' Association	20
Association of Education Committees	5

(from Political and Economic Planning, *Advisory Committees in British Government*, Allen and Unwin, 1960)

This development was logical: these bodies represent important interests and have a much bigger stake than others in the life of the nation. Yet this situation also leads to the possibility that these groups could have more influence on the administration. The representation of small groups in Parliament may therefore to some extent redress the inequality produced by the representation of larger interests in Whitehall. These large interests obviously need to be represented; moreover, advice means only advice, and higher civil servants are not bound – and do not feel that they are bound – to adopt even unanimous suggestions of the advisory bodies. Yet these groups are almost the only ones which will come to the civil servants. Other views, when expressed, as they have to be, through channels which are not officially recognized, are bound to appear to have less of a 'representative' character; they are less likely to be deemed to express the views of the trade, the profession, or the interest.

The problem becomes even more serious when individuals, rather than groups, are considered. In the first place, on the committees, there is a certain tendency for the ministers to appoint the same people to more than one post, as was shown by a survey done by Political and Economic Planning. Interest groups, which are called on to suggest names, are often guilty of the same practice, possibly because few people want to be burdened with jobs on committees. It may be that these people are experts whose value is such that they must be appointed to more than one committee. It does indicate a tendency for 'committeemen' to emerge, however, as a result of the concurring action of interest groups and of higher civil servants.

This tendency also manifests itself when it comes to appointments, not only to advisory committees, but to departmental committees and Royal Commissions. Admittedly the administrators try to select men coming from various walks of life; these committees do not simply represent one vested interest or one point of view. Yet within each of the walks of life which is to be represented, the higher civil service is likely to recommend the appointment of individuals with whom they have already been in contact, whose ways of dealing with administrative affairs are already known and who might, generally speaking, 'fit in' temperamentally with the attitudes of the civil servants. The Conservative government of the early 1960s may have been displeased by the Pilkington report on broadcasting which praised the B.B.C. against commercial television. Yet Sir Harry Pilkington was an example of a private employer involved in several instances in a public activity.

This situation is difficult to avoid: it is easier to blame the civil service for selecting its advisers from a narrow circle than to suggest alternative methods. None the less, the impression which is left by appointments to these committees and commissions usually reinforces the impression which appointments to the permanent consultative bodies leave. The higher civil service is faced, in many of these committees, with people who have already so often been involved in administrative decisions and deliberations that they have become half civil servants and half private individuals. An ill-defined but large sector of administration becomes the responsibility of leading men who, by their profession or training, cannot be said to form a closed group, but who nevertheless have come to be associated with the activities of the administration in such a way that they might be called quasi-administrators, quasi-higher civil servants, and not ordinary 'representatives' of the private interests or of the various shades of opinion.

The same problem arises out of the appointments on the boards of nationalized industries and of other bodies which are run with the help of, if not purely and simply by, private people who are selected by government departments. The inter-mixing between business, and indeed sometimes big business, and the higher civil service has been shown to exist in some nationalized industries and in the Bank of England. The way in which the Bank of England works remains a mystery, which the inquiry about the alleged bank rate leak did not succeed in clarifying. However, it would be difficult to find any profound difference between the personnel of the Board of the Bank of England and the personnel of the Boards of other banks. The important interests of the City, as well as a number of industrial interests, are represented on the Board of the Bank. Similarly, on several Boards of nationalized industries, businessmen are in a majority: the presence of a minority of trade unionists is often the only manifest evidence of the difference between the legal status of nationalized industries and the legal status of private businesses. No doubt in this way the higher civil service comes into contact with many economic interests in the nation and gains an intimate knowledge of the problems and attitudes of leading business-men. But the higher civil service also finds itself faced with a certain 'inner circle' of business which limits the scope of its knowledge of all the interests. Yet it was to enlarge the scope of this 'circle' that interest groups developed and the process of consultation grew.

One is, however, apt to exaggerate these influences and the one-sided character of the information which higher civil ser-vants obtain. The consultative process, and, even more, the influence exercised by individuals on higher civil servants, are not to be considered in a vacuum. In the first place, as already suggested, the influence which some groups have on M.P.s does to some extent redress the overall disadvantages which these groups might have in their dealings with civil servants. In the second place, the pressure which is thus exercised by leaders of large interest groups and influential individuals is contained

Table 33. *Occupations of directors of nationalized industries and of the Bank of England*

| | Nationalized industries | | Bank of England |
	Number	Percentage	Number
Company directors	106	39·0	13
Regular soldiers	5	1·8	–
Senior local government officers	15	5·5	–
Labour, trade unions, co-ops	47	17·2	–
Technicians and professional men	71	26·0	5
Farmers	9	3·5	–
Universities and other voluntary bodies	19	7·0	–
	272	100	18

(partly compiled from data appearing in C. Jenkins, *Power at the Top*, MacGibbon and Kee, 1959, p. 43)

within certain limits. Parliament, as we saw, is not the usual channel which the interest groups use when they want to obtain certain detailed advantages. Yet Parliament remains of considerable importance when interest groups and interests want to obtain rather more than detailed advantages. In the normal way, the large economic interests do not find it necessary to go to Parliament; but in some major instances in the post-war period some more specifically threatened interests, such as the doctors or the road hauliers, had to use, whether they liked it or not, the parliamentary machinery.

We must therefore draw a sharp distinction between normal periods and abnormal situations, between day-to-day activities and occasional crises. When the very existence of an interest is threatened, when for instance several branches of business were threatened by the Labour government of 1945–51, the battle had to be fought on the parliamentary front. No amount of influence which the steel companies might have had on the civil service would have prevented nationalization at the time. It was in Parliament and in front of the public at large that the battle had to be fought. The National Health Service and the Transport bills did not give rise to calm and gentlemanly pressures behind the scenes. They gave rise to bitter opposition in Parliament and it was in Parliament that amendments had to be extracted from the government. More recently, it was finally in Parliament and in the country that the case for commercial television had to be fought.

In normal situations, ordinary M.P.s may be less influential. Big business interests may bypass Parliament or ignore it. But this is because, after all, changes which are promoted or opposed remain of a minor kind. The distinction between administration and politics has been eroded and it becomes fashionable to claim that the distinction is an imaginary one. There are periods, however, when the distinction becomes glaring. It may be true that, in borderline cases, one cannot really know when one begins and the other ends; it is true that, in these circumstances, business and many other interests prefer to use the channel of the civil service rather than to appear in the open and use the political channel. In major difficulties, however, these elaborate contacts with the civil service become plainly unsatisfactory.

Interests – whether formally organized in interest groups or simply made of informally constituted groupings – have developed in Britain a highly complex network of ties with politicians and with the administration. The contacts with the administration are the ones which, in day-to-day life, are the most commonly used. They are better organized by some groups than by others; in general, large, well-established economic and social groups are favoured against the unorthodox and the small organizations. In periods when some interests are more specifically threatened, however, the parliamentary machinery regains its vital importance. There may not be a permanent representation of some large interests in Parliament. It does not follow that a special representation may not have, from time to time, to be established. Indeed, in the last resort, such a special representation can become literally vital to any interest. Interests need permanent administrative links for their daily convenience, but they still need political links in cases of life and death.

CHAPTER NINE

A Ruling Class or an Establishment?

CONTACTS exist between people coming from different walks of life. Politicians see economic and social leaders, economic and social leaders meet civil servants. Some politicians are economic leaders or the spokesmen for economic interests. Civil servants have daily conferences with some politicians, occasional meetings with others. Some of the meetings are formal, pre-arranged; others are casual: they take place in bars or in clubs.

Interlocking membership, formal conferences, and informal talks have become the means by which policy comes to mature. The government may start the ball rolling, but it has to modify its course to rally support and counter opposition. Changes are made long before bills are published and decisions announced. In many cases, pressure is put on the government and action is the result, direct or indirect, clear or concealed, of these outside pressures. Bills, regulations, decisions are the end-product of an incessant flow of information, advice, warnings, which come through the various channels. Politicians, leading bureaucrats, economic and social leaders all play their part.

In such a situation, it seems preposterous to ask who rules Britain and to talk about 'governing' circles. The rule is anonymous, the government is diffused. Everybody seems represented, and apparent authors of plans and decisions are not their real authors. The constitutional and legal machinery might clearly fix responsibility on some ministers: the political practice is a complex network of influences, counter-influences, compromises, arrangements. The process may not be tidy; it is, in one sense, democratic, though perhaps conducive to a form of stalemate. Through consultation with large numbers of interest groups, more than through the political parties, the political system seems to be open to pressures and counter-pressures and those without say seem to have only themselves to blame.

Yet these contacts are made through a number of leaders

who are not drawn at random from the whole of British society. The leaders of the political parties are only broadly representative of the general aspirations of the members and electors of the parties; they often do not come from the same social classes. Leaders of interest groups generally come from the same groups as their members; they have to keep in touch with the demands of the rank-and-file; however, the social gap can often be wide. Moreover, some people have power, not because they are representative of political, social, or economic forces, but simply because they control large economic empires or participate in their control. Although the giants of the economy do not appoint their directors for that specific purpose, these directors play such a large part in the life of the nation that they are often consulted as leaders of interest groups are. Business and cultural 'leaders' can constitute a rather exclusive circle, more than leaders of representative groups can. Because some representatives are different from the people whom they represent, because influential people do not draw their influence from any rank-and-file, the system of consultation cannot be analysed as being simply the natural end-product of a long chain of representation. Power is disseminated in relation to a certain economic structure as well as according to the representative character, real or supposed, of many bodies. the two are juxtaposed, indeed amalgamated.

This is the first reason why one has to analyse the composition of the 'governing' circles. There is yet another reason. Those who take part in consultations and in decisions do not know each other equally well. Contacts and friendships do not only develop in the course of consultation. Some leaders may know each other only because, being political, social, or economic leaders, they have to meet around a table or in a club. Others know each other before becoming leaders: there can be long-standing friendships, family connexions, a common school background. These friendships and connexions can have an influence on the weight of the advice and the nature of the decision. Some are thus favoured by the system, others appear to be at a disadvantage. The governing circles are not anonymous; leaders are not interchangeable.

The process is not entirely democratic. Groups are not entirely open. Personal connexions often count. Do all these characteristics restrict the representative process in such a way that it is, in fact, frustrated? Are those at the top so isolated from the masses that they do not need to respond to the desires of the rank-and-file? Are they divorced from the rest of the population? Are they a class of their own, a 'ruling class?' Are they an 'establishment' or a 'power élite'?

Ruling class, establishment, power élite

Ruling class, establishment, and power élite are three very different notions. The notion of the ruling class is the most rigid, since it describes the governing 'circle' as composed of members of one class, defined in economic or social terms. The theory of the establishment, which is much more flexible, defines the ruling group, not only, nor even perhaps mainly, in socio-economic terms, but in psychological terms as well: members of the establishment are not only those who by birth or by personal advancement have entered a certain class, but also those who have a certain number of attitudes which make them 'acceptable' to other members of the ruling group. The theory is based on the idea of a certain social network, which has its manners, its values, its readily accepted *savoir-vivre*; it is the extrapolation, into the political world, of the sort of code which one expects people to obey when they meet in a drawing-room. The theory of the power élite is probably the least committed about the origins of the group; it does not try to decide by what means people enter the group of rulers, it does not purport to describe this group as being closed to those who do not have the right background or the right accent. It contends only that power is limited to those who have attained top positions in a certain number of groups, political or economic, while the rank-and-file in their own groups and the leaders of other groups do not really influence the course of events, whatever 'power' they may appear to have on paper.

These three theories differ markedly on the nature, on the origin, and also on the size of the group which has 'power'. Yet they are closely related on one point: according to these views, decisions are not the result of the pressures and counter-pressures which take place between *all* the forces existing in society. They are the result of actions and counter-actions taking place within a much smaller group which isolates itself from the rest of the nation, using tradition, secrecy, and even active efforts to frustrate any rebellion of the rank-and-file. In more extreme versions of these theories, representation is a sham, political contests themselves are sham fights. In more moderate forms, leaders and led are only tenuously linked with each other. Society is equipped with springs and shock-absorbers at various key points of the representative process. The leaders are only remotely aware of the roughness of the road and of the depth of the potholes.

There is of course a sense in which these theories are bound to be correct. It is a tautology to say that the government is in the hands of a ruling circle. This is because the political process, particularly in its representative form, is a system by which the views of the rank-and-file become streamlined and thereby modified when they go from governed to government; the representative process isolates the leaders from the led. It gives some scope to the representatives; it gives them time – four or five years – in which to elaborate policies, test their viability, modify them if necessary. During all that time, representatives are necessarily separated from the rank-and-file. There is a break. The only remedy would be to abolish representation altogether. Rousseau had already said so: the British people are 'free' only once every five years; for the rest of the period they are governed by people who belong to a certain group.

The theory is also valid in yet another sense. As we said in Chapter Five, politicians are unlikely to be drawn proportionately from all social groups. The dice are loaded in favour of the middle classes and, indeed, as we saw, rather heavily loaded. This is so because society is what it is, and also because men are what they are. Administrative qualities and political abilities are just not equally distributed. One may hope to better the conditions, one may note that there is scope for improvement. In the last resort, there is a residuum; in this residuum, we will find more rulers than ruled and, as Rousseau also said, democracy is workable only in a society of gods.

Yet given that there are these limits, society may be more or less open. Ruling groups may be more or less isolated and the shock-absorbers may be more or less effective. If the groups at the top are fairly well circumscribed, if it is difficult to enter them, if the family background and the education system are obstacles to social mobility, one is likely to find better ground for the development of an 'establishment'. If somehow the system gives a premium on contacts and friendships, if it is normally accepted that decisions are taken through such contacts, it is more likely that the groups will hold together and that the circle will be relatively closed.

There are, however, three difficulties which beset theories of this kind, even if one introduces some flexibility in the way in which they are invoked. Firstly, the group which is at the top must be a group in the strong sense of the word, it must be a community, with an *esprit de corps* and recognizable attitudes. This class, group, or circle must be different from the mass, not only because it happens to govern, but because of its values. Members of the establishment are allowed to disagree, of course, but they should not disagree on fundamentals.

Secondly, it must not be seriously challenged by other groups outside the establishment. Its rule must be permanent. The establishment cannot just be concentrated in one political party: it must be composed of members of all the parties which have some chance of achieving power. Otherwise, if another party came to power, another establishment would also be in power; there would not be a ruling circle, but, over a period of time, two or more ruling circles.

If one holds the view that there is *a* ruling circle, one must also assert than the opposition between the parties is, in some fundamental sense, irrelevant. There must be more profound unity underneath than there is contest at the surface. One can say that parties, or their leaders, fundamentally agree; one can say that, in Britain, the Labour party and its working-class allies are frustrated from within, because they are dominated by cautious elements who do not really *want* to alter the *status quo* more than superficially. Alternatively, one can say that the ruling group continues to run things behind the scenes, that the establishment keeps its influence and privileges whatever Labour may do in opposition or even in power. In this case, the Labour party remains pure, but irrelevant; in the former case, it can achieve office and even carry some small reforms, but only because its leaders are part of the ruling group, because they do not seriously want to change society and because they spend much time in preventing their own supporters from bursting out and breaking the system.

It is not necessary to decide between these two assertions, but one has to agree with either or both of these viewpoints. If one rejects them both, one also rejects the theory, because it is admitted that a political organization outside the establishment can challenge, with some hope of success, the social and economic power of the ruling group. The ruling group then rules on sufferance, and only for a time. One can perhaps say that a certain group rules at a given moment; one cannot speak, in general terms, of *the* ruling class or *the* establishment.

There is a third difficulty: rule is a vague word, which has to be explained. The theory depends to a large extent on how much power the ruling group can be allowed to have. If the ruling group only administers, if it does not take decisions, but simply waits and sees, its 'power' would clearly not warrant the term of 'ruling group'. Modern representative government includes, as we said, many interest groups as well as the parties. These interests create a kind of equilibrium: one of their chief functions is to try to limit the power of other interests. If the 'ruling' group did not exercise much influence in this process, if it did not modify the equilibrium, it might be in 'office', it would not be in 'power'.

Of these three difficulties, the third is the greatest and it will probably always be the biggest stumbling block of the theory. One can describe and to some extent measure the size of the ruling circle. One can see whether this circle permanently rules, either overtly or behind the scenes. One cannot easily start to define the extent of its 'rule', 'power', or 'domination'. The answer becomes almost entirely one of subjective assessment. It depends on viewpoints; it may depend on ideological postulates or even emotional standpoints. Until these notions are given more adequate and precise definitions, disagreements will probably always occur on the nature and extent of the 'rule' and conclusions drawn will probably remain matters of personal opinion.

The British 'ruling circle'

The British 'ruling circle' is obvious. In most Western countries, ruling groups are an abstract entity, like Wall Street, or are groups hidden behind closed doors, as, it was alleged, the French 200 families. In Britain, the social system, reinforced by the education system, seems to take pride in presenting to all and sundry the names of the members of the ruling circle and the mechanics of their contacts. Nowhere else do 'influential' families seem to take such pleasure in advertising their existence and their size; nowhere else does the education system openly extol the combined advantages of 'breeding' and contacts.

The persistence of a small number of leading families is probably unique, as is the existence of the public schools. It is perhaps natural in a country which did not have any revolution for almost three hundred years, although the absence of revolution has in turn to be explained. It has perhaps to be accounted for by the absence of military occupation and of the political collapse which often ensues; large scale immigration might also have modified the social and political equilibrium, but no such immigration ever took place. The aristocracy had the wisdom to accept new families within its ranks: in return, it succeeded in not suffering the disgrace of being relegated to a museum-like isolation. Social values have continued to recognize the supremacy of the aristocracy. That social supremacy may be challenged; it may be recognized only on the surface and not deeply felt. Yet by the very fact that lip-service is paid to the social superiority of the upper class its members enjoy initial advantages which do not exist to the same extent in other industrial nations. In most developed countries, the aristocrats who remain have to accept appearing bourgeois if they want to succeed. The British upper class may no longer have power *as a class*; its members still can claim as of right that they belong to influential circles if such is their desire. They do not have to gain places *in spite* of their background, as in some Continental countries; their background helps them. It remains for a large number of members of the upper class to use this privilege, and the general position of the group appears well-established. Since a sufficient proportion is talented enough to make a good career, the general claims of the group appear reasonable.

These points are well-known. As for pre-democratic Britain, one can still rather easily trade ramifications of influential families in the upper ranks of the Conservative party, in many financial houses of the City, even in the Foreign Office and in the services. The charts of cousinhoods and intermarriages show connexions which can extend very far. A Conservative prime minister can have a dozen M.P.s, a good number of peers, and several heads of financial houses among his 'family'.

Family connexions are essential to this tightly knit structure. The education network provided by the public schools is also of extreme importance. In the same sectors of society, Conservative party, finance, Foreign Office, to some extent the services, those who went to public schools are at considerable advantage and those who went to the best public schools have the best chance of all. An analysis of C. S. Wilson and T. Lupton conducted in the 1950s showed that Eton produced 30 per cent of Conservative ministers, of the directors of large banks, of the directors of City firms, of the directors of insurance companies. Eton and five other schools (Winchester, Harrow, Rugby, Charterhouse, Marlborough) produced between two-fifths and half of the holders of these posts.

This ruling circle does not, admittedly, remain isolated from the rest of the community. The Conservative party is an integrated society and nowhere is there a gap which would separate the ruling group and the ruling families from the mass of those who are 'ruled'. This 'ruling' circle is only an inner circle. It would be a complete misunderstanding of the nature of the Conservative party to believe that it is composed of two separate groups of rulers and ruled. We hope to have shown, on the contrary, that its great strength lies in the way in which each level comes to be melted into the next. The leadership is usually drawn from a higher social stratum than the rank-and-file, at each point of the hierarchy; yet, at the same time, this leadership responds to the rank-and-file and is connected to it, socially and politically. The chain is never broken. Meanwhile, newcomers are also able to move up by various channels, for example through parallel organizations such as the Young Conservatives. Partly because 'natural' leaders are at the top, partly because newcomers are able to make their way up, the party is not governed – and is not felt to be governed – by an irresponsible clique.

The theory of the ruling circle has thus to be very flexible if it is to describe at all realistically the structure of the Conservative party. Yet the leadership of the Conservative party is composed of many people who have an exclusive background and who are often related. They are intertwined with people who have a large influence in the City. They have also a social prestige – and thereby perhaps influence the social values of the country. They seem thus to constitute the nucleus of an establishment, whose main function is to preserve society in its present form. In other countries an establishment might exist, but the connexions between its members seem to be particularly close in Britain and the group seems likely to be, as a result, more effective.

Moreover, the very flexibility of the notion does to some extent help, rather than frustrate, the power of that establishment. Since there is no clear break between the inner circle and the other circles, its influence may permeate more easily down the line, for instance in the Conservative party; it may also permeate sideways into other groups which might not be directly associated with that inner circle but which might thus become clustered around it in a mysterious way. The civil service and the Labour party do not have many members of that inner circle, defined in terms of families or school background. Yet both of them have some. The establishment could thus become a kind of mysterious freemasonry. Its main hard core could be in the Conservative party, but it would also overspill into other political and social circles. Indirectly, it might extend its influence almost everywhere. The stability of the British social system and of the British political system would be increased; major reforms would at the same time become difficult, if not impossible.

The fundamental 'unity of purpose' of the establishment

In a formal definition, as we saw earlier, the ruling circle, if not perhaps the ruling class, is bound to exist everywhere; in a more specific analysis of British society, the 'establishment' also exists, because families and schools crystallize traditions and enable contacts to take place. But both these notions are only interesting if they also give an account of political power.

Three characteristics, as we said, are necessary to a 'ruling circle' if it is to have real political power. It must have unity of purpose, it must permanently have power, it must be able to rule in the strong sense of the word. The establishment and its inner circle seem to have the first of these three characteristics, although probably not so much because it is an establishment with an inner circle, but because it belongs to the wider group of the middle classes. Particularly if we define it as being concentrated in the leadership of the Conservative party, in financial houses, and in traditional business groups, this inner circle clearly has a certain unity of doctrine. It is conservative-minded. It wants to preserve the social system more or less as it is. It does not want to introduce reforms, except on a small scale and piecemeal.

Yet this fundamental unity of the establishment comes more from the fact that the inner circle belongs to the wider group of the professional and managerial classes, which it represents, than from the fact that it is an 'inner circle'. Moreover, within that circle, it is difficult to sustain the view that there are fewer disagreements than there are among other sections which have the same broad purpose in view. The inner circle is scarcely more a 'group' than is the wider circle of the upper middle and solid middle class.

Family connexions do not seem to explain very much by themselves in Britain. There is no evidence that decisions are taken in a certain way because family links exist within the group. It is not even certain that these families specifically help each other on any major scale. Their members know each other and can therefore by-pass some of the channels of officialdom. But family connexions do not lead to any consistent alignments, politically or otherwise.

Members of these families do not agree any more with each other than they would do if those who hold similar posts were not related. Mr Macmillan seems to have disagreed as much or as easily with Lord Salisbury as if Lord Salisbury was a complete stranger to him. There is not much evidence that the British 'tribes' hold together in the way tribes do in primitive societies. There is clearly some nepotism in British society, but it is not obvious that this nepotism extends beyond the circle of the small family – parents, children, perhaps nephews – any more than it does in most societies.

Mutatis mutandis, the same remarks can be enlarged to the public school background. Boys receive the same kind of training and adopt the same kinds of attitudes, manners, language. Whether this amounts to any greater political 'unity' than would otherwise exist among the members of *these* social classes is very doubtful. It may be said that all these people 'approach' problems in a certain way, but one has to give to 'approach' a pretty technical and almost procedural meaning. They use a certain type of tactics when dealing with each other; they obey certain rules. These rules may well be unknown to outsiders; the establishment may thus perpetuate itself more easily. But this is a question of form rather than of content. The Conservative content of their attitudes is probably not the result of this upbringing: it is much more likely to be the consequence of the upper-middle or simply solid middle-class background of the parents than to be the consequence of the school training. Oxford, admittedly, is often said to turn working-class radicals into Conservative middle-class people, but changes of this kind also happen among non-Oxbridge graduates and, for that matter, among non-graduates as well. We do not know what the proportion of these changes is. Meanwhile, Oxford produces more than a trickle of middle-class radicals. Since the public schools, and particularly the exclusive ones, do not as yet receive many boys from the working class and even the lower middle class, despite scholarships and despite the fact that they always enabled some 'new men' to enter the ruling circles, it is difficult to believe that public school education is the major cause of political attitudes.

If public schools do not necessarily give attitudes to their alumni, they clearly give them contacts and these contacts both facilitate their careers and enable them to have more influence in the posts where they eventually land. The 30 per cent or so of old Etonians whom one finds in a Conservative Cabinet, in banks, in the insurance companies, have greater influence than their numbers warrant, because, being old Etonians, they have more contacts. They supply information about other old Etonians who are influential in other walks of life; they are go-betweens, they are the instruments of compromises in the sectors of British political, social, and economic life in which they are numerous.

This is probably true, but once more it applies to the form rather than to the content of the decisions. In some sectors, an old Etonian is preferable to a grammar school boy, he has an advantage over others. He does not necessarily hold views different from those held by any other individual who might occupy his post. Those who have been through an exclusive public school enjoy an advantage compared to others in the Conservative party, in the financial world, in the foreign service, perhaps in the armed forces. Yet their general attitudes on politics and on the structure of society would probably have been much the same in any case. The establishment is a system of selection – not so much a system by which ideas develop. The establishment consists of people who have certain advantages and hold certain views: their advantage may be due to the fact that they belong to the establishment; but so many of them, in similar positions in this and other countries, hold the same views, that one does not see why these views should exclusively, or even mainly, be due to the existence of an establishment.

The 'permanence' of the establishment

The power of the establishment is real only if it is permanent. There may be sub-establishments within each party or within interest groups. But, if the notion of establishment is to explain the origins of political and economic power, it must go further than just recognizing that there are these various leading circles in the political groups. It must succeed in showing that society is permanently ruled, whatever party is in power, by the same rather exclusive circle or that, if other men come to power, they do not really shake the power of the establishment.

Of course, even in the late 1950s, it was never reasonable to believe that Labour was reduced to electoral impotence; after the 1964 General Election, this view cannot, of course, even be put forward. In reality, both between 1945 and 1951 and since 1964, the establishment has had to accept the fact of a Labour rule. One has, therefore, to look for a less superficial explanation if one is to hold the view that the establishment is permanent. One must presuppose one of the two assertions which we have already mentioned: Labour does not affect the establishment either because it wants to be cautious or because it is condemned only to scratch the surface of the real power of the inner circle.

The Labour party is indeed moderate – and some might say at times impotent – when it is in power, but neither moderation nor impotence can realistically be said to stem from the power of the establishment. The moderation of the 1945–51 Labour government has sometimes been exaggerated. The crises experienced by Britain in the late 1960s have been 'technical', and not forced on the rank-and-file by the power of the establishment. Labour's problem in the 1960s was not at this level.

The political power of the traditional ruling circles is not only weaker when Labour is in power because there are fewer direct contacts between business and the government; it is also positively weakened by the actions and attitudes of the Labour government. Unions increase their influence; business sees its power decline. In 1945–51, the Conservatives fought very strongly many nationalization measures, although they objected only moderately to some of the very early ones, such as the nationalization of the mines and of the Bank of England. Businessmen may have been called to sit on Boards of nationalized industries and members of the City élite may have been called on to sit on the Board of the Bank of England; business interests may have accommodated themselves to the situation while

Labour leaders perhaps did not realize the extent of their concessions: in the long run, business perhaps did not suffer as much damage as was thought. Yet originally these long-term results were scarcely forecast. Indeed some of the 'damage' was 'repaired' only because the Conservatives came back to power and not because business was able to maintain its influence under the Labour rule.

On this plane, what is true is that the Labour party has not tried to eradicate the *social prestige* of the traditional ruling élite while it was diminishing its political and economic power. Labour did not do so because it cannot very well do so by Acts of Parliament. It may have considered in 1945–51 that that social prestige would suffer from the attack on the economic power, because social prestige seemed to be attached to economic power, at any rate in a general way. This judgement may have been wrong, although even the social prestige of the establishment did somewhat suffer at the time. Moreover, the establishment succeeded in maintaining its prestige because the first postwar Labour government did not last long enough for the social effects of its measure to be more than passing. But, even if the establishment has, in the field of social prestige, a 'permanent' strength, that permanent social supremacy must be sharply distinguished from permanent political and economic power.

The moderation of the 1945–51 government does not therefore justify the theory of the establishment, while the difficulties of the 1964 and 1966 governments were not created by the establishment. In all cases, the establishment accepted government rule, as did, in most cases, the largest section of the trade union movement. Reform was impeded or limited during the late 1960s, possibly because the Labour government was technically ill-equipped (or ill-advised) about economic measures, possibly because of the magnitude of the problem. But, had Labour not been so embroiled in these difficulties, it would have remained moderate. It would have done so because both Labour electors and Labour leaders agree broadly on the aims and means of reform. The division between extreme and moderate Socialists is a deep-rooted and long-standing one: it exists among electors and in the constituency organizations. Whether Labour leaders are middle class and had a public school education is, in this respect, immaterial. Moderate socialism was perhaps to some extent out of sight in the dramatic conditions of capitalism in the early thirties; even then, it was still widely supported. Since the late 1940s, it has been, once more, the short- and long-term aim of the majority of the electors and of a good number of members. Indeed it is significant that the criticisms of Labour have not been, in the main, on grounds of 'betrayal', even during the most serious economic crises which the Labour government of the late 1960s had to face.

If the moderation of the Labour party is thus considered as a form of 'impotence', it cannot be because the leaders of the party have successfully imposed on the electors a moderation which these electors rejected. It is among the electors themselves, in their general approach to the structure of society, that the cause has to be found. By and large, the British electorate and the Labour electors in particular do not consider as 'impotence' the rather piecemeal reforms which the Labour party has put forward and seems determined to put forward in the future. In the light of a certain interpretation, this may of course mean that the establishment does maintain its position or that it has only to endure minor encroachments to its permanent rule. In another interpretation, it simply means that British electors, including Labour electors, do not conceive the power of the establishment as being all or nothing, but that they think that these 'minor modifications' are, in practice, determining changes in the structure of the nation.

The 'rule' of the establishment

The role of economic conditions in general in the 1960s also shows the limits of the 'rule' which the establishment can impose. Rule has to be conceived narrowly. The Labour party is reformist; it has not eradicated the social prestige of the establishment; it does not even attempt to abolish altogether the power of business. But the inner circle of the Conservative party, in so far as it represents the 'hard core' of the establishment, also does not find it practicable to rule without reference to many outside forces.

The Conservative leadership does not only have to take into account the views of its rank-and-file and to expect to see some of the 'new men' move up towards the top of the party. It does not only have to take into account the forces of the opposition, of the trade unions and of the Labour party itself. It also has to take into account the views and proposals of groups in big business which do not strictly belong to the establishment. In large industrial concerns, the proportion of self-made men is large and that of people coming from exclusive public schools relatively small. The contacts which exist between the new managerial groups and the Conservative party are much more contacts based on a *quid pro quo* than contacts based on a life-long acquaintance such as the ones which one might find between the Conservative party leaders and some of the financial leaders. There are some cases of long-standing personal connexions. There are more cases when the leaders belong to two entirely different worlds. This situation prolongs and follows the situation which we encountered in Parliament: the businesses which are represented in Parliament are not normally the very large businesses. Big business tends more and more to have its own élite, which is not recruited from the traditional circles but grows within the firms. The conjunction between the managerial world and the Conservative party is a conjunction of interests between two groups which need each other and not a more profound, obscure, permanent conjunction of people who belong to the same fraternity.

Admittedly, through the influence which the large banks exercise on the British economy, the personal ties are perhaps in some cases closer than they might have been. However, these contacts do not equally apply to all the giants of the economy. The integration between the managerial world and the Conservative party, assuming that it was very marked in the past, is in the process of diminishing. It is close in the financial world; it is not so close in those organizations where the 'managerial revolution' has enabled 'technocrats' to come to the top or where powerful businessmen have personally built their own empires. It may be that some of the latter will eventually be attracted by the world of politics; it is unlikely that the former will so easily agree to be integrated in the political organization of the Conservative party.

The growth of the private technocracy is paralleled by the increase in the size and influence of the public bureaucracy. We noticed that this bureaucracy never was, and is less than before, personally or even educationally connected with the ruling circles which constitute the traditional nucleus of the establishment. Admittedly the members of this bureaucracy are perhaps not as influential in Britain as in other countries. However, around them, one sees the gradual development of a kind of third force in British social and economic life, which is not as concerned with political matters and is not as strictly associated with, or aligned to, the political circles as the more traditional forms of business or the representatives of organized labour.

Political power and the establishment

The establishment exists. It is a larger group than the inner circle of the families and of the exclusive public schools. It is a kind of outer circle, somewhat vaguer, but also somewhat more open than the inner circle. It exists probably because the inner circle exists; it exists probably because the general social values remain, as we have said so often, organized more hierarchically in Britain than in other industrial countries.

Yet Britain's difficulties in the late 1960s have clearly shown that the establishment is not the only repository of political power. The real strength of the establishment is one of social prestige, as is that of the inner circle; it is not political. Because the establishment is associated with social prestige, and is based on the acceptance of certain social values and on contacts, it has some indirect influence on the political forces. It does not create political power, however. It does not seem to influence very markedly the balance of forces in British society, even when the Conservatives are in power. It probably helps to hold the Conservative party together and contributes to its integration. Yet, even so, the establishment largely operates outside the circle of political power: it imposes a kind of language, a code of manners, but does not primarily give strength and vitality to the political organs.

The two main spheres of influence represented by the two parties, as well as the new third force of the technocratic and managerial groups, are unequally permeated by the spirit and the reality of the establishment. The traditions and codes are different. The ways in which one achieves power and leadership differ very markedly. In the Conservative party, in the more traditional sectors of finance and industry, the road to power is often open to those who have a good background and the 'right' education. In the Labour party, power and influence can be attained if one has the 'right' background, but a life-long work for the cause is still the most natural way of getting to the top; it is perhaps more necessary to those who have the 'right' background than it is to the others. In the new managerial groups, the emphasis is on meritocracy, still to some extent allied with 'character-training' in the bureaucracy, probably much less diluted in that way in the world of private technocrats.

The notion of establishment or of ruling circles is superimposed on these divisions and on these modes of acquiring influence. It is a social network which cuts across the groups. Its presence is naturally more felt in the Conservative party, since the Conservative party is the party of tradition. But the advantages which the establishment gives are mainly individual. It helps in a career but it really helps in a career in the Conservative party and in traditional business only. The establishment gives social influence and prestige, but members of the establishment do not have political or economic power *because* they are members of the establishment. They have political or economic power because they belong to some political or economic group which has a stake in the life of the nation. All these groups are not, as we saw, equally based on the representative principle; some do not operate at all on the basis of representation. But their leaders, whether they are representatives of a rank-and-file or not, are more than just members of the establishment or of its inner circle. They are members of a political or economic sphere of influence. They can shape the future of British society, but within the framework of the constraints which the country as a whole has to face.

CHAPTER TEN

Conclusion

INVESTIGATIONS on the social bases of politics started only recently and, as was to be expected, many conclusions are tentative or provisional. We do not always know the relative strength of the social forces which compose the parties and we do not know the differences which may exist between various parts of the country. Other conclusions are tentative because the statistical or other instruments with which we can analyse society are still not very sharp. They do not enable us to understand motivations and to weigh with precision the influence of personal connexions or of a common background. We might be able to increase our knowledge: but we will probably always be hampered by difficulties of method and difficulties of interpretation, until and unless new techniques are discovered.

A few conclusions are perhaps more firmly established, however. We may not know 'why' people vote; we know that people do distinguish sharply between their opinions on issues, however important these issues are, and their allegiance to a political party. We know that, in this respect, the old Burkeian theory of representation becomes once more valid in a different way, not simply because politicians and parties have to be given some independence of action, but because the people at large expect parties to have that independence of action. When they vote for a party, electors seem concerned with general images of that party and the other parties. These images are related, not to policy, but to some long-term social aim. It is perhaps exaggerated to present the cleavage too sharply: not all Conservative electors feel that there is 'one nation' and not all Labour electors want a 'classless society' to come about. On the whole, however, the main divisions run along these lines and they will probably continue to run along these lines for some time, whatever the Conservative and Labour parties may do in the short term. There may be a gradual change; more people may come to think that the class structure is, on the whole, satisfactory; more people may come to think that the Conservatives will eventually abolish, or substantially diminish, the class differences which at present exist. We do not know as yet whether these trends exist. We do not know whether they will develop in the future. We do not even know how much images of this kind are affected, in the long run, by policies and by the propaganda of the mass-media.

We do know, however, that, for the time being, these broad class images constitute an important cleavage between the electors of the two main parties. We also know that these images generally coincide – although they do not always coincide in detail – with an objective division of society into social groupings which we may or may not call 'classes', but which have social reality. Many social groups in British society do not have political cohesion – they probably do not have social cohesion either : this is particularly true of the lower strata of the middle class and of some sections of the manual working class. Those who belong to these 'groups' seem to be politically divided, almost at random, between Conservatives and Labour, and the Liberals have also made many inroads in these sections of the community. Whether the Liberal advance within these groups is permanent or not is, of course, impossible to tell even after about a decade of 'revival'; but it is interesting to note that it is among these groups that the Liberal party has found it easier to make a breakthrough. In order to 'understand' the political behaviour of these groups, we need to know more about the role of family background, about the influence of social and geographical environment and about social psychology, particularly in these sections of the community.

Other sections do not present us with the same difficulties. They constitute the backbone of the two main political parties. The voting behaviour of the solid middle class and the voting behaviour of the manual workers who are trade unionists have a considerable degree of cohesion. Among the solid middle-class groups, the Conservative party is predominant and the Labour party is often reduced to a very small and almost insignificant minority. Among trade unionists, the Labour party has much the strongest appeal of all the parties. A Conservative minority exists, but, by and large, the Labour party has remained 'the' party of the trade unionists, not only in the imagery of politics, but also in the reality of voting behaviour.

The social attitudes and the social values of the solid middle class and of the trade unionists are very different indeed. As a result, the general structure of the two parties has profound differences. Both parties – but more precisely the Labour party – have had to adjust themselves to the parliamentary and Cabinet system of government. They have therefore had to resemble each other to some extent, particularly at the parliamentary level. Yet the parties also reflect the social characteristics of the mass of their respective electors, of their members and of their active membership in particular. They perhaps reflect the characteristics of these electors and of these members more than one would have expected, since the main functions of the parties is to form the government or to be ready to form an alternative government. The idea of hierarchy, or of 'deference', remains in the Conservative party. It is a hierarchy which is accepted, not imposed. It is a hierarchy in which the top elements 'naturally' emerge from a rather restricted group, but where the top elements remain aware of the desires and ambitions of the mass of supporters. The Labour party is based on a certain sense of equality or solidarity: the debates which take place within the party may often be acrimonious; this is not inconsistent with equality and the acrimony is indeed probably partly due to that equality. Unlike the old Liberal party, the Labour party does not have 'natural' leaders, nor does it even have a social group from which natural leaders could emerge. Leaders, in the Labour party, have to come forward by a process of competition.

This competition is often obscure in detail; it differs from one situation to the next, but it exists. Admittedly it is not open to all on equal terms, in the Labour party any more than in other organizations. Some trade unionists and some middle-class recruits – who normally come from the intelligentsia and not from all sections of the middle class – have a clear advantage. The advantage of the trade unionists is to be expected in a party in which trade unionism is the main badge and where trade unionists form the hard core of the electors and of the local members. The advantage of the middle-class 'intelligentsia' is not 'normal' in the same way; it is normal if one considers the practical necessities of administration which face the Labour party. It seems difficult to see how this bias could be avoided. Those who benefit from it do not, in any case, belong to a 'natural' leadership; they benefit from it because of their specialized training and not because of the recognition of their social superiority.

The opposition between the two types of attitudes must not be exaggerated. It is deep-rooted in many other industrial societies. What, however, is peculiar to Britain is the way in which these attitudes are jointly embodied both in the social structure and in the political structure. The social structure of the middle class is repeated with its refinements in the Conservative party; the same refinements cannot usually be found in all 'middle-class' parties, either because these parties are full of professional politicians or because the forces of the 'right' are divided between many political parties. It may be felt that the perpetuation of this social and political 'hierarchy' is not to the advantage of Britain. Yet it is probable that the embodiment of this sense of hierarchy into a political organization corresponds to a necessity, since the respect of class differences and the desire for a social hierarchy remain alive in our societies. These feelings become tamed in the process. If the right was not integrated, the social groups among which these feelings are common might well be politically unstable and socially dissatisfied, and they might well favour a more authoritarian form of government.

This conclusion is debatable. What is not debatable is that this hierarchical social and political structure exists in some, but not in all, corners of British society. These other corners have their importance and their influence. The Labour party has rarely been in power since its creation. As a result, one often equates the 'dominant' groups and circles of British society under Conservative rule with the 'dominant' groups and circles of British society under any kind of political rule. This may have been logical for those who believed before 1964 that Labour would never be returned. But since a Labour victory was proved possible, one must also accept that the 'dominant' forces are not exclusively confined within the spheres of Conservative predominance. This does not mean that Labour will ever wholly upset the equilibrium: on the contrary, it can be stated that Labour will never upset the whole equilibrium, any more than the Conservatives or, for that matter, any other political party. On elections and the electoral process, two schools of 'thought' (or rather two somewhat impressionistic views) have often been presented. One paints the political process in terms of clear-cut alternatives, of 'radical' changes in the approach to political problems. As we saw, this view is mistaken, since there are many interests in and around politics against which the political parties can do very little, short of introducing some form of veiled or overt authoritarian rule. But the other extreme view is equally mistaken. It is sometimes suggested that the 'system' cannot change anything and that 'revolutionary' action is the only alternative, as elections do not provide a choice. 'Revolutionary' action is more mythical than real and, the more complex society becomes, the more 'revolution' is an exaggerated word which by-passes the realities of interest groups, of men's occupations and of socio-economic functions.

What is true is that elections do affect the balance of power to some, but only to some extent. The balance of power was affected by the return of Labour in 1945, of the Conservatives in 1951, of Labour again in 1964. Some groups, financial or industrial, which increase their influence under the Conservatives tend to be affected by the return to power of Labour, however moderate it might be. Some financial and commercial circles have close connexions with Conservative leaders: they do not have the same close connexions with Labour leaders; they are unlikely ever to acquire them, because, if they were to try, they, and not only the Labour leaders, would 'betray' the cause of their party. Conversely, the close connexions which exist between Labour leaders and the trade unions constitute a counterbalancing force which leads the Labour leaders to a different sphere of influence of British politics. The return of one party to power, rather than that of the other, thus sets the tone of political life by determining, not what the cards are, but what each hand will be.

Elections are, in the strong sense of the word, a deal: they give opportunities to some and diminish the opportunities of others.

Admittedly the political process is not static. In the very short run, elections do not modify very much the power of interest groups and only slightly change their relative position. Over a longer period, after a few years, the balance of forces can appreciably shift, as if the results of the previous deals did affect the status and reputation of some of the players. The strength of the trade unions in the nation diminished in the 1950s. Business and financial circles did not only provisionally come nearer to the centres of power. Their influence became more rapidly accepted than it was in the late 1940s. They seemed to be part of the 'natural' process of government. This might not have happened so easily, however, if the perpetuation of the rule of the Conservative party had coincided with grave social discontents. In a social and economic situation such as that of the 1950s, where, on the whole, the mixed economy managed by the Conservatives has been *felt* to be materially advantageous to many groups in the community and where, as a result, the area of discontent has been limited, objections to the power of the 'ruling groups' have not been widely voiced. The social position of financial and business groups has been buttressed. The contrary would have been, in fact, very surprising. Yet this situation is neither 'normal' nor 'necessary'. The return of Labour in 1964 has to some extent shifted the emphasis away from business: more stress is given to problems of planning, of wage structure, of relative rates of pay. Thus the other 'spheres of influence' are slowly playing a larger part, though they clearly do not and will not abolish the role of the business circles.

The general balance of forces is, therefore, modified by electoral results, even though it has become fashionable to consider that interest groups, in the forefront or behind the scenes, 'dominate' the whole of society. Yet, at the same time, other changes take place in the very fabric of British society. In present-day Britain, the traditional hierarchy probably becomes less influential as a result of the appearance of new industrial forces, while the 'working classes' may be losing some of the traditional characteristics with which they were, for many decades, associated. The integration of the business and financial groups with the Conservative party is perhaps also being modified. It is not yet modified very conspicuously; managers of big businesses continue, and will continue for a long time, to help the Conservative party and feel at home in the Conservative party. None the less, while the country may be becoming less 'working class', its social hierarchy may also be beginning to crumble. Since the movement is in process, one is easily apt to overestimate – but perhaps also to underestimate – the magnitude of the changes. In the well-publicized transformation of working-class attitudes there is certainly an element of overestimation; in some of the changes which take place 'at the top', particularly in large-scale industry, there might equally be some exaggeration. Yet some of these movements are real and some have an influence on the political system. It is probably not by chance that these changes seemed to emerge on the political front in the form of 'independence' from the two major parties: the failures of successive governments are not the only sources of this new 'independence'. Shattering by-election defeats and periodic Liberal gains (as well as successes of Nationalist parties) are signs of deeper changes in the fabric of British politics.

The overall result remains difficult to predict, however, particularly in a country like Britain. Whatever may happen temporarily to parties in the short-term, whatever gains they may make as a result of their opponents' failures, new classes and new attitudes will have to be integrated: the relationship with the 'new' middle-class – and indeed the 'new' working-class – has to be re-examined by all political organizations. If this integration takes place, Britain will have once more proved the strength of her political and social system, and she will once more leave sociologists and students of politics with ample scope for prolonged meditations.

Bibliography

ALTOUGH the subject is relatively new, the number of books on the social structure of politics is already large, and the number of articles is larger still. The books mentioned here are only a selection of these works. We have concentrated on books on elections and party structure, since these problems were at the centre of this sociology of politics. On the social structure, we mentioned only a few general works and a certain number of recent 'case-studies'. On 'interests' and the civil service, we mentioned the works which were primarily concerned with the representative problem and with the relationship between politics and the other forces which influence British politics.

Many important findings are in the form of articles, not of books. We thus mention a number of articles, but only when they give information which cannot be found elsewhere. We refer here to five journals: *Political Studies*, the *Political Quarterly*, the *British Journal of Sociology*, the *Manchester School of Economic and Social Studies*, and the *Sociological Review*.

General

SIR I. JENNINGS, *Party Politics:* I *Appeal to the People*, C.U.P., 1960; II *The Growth of Parties*, C.U.P., 1961; III *The Stuff of Politics*, C.U.P., 1962

G. WALLAS, *Human Nature in Politics*, Constable, 1908

G. C. MOODIE, *The Government of Great Britain*, Crowell Comparative Government Series, Crowell, New York, 1961

R. ROSE, *Politics in England*, Faber and Faber, 1965

R. ROSE, ed., *Studies in British Politics*, Macmillan, 1966

Social structure

A. M. CARR-SAUNDERS, D. CARADOG-JONES, and C. MOSER, *Social Conditions in England and Wales*, O.U.P., 1958

D. C. MARSH, *The Changing Social Structure of England and Wales*, Routledge and Kegan Paul, 1958

D V. GLASS, ed., *Social Mobility in Britain*, Routledge and Kegan Paul, 1954

G. D. H. COLE, *Studies in Class Structure*, Routledge and Kegan Paul, 1955

J. HALL and D. CARADOG-JONES, 'Social Grading of Occupations', *British Journal of Sociology*, 1950

BIBLIOGRAPHY

P. WILLMOT and M. YOUNG, 'Social Grading by Manual Workers', *British Journal of Sociology*, 1956

A. F. DAVIES, 'Prestige of Occupations', *British Journal of Sociology*, 1952

H. PEAR, *English Social Differences*, Allen and Unwin, 1955

J. E. FLOUD, A. H. HALSEY, and F. M. MARTIN, *Social Class and Educational Opportunities*, Heinemann, 1957

C. A. R. CROSLAND, *The Future of Socialism*, Jonathan Cape, 1956

R. HOGGART, *The Uses of Literacy*, Penguin Books, 1960

B. JACKSON and D. MARSDEN, *Education and the Working-Class*, Routledge and Kegan Paul, 1962

J. WILSON, *Public Schools and Private Practice*, Allen and Unwin, 1962

R. WILKINSON, *The Prefects*, O.U.P., 1964

Report of the Central Advisory Council for Education (Crowther Report), *15 to 18*, H.M.S.O., 1960

R. LEWIS and A. MAUDE, *The English Middle Classes*, Penguin Books, 1953

F. ZWEIG, *The British Worker*, Penguin Books, 1952

R. LEWIS and A. MAUDE, *Professional People*, Phoenix House, 1952

Political and Economic Planning, *Graduate Employment*, Allen and Unwin, 1956

R. LEWIS and R. STEWART, *The Boss*, Phoenix House, 1958

R. V. CLEMENTS, *Managers*, Allen and Unwin, 1958

D. LOCKWOOD, *The Blackcoated Worker*, Allen and Unwin, 1958

P. WILLMOT and M. YOUNG, *Family and Kinship in East London* (Bethnal Green), Routledge and Kegan Paul, 1957; Penguin Books, 1963

Family and Class in a London Suburb (Woodford), Routledge and Kegan Paul, 1960

W. W. WILLIAMS, *Sociology of an English Village* (Gosforth), Routledge and Kegan Paul, 1956

M. STACEY, *Tradition and Change, a Study of Banbury*, O.U.P., 1960

Mass Observation, *Puzzled People*, Gollancz, 1947

T. HARRISON, *Britain Revisited*, Gollancz, 1961

Elections and parties

R. T. MCKENZIE, *British Political Parties*, Heinemann, 1963

BIBLIOGRAPHY

I. BULMER THOMAS, *The Party System in Great Britain*, Phoenix House, 1953

The Growth of the British Party System, 2 vols., J. Bauer, 1965

S. BEER, *Modern British Politics*, Faber and Faber, 1965

R. B. MCCALLUM and A. REDMAN, *The British General Election of 1945*, O.U.P., 1947

H. G. NICHOLAS, *The British General Election of 1950*, Macmillan, 1951

D. E. BUTLER, *The British General Election of 1951*, Macmillan, 1952

The British General Election of 1955, Macmillan, 1955

D. E. BUTLER and R. ROSE, *The British General Election of 1959*, Macmillan, 1960

D. E. BUTLER and A. H. KING, *The British General Election of 1964*, Macmillan, 1965

D. E. BUTLER and A. H. KING, *The British General Election of 1966*, Macmillan, 1966

A. J. ALLEN, *The English Voter*, English Universities Press, 1964

R. R. ALFORD, *Party and Society*, John Murray, 1964

L. D. EPSTEIN, *British Politics in the Suez Crisis*, Pall Mall Press, 1964

M. BENNEY, A. P. GRAY, and R. H. PEAR, *How People Vote* (Greenwich), Routledge and Kegan Paul, 1956

J. BONHAM, *The Middle-Class Vote*, Faber and Faber, 1954

I. BUDGE, *Scottish Political Behaviour*, Allen and Unwin, 1965

A. H. BIRCH, 'The Habit of Voting', *Manchester School*, 1950

A. H. BIRCH and P. CAMPBELL, 'Voting Behaviour in a Lancashire Constituency' (Stretford), *Brit. Journ. of Soc.*, 1950

P. CAMPBELL, D. V. DONNISON, and A. POTTER, 'Voting behaviour in Droylsden', *Manchester School*, 1952

R. S. MILNE and H. C. MACKENZIE, *Straight Fight* (Bristol North-East), Hansard Society for Parliamentary Government, 1954

Marginal Seat (Bristol North-East), Hansard Society for Parliamentary Government, 1958

A. H. BIRCH, *Small-Town Politics* (Glossop), O.U.P., 1959

R. T. MCKENZIE and A. SILVER, *Angels in Marble* (Conservative working-class vote), Heinemann, 1968

E. A. NORDLINGER, *The Working-Class Tories*, MacGibbon & Kee, 1967

F. BEALEY, J. BLONDEL, and A. McCANN, *Constituency Politics*, Faber and Faber, 1965

BIBLIOGRAPHY

J. BLONDEL, 'The Conservative Association and the Labour Party in Reading', *Political Studies*, 1958

E. G. JANOSIK, *Constituency Labour Parties in Britain*, Pall Mall, 1968

M. ABRAMS, R. ROSE, and R. HINDEN, *Must Labour Lose,?* Penguin Books, 1960

N. DEAKIN, *Colour and the British Electorate*, Pall Mall Press, 1965

S. M. LIPSET, *Political Man*, Heinemann, 1960

J. TRENAMAN and D. McQUAIL, *Television and the Political Image* (two Leeds constituencies), Methuen, 1961

J. G. BLUMLER and D. McQUAIL, *Television in Politics*, Faber, 1968

R. ROSE, *Influencing Voters*, Faber, 1967

LORD WINDLESHAM, *Communication and Political Power*, Cape, 1966

T. CAUTER and J. S. DOWNHAM, *The Communication of Ideas* (Derby), Chatto and Windus, 1954

H. J. EYSENCK, 'Primary Social Attitudes', *British Journal of Sociology*, 1951

The Psychology of Politics, Routledge and Kegan Paul, 1954

National Union of Conservative and Unionist Associations, *Annual Conference Reports*

Conservative and Unionist Central Office, *Organization Series*

Labour Party, *Annual Conference Reports*

Constitution

M. HARRISON, *Trade Unions and the Labour Party*, Allen and Unwin, 1960

K. HINDELL and P. WILLIAMS, 'Scarborough and Blackpool', *Political Quarterly*, 1962

R. ROSE, 'Who Are the Tory Militants?', *Crossbow*, Autumn, 1961

Political Quarterly, Special number on the Labour Party, January 1953

Special number on the Conservative Party, April 1953

Special number on the Liberal Party, July 1953

Special number on British Attitudes to Politics, January 1959

Selection of Parliamentary Candidates, July 1959

Special number on the Labour Party, July 1960

Special number on the Conservative Party, July 1961

Parliament

SIR I. JENNINGS, *Parliament*, C.U.P., 1957

BIBLIOGRAPHY

J. F. S. Ross, *Parliamentary Representation*, Eyre and Spottis-woode, 1943

Elections and Electors, Eyre and Spottiswoode, 1955

N. Nicholson, *People and Parliament*, Wiedenfeld and Nicolson, 1958

P. G. Richards, *Honourable Members*, Faber and Faber, 1959

A. Ranney, *Pathways to Parliament*, Macmillan, 1965

R. J. Jackson, *Rebels and Whips*, Macmillan, 1968

S. E. Finer, H. B. Berrington, and D. J. Bartholomew, *Backbench Opinion in the House of Commons, 1955–1959*, Pergamon Press, 1961

F. M. G. Willson, 'Routes of Entry of New Members in the British Cabinet', *Political Studies*, 1959

Interests and interest groups, civil service, web of government

R. M. MacIver, *The Web of Government*, Macmillan, New York, 1947

S. E. Finer, *Anonymous Empire* (groups), Pall Mall, 1965

B. C. Roberts, *Trade Union Government and Administration*, Bell, 1957

V. Allen, *Power in the Trade Unions*, Longmans, 1954

Trade Union Leadership, Longmans, 1957

H. A. Clegg, *General Union*, O.U.P., 1954

H. A. Clegg, A. J. Killick, and R. Adams, *Trade Union Officers*, Blackwell, 1961

J. Goldstein, *The Government of British Trade Unions* (the T.G.W.U.), Allen and Unwin, 1952

A. Flanders and H. A. Clegg, *The System of Industrial Relations in Great Britain*, Blackwell, 1956

Political Quarterly, Special number of Trade Unions, January 1956

C. Ostergaard, 'Parties in Co-operative Government', *Political Studies*, 1958

Political and Economic Planning, 'Trade Union Membership', *Planning*, vol. 28, No. 463, July 1962

Political and Economic Planning, *Industrial Trade Associations*, Allen and Unwin, 1957

S. E. Finer, 'The Federation of British Industries', *Political Studies*, 1956

C. H. Copeman, *Leaders of British Industry*, MacGibbon and Kee, 1955

P. Self and H. Storing, *The State and the Farmer*, Allen and Unwin, 1962

BIBLIOGRAPHY

H. ECKSTEIN, *Pressure Group Politics* (The British Medical Association), Allen and Unwin, 1960

J. B. CHRISTOPH, *Capital Punishment and British Politics*, Allen and Unwin, 1962

A. POTTER, *Organised Groups in British National Politics*, Faber and Faber, 1961

J. D. STEWART, *British Pressure Groups*, O.U.P., 1958

A. ROTH, *Business Background of M.P.s* (editions appear yearly), Parliamentary Profiles Ltd, London

H. H. WILSON, *Pressure Group* (Commercial Television Campaign), Secker and Warburg, 1961

S. E. FINER, 'The Political Power of Private Capital', *Sociological Review*, 1955 and 1956

Report of the Committee on the Civil Service (Fulton Report), H.M.S.O., 1968

R. K. KELSALL, *Higher Civil Servants in Britain*, Routledge and Kegan Paul, 1955

W. J. M. MACKENZIE and J. W. GROVE, *Central Administration in Britain*, Longmans, 1957

S. P. HUNTINGDON, *Changing Patterns of Military Politics*, Free Press, New York, 1962

Political Quarterly, Special number on the Civil Service, October 1954

Political and Economic Planning, *Advisory Committees in British Government*, Allen and Unwin, 1960

C. JENKINS, *Power at the Top* (nationalized industries), MacGibbon and Kee, 1959

Who runs Britain?

The Twentieth Century, 'Who Governs Britain?', October 1957

H. THOMAS, ed., *The Establishment*, A. Blond, 1959

J. PLAMENATZ, 'Electoral Studies and Democratic Theory', *Political Studies*, 1958

C. S. WILSON and T. LUPTON, 'The Social Background and Connections of Top Decision-Makers', *Manchester School*, 1959

E. P. THOMPSON, *Out of Apathy*, Stevens, 1960

W. L. GUTTSMAN, *The British Political Elite*, MacGibbon & Kee, 1963

A. SAMPSON, *Anatomy of Britain Today*, Hodder and Stoughton, 1965

KINGSLEY MARTIN, *The Crown and the Establishment*, Hutchinson, 1962; Penguin Books, 1966

Index